THE
BLUE BOOK
OF
SAILING

THE BLUE BOOK OF SAILING

THE 22 KEYS TO SAILING MASTERY

Adam Cort

Camden, Maine ✦ New York ✦ Chicago ✦ San Francisco ✦ Lisbon ✦ London ✦ Madrid ✦ Mexico City ✦ Milan
New Delhi ✦ San Juan ✦ Seoul ✦ Singapore ✦ Sydney ✦ Toronto

The McGraw·Hill Companies

1 2 3 4 5 6 7 8 9 FGR FGR 2 1 0 9

Library of Congress Cataloging-in-Publication Data is available.
ISBN 978-0-07-154799-4
MHID 0-07-154799-1

Questions regarding the content of this book should be addressed to
www.internationalmarine.com

Questions regarding the ordering of this book should be addressed to
The McGraw-Hill Companies
Customer Service Department
P.O. Box 547
Blacklick, OH 43004
Retail customers: 1-800-262-4729
Bookstores: 1-800-722-4726

Illustrations by Joe Comeau unless indicated otherwise.

THIS BOOK IS DEDICATED TO MY WIFE, SHELLY,

AND OUR DAUGHTER, BRIDGET.

CONTENTS

INTRODUCTION

PEARL S. BUCK, author of *The Good Earth*, wrote, "To know how to do something well is to enjoy it." Nowhere is the truth of this maxim more evident than in sailing. If there is anything more satisfying than bowling along under sail in a fresh breeze, it's bowling along under sail in a fresh breeze while serenely assured of your boat and your abilities.

Has the wind kicked up since you cast off from the marina? No problem. You know what your boat will handle and how to rig for a blow. Are you cruising in strange, reef- and wreck-strewn waters? No worries. You know where you are and how to pick your way safely through. Do you face a difficult downwind approach to a tight berth at a crowded fuel dock? Again, not a problem. You proceed with alert confidence, knowing how your boat performs under engine power and how to maneuver in close quarters with the help of dock lines.

In each case your sense of well-being springs not just from the ability to follow a sequence of procedures, but from a deep understanding of your boat and its sailing qualities. The forces inherent in each situation present themselves to your mind's eye. You know what will happen before it happens. You know what the wind is doing now and what it is likely to do one hundred yards ahead. You take the correct precautions, and you make the necessary preparations. You know which maneuvers are possible and which are not. You know the alternatives and how to execute them.

It was with this kind of sailing in mind that I wrote this book. My goal is to bridge the gap between basic sailing skills and true sailing knowledge. Most books treat sailing and seamanship as a suite of unconnected scenarios, each one requiring a unique solution. Readers are given what's and how's, but there is little if any discussion of why particular solutions are necessary. My intent is to dig a little deeper so that the what's and how's make more sense. Why do sails set and trim as they do? Why are modern sails cut in triangles? How do keels generate lift when sailing to windward? Why does one boat sail faster to windward than another of similar size, sail plan, and appearance?

In the first couple of chapters we inventory the basic sailing maneuvers— things like tacking, jibing, and points of sail. The goal is not to teach these skills so much as to catalog and classify them as the starting point for what follows.

The remaining chapters explore the reasoning behind those skills and maneuvers, examining everything from why sailboats look the way they do to why they don't (usually) tip over. Chapter 5, for example, discusses how to steer a sailboat using only its sails, then goes on to explore how this skill can be employed to increase speed and comfort when steering with a rudder. Chapter 6 looks at the qualities of various rope constructions, the effects of friction, and how those two characteristics come into play when executing an effective sailing knot. Chapter 15 examines why so many contemporary sailboats are equipped with two sails, as opposed to three or more as was often the case in the past.

We'll delve beneath the surface—both figuratively and literally. We'll examine the reasons behind things sailors take for granted. We'll look at aspects of sailing that will surprise even many longtime sailors. At first glance the chapters in the table of contents may look like distinct and separate entities, but our focus on hidden principles—the cause-and-effect levers behind the curtain—will provide a common thread.

While it's possible to learn the fundamentals of sailing in an afternoon, you can spend the rest of your life becoming a complete sailor. The journey is entirely optional. Many of us sail for years, quite happily, without progressing beyond the "practiced novice" phase, and there's absolutely nothing wrong with that. But once you commit to the journey, you'll never tire of it. Gaining a better understanding of the art and theory of sailing isn't just a matter of utility. It's also deeply satisfying. The process is its own reward. I am still on that journey, and I've enjoyed every tack of it. In sailing—as in all things that speak directly to the human spirit—the journey is as important as the destination.

KNOWING THE ANGLES

How Wind Apportions the World

ONE OF THE great things about sailing is that it can be incredibly satisfying even if you don't really know what you're doing. I was born in Boston and got my first taste of sailing aboard a little dinghy named *My Yacht* that my grandparents kept on the beach near their house on Marblehead Neck. My earliest memory afloat is of steering *My Yacht* back to the beach from Roaring Bull Rock, just off Tinker's Island, keeping the starboard shroud lined up with the east end of the causeway. I had little idea what I was doing or why, but I loved every minute of it.

Then my parents moved the family to Bloomington, as in . . . Indiana.

For the next eight years, except for an annual two-week pilgrimage to visit my grandparents, the only way to satisfy my growing interest in sailing was to read everything I could get my hands on. *Sailing* magazine, *Sail* magazine, *National Fisherman*, the entire Horatio Hornblower saga, a shelf full of books on sail shape and racing, *The Last Grain Race*, and on and on—a sailor in exile, I devoured them all with the dedication of a cloistered monk, even when I wasn't entirely sure what I was reading. When we moved to Cleveland and I found myself in close proximity to Lake Erie, I was surprisingly well prepared for that city's thriving racing scene. Of course it took some time to put all that book learning into practice, but it all made sense. That was the main thing.

For all their apparent complexity, sailboats are refreshingly straightforward creatures, and the same can be said for the principles that make them work. Better still, thanks to the generations of accumulated knowledge that goes into their design and construction, the vast majority of sailboats are wonderfully sturdy and forgiving even when handled by the clumsiest of neophytes. It's as if they *want* to take us sailing, like a frisky horse looking for an excuse to romp.

So let's get started.

Beating, Running, and Reaching

When it comes to sailing, the single most important thing to know is your *angle of sail*, or what mariners traditionally called their *point of sail*. (There were thirty-two points on the traditional compass card, with one point comprising $11^1/_4$ degrees—a bit of esoterica few sailors bother to learn anymore.) That is, you need to know whether you're on a run, a reach, or a beat. These terms refer to the angle of the wind relative to the direction in which your boat is moving. Whether you're daysailing, racing around the buoys, or battling a storm, this concept cuts to the vital core of sailboat motion, efficiency, and even safety. Even if you're sailing for the first time, to know what angle of sail your boat is on is to pump a sailor's blood through your veins.

A boat is *beating*, or sailing *close-hauled*, when it's sailing as close as possible to the direction from which the wind is blowing. A good boat can sail to within 45 degrees of the wind before its sails start flapping and it slows down. If you turn much closer to the wind than that, your sails will lose all drive and your boat will grind to a halt. Without forward motion there will be no flow of water over the rudder, and the rudder will no longer steer the boat. The boat is then likely to turn its bow into the wind and remain that way, at which point it's said to be *in irons*—drifting *head to wind* without steering control. Some high-performance racing boats can sail a little closer than 45 degrees, but only under ideal conditions and certainly not in big waves.

Keep in mind that, to be beating, a boat must be sailing as close to the wind as possible. A good helmsman will not just sail a straight-line course

Whether you are daysailing, racing around the buoys, or battling a storm, angle of sail cuts to the very heart of sailboat motion, efficiency, and safety. (Alison Langley)

but will continually adjust his heading to take advantage of every favorable wind shift and to make grudging concessions to every unfavorable one. This angle of sail tests boats and sailors like no other. A heavy-weather beat can be both physically punishing and emotionally exhilarating. It's what defines modern sailboats and sailors. Crack off just a few degrees from close-hauled, ease the sails a little, and you're no longer on a beat.

At the other end of the wind-angle spectrum is sailing on a run, or *running*. A boat is on this angle of sail when it's heading directly downwind, or away from the wind. If the wind is blowing from the north, you'll be running when you sail south with the wind blowing from directly astern. In practice, the definition of this angle of sail is a bit more forgiving than beating, but when the wind is more than 10 degrees or so from being directly astern, strictly speaking, you're no longer on a run. Think of it as running away from the wind. What could be simpler?

Finally, there is *reaching*. This angle of sail—or angles, really—encompasses every possible course between a run and a beat. Because this constitutes a pretty wide arc—on both sides of the boat you're talking about some 125 degrees—sailors break it into three more manageable chunks.

The first, which largely defines the other two, is the *beam reach*. On this angle of sail the wind is blowing directly from the boat's side, or beam, at right angles to the boat's direction of travel. (A boat's beam is the width of its hull measured at the widest point—a term derived from the sturdy transverse members used to hold together old-time wooden sailing ships.) If the wind is blowing from forward of the beam—i.e., from a direction between 45 and 90 degrees off the bow—the boat is said to be sailing on a *close reach*. In other words, it's sailing somewhere between a beat and a beam reach. Similarly, if the wind is coming from aft of the beam but not directly over the stern—i.e., from somewhere between 90 and 170 degrees off the bow—the boat is said to be on a *broad reach*. In other words, it's sailing somewhere between a beam reach and a run.

And that's it. You now have the means of defining the primary relationship of a sailboat to its world in pretty much any situation imaginable.

Maritime Relativity

The importance of knowing a boat's angle of sail can't be overemphasized. Where do you want to go? What is the best way to get there? Is it even possible to get there, and if so, will your route be a safe one? Such questions are impossible to answer if you don't take into account both your present angle of sail and the angle you will need to sail in the event of a future course change.

Let's say, for example, that you want to sail to a small island a couple of miles seaward from the marina. The first thing you need to do is figure out where the wind is blowing from and therefore what angle of sail you will be on when you point your bow in the island's direction. Will you be on an easy run or broad reach, or will you have to sail close-hauled, or will it be impossible to point your bow at the island even when close-hauled?

This same way of thinking applies when crossing oceans. Sea captains often sail great looping courses, as opposed to the shortest distance between two points, in their search for favorable sailing angles that will ensure an easy passage.

The clipper ship captains of the mid-nineteenth century, for example, would sail hundreds of miles east from Boston and New York before turning south for Cape Horn, at the southernmost tip of South America. They did this because it allowed them to sail an easy broad reach through the prevailing westerlies of the North Atlantic's temperate latitudes. Then, after turning south, they remained on a broad reach while riding the northeast trade winds to the equator. The alternative—sailing directly southeast—would not only

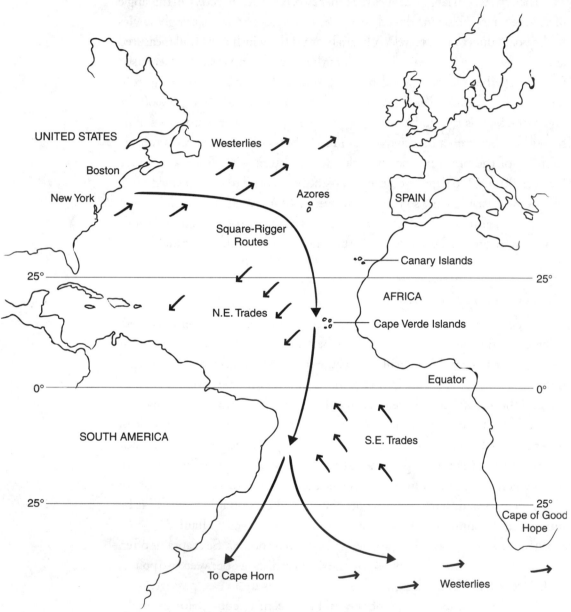

Square-rigger captains bound from the United States for Cape Horn or the Indian Ocean via the Cape of Good Hope would sail hundreds of miles east before turning south to ensure they would enjoy favorable sailing angles for as much of the passage as possible.

have meant contending with the light winds that plague the North Atlantic's central gyre. It would also have meant sailing a close reach through the trades, something clipper ships, which could sail no closer than 60 or 70 degrees off the wind, did poorly despite their vast spreads of canvas.

Similarly, the vast majority of modern circumnavigators prefer to sail from east to west to take advantage of the easterly trade winds north and south of the equator. They also carefully time their journeys for the seasons that are most likely to bring tailwinds and fair weather. The expression "gentlemen never sail to windward" sounds snooty but reflects ocean-voyaging reality. Beating into a stiff headwind can be a barrel of fun on an afternoon in a sheltered bay, but beating your way across an ocean is another matter entirely. "Fair winds and following seas," goes the sailor's benediction—for good reason.

Angle of sail also plays a role in the design and construction of sailboats. In Maine, for example, fishermen and sailors transporting small cargoes of timber, cod, and salt long relied on the fore-and-aft schooner rig because it allowed them to sail closer to the wind than the square rig it supplanted (though not close by modern standards). They did this because of the prevailing westerlies in the area. Sailing east from Boston to, say, Rockland meant easy reaching conditions. That's why sailors refer to Maine as being "down east." Going the other direction, however, was an entirely different matter and required a rig that was good for beating.

Similarly, modern America's Cup boats are extremely slender so that they will sail to windward well. In fact, these boats are so finely tuned that they can sail closer to the wind than 40 degrees. Boats that compete in long-distance events such as the Volvo Ocean Race, on the other hand, will often spend days or even weeks sailing on a broad reach. The same goes for the big 50- and 60-foot boats sailed by "extreme" solo sailors in around-the-world events like the VELUX 5 Oceans race and the Vendée Globe. These boats are often built wide and shallow in order to skim across the water downwind, sometimes even surfing down waves like oversize racing dinghies.

A 12-meter yacht employs a narrow hull shape optimized for sailing to windward. (Billy Black)

An Open 60 has a broad, shallow hull optimized for sailing downwind. (Billy Black)

Where's Your Lade Board?

Left and right mean different things depending on what direction you happen to be facing. Ashore this is rarely a problem, but precise communication is often critical aboard a sailboat. If a crewmember facing aft is asked by a skipper facing forward to untie the "left-hand" line, the crew's justified response is, "Whose left?"

To solve this problem, sailors long ago replaced right and left with starboard and port—or larboard, as the latter is sometimes known. Something on the left side of the boat as you face forward—whether it's aboard the boat or across the water—is said to be to *port*. Something on the right side of the boat is to *starboard*. The port side will be to your right if you turn and face the stern, but it's still port. If you ask a crewmember to untie the port halyard, there should be no confusion about which halyard to untie. If there are two halyards to port, it should be understood that you mean the one that's *farther* to port.

According to etymologists, starboard comes from "steer board." In the days before Europeans figured out how to make rudders, the Vikings steered their longships with an oar mounted on the right side when facing forward—i.e., the starboard side. It made obvious sense when tying to a dock to position the boat so its *other* side, the one unencumbered by the oar, rubbed against the stone facing or pilings. That side therefore came to be known as the lade-board or larboard side, the side across which a cargo was loaded. The word *port* came into use in the 1700s and 1800s to remedy the fact that starboard and larboard sound deceptively similar when shouted through a gale of wind.

The concepts of port and starboard are especially useful when referring to the direction from which the wind is blowing relative to a boat's direction of travel. For example, if the wind is arriving over your boat's port side, the boat is said to be on *port tack*. When the wind approaches from starboard, your boat is on *starboard tack*. Beat, reach, or run, port tack is port tack and starboard tack is starboard.

If you're having trouble visualizing which tack is which, just look at the boom. It will always hang over, or point, toward the side opposite the boat's tack—i.e., away from the incoming wind. When a boat is on starboard tack, its boom will be to port of the boat's fore-and-aft centerline. When a boat is on port tack, the boom will be starboard. This rule of thumb is especially useful when figuring out the tack of a boat that's running. Because the wind on this angle of sail is coming from astern, boom orientation means everything when determining the boat's tack—or its *jibe*, as some sailors call an off-the-wind tack. If a sailor tells you he approached an island on starboard jibe, you'll know he was sailing a broad reach or run with his boom to port.

Windward and Leeward

Another important concept is windward versus leeward (pronounced *loo-ward*). Anything upwind of you—anything between you and the direction the wind is blowing from—is to *windward*. Anything downwind of you is to *leeward*. To alter your course more to windward is to sail *higher*. To turn more to leeward is to sail *lower*.

The windward-leeward dichotomy is critical to any number of situations—especially in extreme conditions—because of a boat's tendency to drift downwind when the going gets rough. It's also important because the air immediately to leeward of a boat, dock, island, or any other object

course actually sailed

course steered

Leeway is the difference between the course steered and the course actually sailed. All boats make leeway, especially when sailing to windward. (Billy Black)

will be more turbulent and move at a slower velocity—which can be a good thing when seeking shelter from a storm but not so good when racing or when sailing through a crowded marina. Even in moderate conditions, you should keep track of whether objects—ledges, islands, docks, moored boats, and the like—will be to windward or to leeward when you sail past. Except when sailing directly downwind, all sailboats make *leeway*—slide a bit to leeward—so it's always a good idea to leave yourself a little extra room when passing to windward of an object.

Let's say you're sailing to an island a couple of miles offshore, and your course will take you past a rock marked by a green daybeacon (a pole topped by a green triangular board). Heading toward the island, you find that the wind is about 60 degrees off your port bow, which means that unless the wind changes (always a possibility), you will be able to sail to the island on a close reach on port tack. The question then becomes, should you leave the rock to port (i.e., pass to the right of the rock so that it's on your port side as you sail past) or to starboard? To the uninitiated, this question may seem academic. What does it matter as long as you don't hit the rock? To a sailor, however, the two choices couldn't be more different. In leaving the rock to port, you will be passing to leeward of it, whereas leaving the rock to starboard will mean passing to windward of it, which could result in serious problems should something go wrong.

And we're not talking about something truly catastrophic here, like the mast falling down. It could be something as simple as a sudden wind shift or getting tangled up in a stray lobster pot or fishing line—rocks being especially common in "lobstery" places such as Massachusetts and Maine. What if the wind dies and your engine refuses to start, leaving you

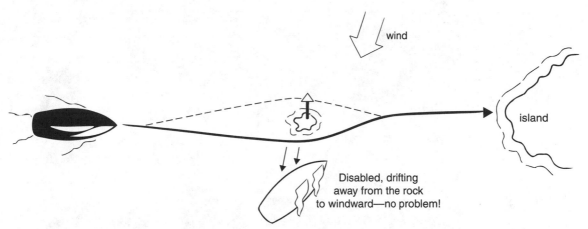

wind

island

Disabled, drifting
away from the rock
to windward—no problem!

By passing to leeward of an obstruction—in this case, "leaving it to port"—the skipper ensures a wide margin of safety in the event something goes wrong.

at the mercy of the residual waves and swells? (Smart sailors continually play these kinds of what-if games as they sail along.) Sailing just to windward of the rock leaves you little if any margin for error.

If on the other hand you pass to leeward of the rock, the world looks completely different. Now if something goes wrong, you will move farther away as you drift downwind, downcurrent, or downsea—unless of course the wind shifts 180 degrees, but some what-ifs are more improbable than others.

In days of old, when ships didn't sail anywhere near as well to windward as boats do today, the very idea of a *lee shore*—a shore in close proximity to leeward—was enough to strike fear into the heart of even the stoutest sailor. Many a ship was wrecked because it couldn't claw its way to windward off a lee shore in a blow. Many were the seemingly sheltered anchorages that became traps when the wind swung around and began to whistle in through the entrance. Anchors dragging, lee-shore breakers drawing closer by the minute, a ship caught in this situation would have little choice but to raise sail and attempt to beat its way to sea through the storm. For a ship embayed like this, the chances of survival were often all too slim.

Note that no mention was made of compass headings or bearings in any of the above situations, yet you still (hopefully) saw vivid pictures in your mind's eye of the conditions described. On the water, even port and starboard can become superfluous. A helmsman facing a rock just ahead probably wouldn't announce that he planned to leave it to port or starboard. Instead, he would announce his intention to go high—to windward—or low—to leeward.

Making Your Intentions Clear

In a racing situation few skippers will say they are going to pass to port or starboard of another boat on a collision course. Instead, they will tell the crew they want to pass ahead of or behind another boat, or "above" to windward, or "below" to leeward. The goal, as always, is clear, unambiguous communication. "Port," for example, could refer either to the other boat's port side or your own. Windward, on the other hand, is always windward, and leeward is always leeward. (Billy Black)

The same is true in a busy harbor or on a crowded race course: Few skippers will say they're going to pass to port or starboard of another boat on a collision course. Instead, they will announce their plan to pass in front of or behind another boat, or to windward or leeward. The goal, as always, is clear, unambiguous communication. Are you going to port or leaving the rock to port? Do you mean your port or the other boat's port? By the time the crew is able to sort things out it may already be too late. Windward, on the other hand, is always windward. Leeward is always leeward. By saying that you plan to steer higher or lower, to windward or leeward, you also forewarn the crew that the angle of sail will soon be changing. They will be mentally prepared to adjust the sails, if necessary, to maintain boat speed.

Experienced sailors are continually aware of their angle of sail, often to within a few degrees. This awareness is as deep-set and profound as their sense of balance, as natural and subliminal as breathing. It's the way they see the world. It's what ties things together. It's what gives whatever else might be out there—waves, shoals, docks, lighthouses, other boats—their context and most immediate meaning.

GETTING WHERE YOU WANT TO GO

*And Why Sailing Close-Hauled
Is Fundamentally Different*

BIOLOGISTS ONCE believed that ontogeny recapitulates phylogeny. In other words, every organism recreates its entire evolutionary ancestry as it develops in the egg or womb. Think of a human fetus looking like an amoeba, then a fish, and later a mammal as gestation progresses. Alas, this hypothesis has long since been disproved, but it still serves as a nifty way of talking about how sailboats do what they do.

Sailing Downwind

Somewhere in the dim recesses of time, some intrepid boater hoisted his or her first sail. Undoubtedly it consisted of little more than a scrap of hide or crude fabric. Maybe the world's first sailor used a stick to hold up said scrap. Who knows, the first sail may have been as simple as a palm frond or leafy branch.

Whatever sail our clever forebear hoisted, the boat in question—probably a simple dugout or log raft—undoubtedly started sailing downwind, on a run. The lack of a rudder or any kind of keel to resist drifting to leeward would have made it pretty much impossible to pursue

2

16

any other course. Raise sail. Watch your boat gather way. Relax. Have a sip of pomegranate juice and enjoy the ride. That's pretty much all there was to it.

Amazingly, some five or six thousand years later, downwind sailing remains pretty much the same. Even pomegranate juice appears to be making a comeback. To sail on a run, or *dead downwind* as many sailors call it, hoist sail, point your bow in the direction toward which the wind is blowing, and steer as necessary to keep yourself moving in a straight line. There's no need to worry about any subtleties of sail trim—simply let out the mainsail, jib, and any other sails you may have aboard—mizzen, topgallant, staysail anyone?—until they're either perpendicular to the wind or as close to perpendicular as they can get before fetching up against something fixed, like a spreader or a shroud. The idea is to project as much surface area as possible to the wind, which then blows your boat along like a dry leaf.

Of course, a dry leaf's options are limited, and it probably wasn't long before prehistoric sailors grew tired of sailing only dead downwind. One of them must have begun sticking his or her paddle in the water at various points along a boat's hull to see what would happen. The result was that the boat—the dugout, canoe, coracle, or whatever it may have been—started moving at an angle to the wind. Incredible! As if by magic, the boat was sailing on a broad reach.

Once again, things are not much different today, just a lot easier thanks to today's "paddles"—i.e., rudders, centerboards, keels, and various other *underwater appendages*. Steering a reach is like steering a run—or like driving a car, for that matter—just point your bow and go. Sail trim is easy too—just keep adjusting your sails so they remain perpendicular to the wind, the same as on a run. Surface area is still the name of the game. Your boat is still pretty much a dry leaf, albeit one with a modest sense of direction.

Steer a little higher, though, so that your angle of sail approaches a beam reach, and things start to get interesting. The steering remains straightforward, but sail trim gets trickier because you're no longer simply squaring your sails to the wind. Think about it. If you position your sails so that they're perpendicular to the wind on a beam reach, they will be parallel to the boat's centerline. In that position they will do little more than try to blow the boat sideways. Where's the sense in that?

The solution is to let each sail out until a "bubble" begins to form in its leading edge. This tells you that the sail is starting to *backwind*—that is, the approaching wind is no longer flowing smoothly over the sail's windward and leeward surfaces. When you see this, sheet back in just enough to make the bubble disappear. The curved leading edge is now angled so that the wind passes smoothly over both the windward and leeward sides of the sail, hugging its curved midsection before finally passing without fuss off the trailing edge. The sail is now ideally angled to channel the wind's energy into forward motion.

Sailing to Windward

Alas for Stone Age sailors—and most pre-Industrial sailors as well—it's at this point that things *really* started to get complicated. With a few notable exceptions, such as Polynesian multihulls and Viking longboats, it would be centuries before most sailing craft could sail any closer to the wind than a beam reach. The right sails, keels, and hull shapes had yet to be developed. Luckily, today's sailors—being the beneficiaries of centuries of trial-and-error evolution—can sail closer to the wind with ease.

Steering on a close reach remains a simple matter of aiming the bow where you want to go—just as on a beam reach, broad reach, or run. As you're doing so, keep an eye on those sails. The closer to the wind your boat is sailing, the closer to the boat's fore-and-aft centerline you'll have to trim the sails to keep them from backwinding, or *luffing*. Eventually you'll reach a point—ideally when you're sailing about 45 degrees from the wind's direction of approach—at which the sails are so close to the boat's centerline that you can't pull them in any more. Congratulations, you're now on a beat!

It's at this point that the helmsman's job becomes a bit more complicated. On a reach, it's the crew's job to adjust the sails to the conditions—trimming or easing in response to wind shifts. The person at the helm simply keeps the boat moving in a straight line. As soon as the boat is on a beat, though, the roles are reversed. Now, once the sails have been sheeted in, the crew leaves them there and it's the helmsman who must play the shifts. The goal when beating is always to sail on a close-hauled course, as close to the wind as possible while maintaining the greatest possible speed. Even the best close-hauled course represents a compromise between speed and heading. Sometimes a helmsman will *pinch* up a little, sacrificing a fraction of a knot to sail a few degrees higher than normal. On other occasions it makes sense to *foot* off a little, sacrificing a little pointing ability to generate a tad more boat speed.

Use your sails as a guide, just as your trimmers watch the sails when you're reaching. If the sails start backwinding, you're sailing too high. Steer a little

Different Angles, Different Responsibilities

On a reach, it's the crew's job to adjust the sails to the conditions—trimming or easing in response to wind shifts. The person at the helm simply keeps the boat moving in a straight line. On a beat, the roles are reversed. Now the crew trims the sails in, and it's the helmsman who must play the shifts, making the necessary small course adjustments to ensure the sails are drawing at maximum efficiency. The boat to the right of center is on a broad reach with the spinnaker set, and the crew is busy trimming sail. The other boat is close-hauled, and the crew is hiking out on the windward rail, serving as a kind of movable ballast. (Billy Black)

away from the direction of the wind. If your sails have been full and taut for a while, try sailing a few degrees higher to see what happens. Are they still pulling like a team of contented Clydesdales? Excellent! Try sneaking up a couple of degrees more. Keep pushing that envelope until you get a little backwind going. Then steer back down until the sails are full again. Can you feel them pull and feel your boat respond? Good. Now wait a bit, and then start the cycle again. Bear in mind that the jib is a more reliable indicator than the main, because the latter may suffer some unavoidable backwind from the jib. If you keep your adjustments small enough, you'll never induce enough luffing in the sails to sacrifice boat speed. That's the way! Russell Coutts, eat your heart out!

Flip-Flopping

Once you've mastered the art of keeping your boat moving on any angle of sail between a run and a beat, all that remains is to maneuver your boat from port to starboard tack by tacking or jibing.

Tacking, or coming about, involves switching from a close-hauled course on one tack to a close-hauled course on the other by steering the boat through the eye of the wind. In other words, the helmsman turns the boat so that the bow sweeps through that 90-degree sector (45 degrees on either side of the true wind direction) where it can't otherwise go. This is possible because the boat's momentum keeps it moving until the sails can fill and start working again on the other side.

Of course, a boat's momentum isn't going to keep it moving directly into the wind forever, so the tack needs to be completed expeditiously. Otherwise your boat might get bogged down midway through in the condition described as being in irons. Wide, heavy cruisers, for example, can sometimes get into trouble in choppy conditions, when waves slapping their bows impede forward progress. A steep chop can also become a problem aboard smaller, lighter boats with minimal inertia.

Larger, narrower boats, on the other hand, like the 12-meter boats that used to compete for the America's Cup, can be maneuvered through a tack much more slowly. In fact, it was—and still is—a common trick among America's Cup skippers to sometimes fake each other out by steering midway through a tack, then suddenly returning to their original heading. Try that with a lightweight dinghy in a seaway!

To execute a tack, the skipper or helmsman first calls, "Ready about," "Prepare to tack," or something along those lines—the main thing is to use the same expression consistently so there will be no confusion in blustery conditions when the warning may be hard to hear. Once the crew is ready, the helmsman begins the turn and the crew casts off the loaded jibsheet as the jib backwinds and starts luffing and shaking its way to the other side. When the jib nears the end of its journey across the foredeck, the crew trims in the new sheet. In a fresh breeze this trimming is easier to accomplish if it is done before the tack is completed. Otherwise, it can be an absolute bear getting the jib all the way in.

The mainsail, on the other hand can be pretty much ignored. Though there are two jibsheets, one of which must be activated and the other idled with each tack, there is only one mainsheet attached to the main boom. As the boat turns through its tack, the sail, the boom, and its attached sheet shift from one side of the boat to the other like a weathervane. Because the angle of the boat relative to the wind will be the same on the new tack as it was on the old, the mainsheet setting will also be the same, so it doesn't need to be adjusted unless it's sheeted from windward of amidships—a subtlety we'll return to later.

This is another area in which modern sailors have a tremendous advantage over the sailors of the past. Consider the proas of Melanesia: With their narrow hulls, lithe outriggers, and lateen-style sails, these small speedsters were a source of wonder to European explorers like Captain Cook. But changing tacks could be problematic, to say the least. Instead of steering the bow through the eye of the wind, the helmsman steers away onto a reach until it's the stern—not the bow—that points toward the approaching wind. The crew then shifts the sail around so that the boat starts sailing stern-first on the new tack. Because these boats are double-ended, with a sharpened tip on either end, they sail equally well in either direction. To complete the maneuver, the helmsman simply moves the steering paddle from the old stern to the new stern, and the boat is on its way.

Tacking a square-rigger was even more problematic. Among other things, because these ships could sail no closer than 60 degrees off the wind, tacking meant sweeping through a turn of at least 120 degrees. Compare that to the 90-degree tacking angles of modern sloops. In addition, even with their towering masts and acres of sail, square-riggers lacked the momentum to complete a tack before stopping dead in the water. As a result, they needed to be cajoled through a tack by various means, including backwinding the jib and other sails up in the bow and overtrimming the fore-and-aft-rigged spanker in the stern—that is, trimming it to windward of the ship's centerline. More often than not, the ships would even start drifting backward, with the rudder hard over to pull the stern around until the bow was pointed in the right direction. The process could take 5 or even 10 minutes, assuming everything went as planned—not counting all the adjusting and tweaking that had to be done afterward to get all those sails drawing efficiently again!

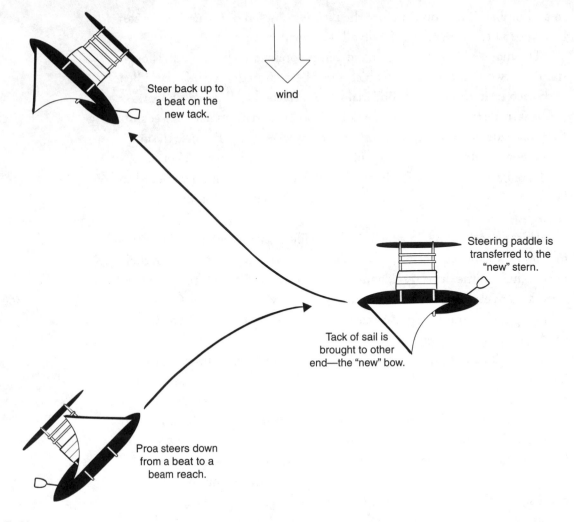

Steer back up to
a beat on the
new tack.

wind

Steering paddle is
transferred to the
"new" stern.

Tack of sail is
brought to other
end—the "new" bow.

Proa steers down
from a beat to a
beam reach.

Tacking a proa.

In many situations—such as storm seas that would quickly stop the ship in its tracks—tacking a big square-rigged vessel became physically impossible. Instead, their captains would *wear ship*, which meant steering down from a beat to a run, then jibing around to a broad reach on the other tack. Once that was done, the helmsman could steer back up through a beam reach and close reach until the ship was once again close-hauled on its new tack. With all sail set, this maneuver would have been something to see, but it wasn't an efficient way to make progress to windward.

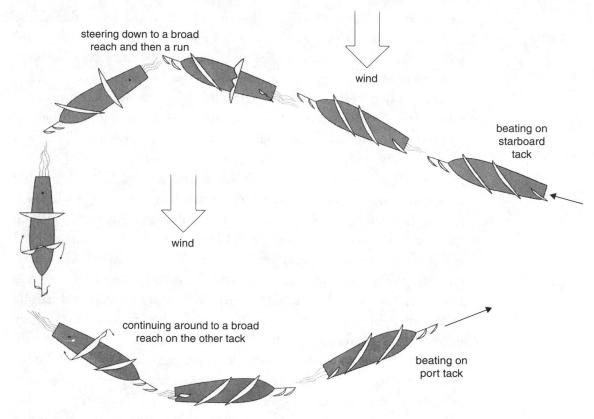

steering down to a broad
reach and then a run

wind

beating on
starboard
tack

wind

continuing around to a broad
reach on the other tack

beating on
port tack

A seagull's eye view of a three-masted bark wearing ship.

Jibing

In contrast with pretty much everything else, jibing is one maneuver that can be trickier today than it was in the past. Jibing from one tack to another on a square-rigged vessel is nearly effortless, since on a run the yards are already squared to the wind. Jibing a fore-and-aft-rigged vessel, on the other hand, requires swinging the main boom from all the way out on one tack to all the way out on the other—nearly 180 degrees. On a small boat in light conditions this task isn't especially daunting, but aboard a larger boat in a strong breeze, that big, heavy boom swinging overhead is a force to be reckoned with. It's vital that the crew restrain that force by first hauling in the sail with the mainsheet as the boat starts its turn. Once again, the skipper needs to make his or her intentions clear by calling out, "Prepare to jibe!," and then, "Jibing!," so that everyone will be prepared.

The crew then eases around the boom and sail to the other side as the boat steers onto its new heading. Only by keeping the rig under control will you be able to avoid unwelcome excitement, possibly even breaking equipment or causing injury. An uncontrolled jibe in a small boat in heavy air can easily cause a capsize. Fortunately, jibing the headsail is substantially easier. Simply ease it out as the boat steers down to a run. Then, as it collapses to the centerline, take in on the other sheet. Once the turn is complete, trim in for your new heading.

I recall one unplanned jibe aboard a sloop-rigged C&C 41 during a race on Puget Sound that drove this point home in a way I will *never* forget. A black squall was rushing up from astern, but we decided to keep up all sail—including a beautiful and extremely large white-and-red spinnaker—hoping we could carry it to the turning mark before things got ugly. As the seconds ticked away, the storm's leading edge overtook boat after boat behind us, heeling them over, blowing out sails, and causing spectacular jibes left and right. Just as we were about to round the turning mark, our luck ran out. Boom! The wind hit us like a damp, icy wall. Instantly the boat heeled over onto its beam ends, its mast nearly parallel with the water. At the same time we slewed around, completely out of control, until we found ourselves sailing a new tack. Instantly, the main jibed itself with the entire force of the storm behind it. One moment it was fully extended against the port-side spreaders, and the next it was fully extended to starboard. The speed with which it swung over the cockpit was incredible, rivaled only by the crash as it fetched up against the mainsheet. Anyone unlucky enough to have had his head at boom height during that jibe would not have survived.

It was for this very reason that deep-sea sailing ships continued to carry square sails well into the twentieth century, rather than switching to more efficient fore-and-aft schooner rigs. The prospect of having to jibe a schooner with two, three, four, or even more big booms was enough to give even the staunchest windjammer captain pause for thought.

For this same reason, Sir Chay Blyth's Global Challenge fleet always sails from east to west around Cape Horn and the Cape of Good Hope, *against* rather than with the prevailing winds in the Roaring Forties. The Global Challenge boats are crewed by paying amateurs, and it's safer, albeit slower and more physically punishing, for these nonprofessionals to sail to windward than to try to control a 70-foot racing boat careering downwind

Going Around the World the Hard Way

One of the reasons Sir Chay Blyth's Global Challenge fleet sails from east to west—against rather than with the prevailing winds in the Roaring Forties—is that it is safer for the nonprofessionals making up the race's crews to sail to windward rather than to try to control a 70-foot racing boat careering downwind through near-hurricane blasts and mountainous seas. An uncontrolled jibe in such conditions could easily prove fatal to a boat and its crew.

through near-hurricane blasts and mountainous seas. An uncontrolled jibe in such conditions could easily prove fatal to a boat and its crew.

Zigzagging to Glory

The other advantage of tacking is that it allows you to switch from one tack to the other without losing any ground to windward. If you're on a deep-sea voyage covering thousands of miles, executing a big loop to leeward during a rare jibe is no great loss. But when you're sailing up a narrow channel against the wind or trying to return to a snug harbor in an engineless boat at the end of the day, tacking rather than jibing can make the difference between getting where you're going and having to accept a tow.

For me, navigating a zigzag course directly to windward—into the eye of the wind (or into its teeth, if the wind is strong)—is the ultimate expression of competent sailing. Few things are more satisfying than throwing in a series of smart, well-executed tacks as you make your way toward an upwind destination—whether it be a racing mark, a permanent navigation buoy, or the end of a harbor breakwall. It takes skill, smarts, and perseverance, not to mention, in some cases, a good deal of hard work. Granted, it would be a lot easier just to fire up the engine, but what's the hurry? What could possibly be better than the challenge before you? No matter how many times you've done it, a well-executed sail to windward confers a feeling of accomplishment that simply can't be beat.

HOW TO SEE THE WIND

3

Observing What You Can't See, Divining What You Can't Know

ONE OF THE TRULY magical—and vexing—things about sailing is that your progress is wholly dependent on something that is both invisible and notoriously fickle. Deepwater cruisers rave about the steady, reliable trade winds of the tropics, and for good reason. A breeze that never—or at least rarely—lets you down is undoubtedly one of the prerequisites of a sailing heaven.

Luckily for those of us who don't happen to be passagemaking in the Caribbean, there are a number of ways to figure out which way the wind is blowing. This is true both of the wind around your boat and the wind farther away, on the horizon and beyond. The way some old salts can anticipate what the wind is going to do may seem utterly incredible, but don't be fooled. It isn't magic, just a matter of opening your eyes. The wind itself may be invisible, but there are signs everywhere letting you know what it's up to. You just have to know what to look for. As Sherlock Holmes admonished poor, befuddled Doctor Watson in *A Scandal in Bohemia*, "You see, but you do not observe. The distinction is clear."

What to Look For

First and foremost, sailboats themselves are excellent wind indicators. By looking at the way another boat's sails are trimmed, you can infer the wind direction in its immediate vicinity. By paying attention to its angle of heel, you can infer the wind's strength. Many racing sailors will actually use their boats like giant wind vanes in the last couple of minutes before a race. While sailing along the starting line—which is generally delineated by a fixed buoy at one end and the anchored race committee boat at the other—they will round up so that the sails are flapping and blowing directly aft, at the same time noting their compass heading. The result is a precise indication of true wind direction—although it comes at a price, given that all that flapping and banging can quickly damage today's stiff, high-performance sailcloth.

Watching the way another boat has its sails trimmed allows you to infer the wind direction in its area. You can also deduce wind strength by watching the other boat's angle of heel. (Stephen Gross)

Like angle of sail, a sense of wind direction eventually becomes almost instinctive.

Sailboats are also generally equipped with various onboard wind indicators, making it possible to gauge the wind at a moment's notice. The simplest of these are nothing more than a couple of pieces of yarn or strips of orange nylon cloth attached to the port and starboard shrouds. Tied, taped, or clipped a few feet above the deck, these *telltales* can easily be seen by the helmsman and crew no matter what the angle of sail or heel.

Most midsize and large boats also carry a masthead wind indicator—basically an arrow that points into the wind and is often called a Windex after the most popular brand—while some dinghy sailors will attach an indicator on a small bracket sticking out in front of the mast. High-performance catamaran sailors often carry a small wind indicator on the bridle that spans the two hulls forward and anchors the forestay.

Of course, many of today's racing boats and even cruisers also carry sophisticated electronic instruments that sense wind velocity and direction to within a single degree. Unless you're trying to wring out the last fraction of a knot on the race course, however, this kind of data is of dubious value. Many sailors—myself included—believe that only by keeping things simple can one truly master the art of sailing. Many smokers, for example, have claimed that lighting up can be a huge help in identifying what a light breeze is up to (not that I recommend taking up smoking for the sake of boat speed). Similarly, I once saw a beautiful Sydney 41 racing sloop named *Scout* with what appeared to be a long, tapered pheasant's tail feather mounted a few feet over the transom. According to *Scout*'s skipper, it helped him determine the correct jibe angles when sailing downwind.

Then again, if you're feeling adventurous, why not try sailing without any wind indicator at all? Again, your entire boat is a wind indicator. Granted, it's a wind indicator that works best when your sails are trimmed correctly and you're underway, but isn't that the point of the exercise?

When I was a kid, we were forever losing our shroud telltales or breaking the masthead indicator on my family's sturdy old Ensign. Come race day we'd be sure to deploy a telltale or two, but sailing by the seat of one's pants was *de rigueur* for daysailing.

It was the same with *Goose*, my 19-foot Lightning. She was old, and since I didn't intend to race her, I never bothered rigging telltales. I'm glad I didn't, because it made me a more intuitive sailor. Like angle of sail, a sense of wind direction eventually becomes almost instinctive. You don't need to look at a bit of yarn or a plastic arrow to know that the wind is coming from, say, slightly over your shoulder as you're steering a broad reach. You don't need electronics to sense that you're losing power as you head up a few degrees and that you need to either head back down or sheet in a bit.

Think of sailing without a wind indicator as a way of developing your muscle memory.

Young golfers develop muscle memory. They can leave the game for years and come back to it with an uncanny, effortless swing still intact. Muscle memory is harder for adult learners to acquire—we tend to overthink things—but golf pros have developed exercises that help. Think of sailing without a wind indicator as a way of developing your muscle memory. *Goose* never sported a single Windex, streamer, or telltale the entire time I owned her, and I never once rued their absence.

Take a Look Around

We've figured out how to keep track of the wind in our immediate vicinity. Now let's broaden our wind sense a little by figuring out what it's doing a little farther away. This question is far from academic. Knowing what the wind is doing elsewhere can give sailors valuable insights into the conditions they themselves might soon be experiencing.

Fortunately, like boats themselves, the sailing environment is replete with clues, especially near shore, where 99 percent of us do 99 percent of our sailing. Smokestacks, flagpoles, leafy trees, and other indicators dot all but the most featureless of shorelines. Urban shorelines in particular often yield a wealth of wind data. The same goes for many marinas and harbors.

Growing up in Cleveland and living as an adult in Milwaukee and Chicago, I have spent countless hours sailing along shorelines replete with wind indicators large and small. One of my favorites in Milwaukee was a beachfront flagpole immediately north of the Milwaukee Community Sailing Center and the Milwaukee Yacht Club. Perched on a spit that jutted a good 30 or 40 yards into Lake Michigan, it could always be relied on to provide a forecast of what to expect when sailing back toward the marina.

At the other end of the harbor were the flagpoles of the South Shore Yacht Club and the Coast Guard station. Better still, looming over the mouth of the Milwaukee River, smack-dab in the middle of the city, was a towering smokestack that continually belched clouds of gas and steam. The thing probably wasn't doing the regional air quality any favors, but it worked wonderfully as a wind indicator.

What Are the Neighbors Up To?

Yet another way to figure out what the wind is up to is to check out other sailboats in the area. Again, sailboats are natural-born wind indicators, so pay attention to what they have to say.

Do boats to windward of you seem to be having an easier time keeping their sails full in drifting conditions? A new breeze will often fill in to windward and then spread downwind, so there's a good chance a little wind will soon be coming your way. Similarly, if a boat to windward is on its ear, you may want to be ready to ease out your mainsheet. If a boat ahead seems to have sailed into a "hole," with its sails hanging limp, you would be well advised to give his inadvertent parking lot a wide berth.

I have always taken an almost perverse pleasure in figuring out what the wind is doing to other boats, especially when I'm racing. Once I was sailing on Green Bay on a friend's Rogers 26, and we were quite comfortably dead last as we rounded Chambers Island, midway through the annual 100 Miler race. Luckily, as the sun started to go down, the wind sank with it, and in no time a good part of the fleet had sailed under spinnaker right into a big hole alongside the Michigan shore. By staying clear and aiming for those boats that still had a little pressure in their sails, we managed to keep our spinnaker drawing and in no time found ourselves back in the middle of things.

A little later, a new breeze having filled in from the southwest, the fleet was barreling along under spinnaker on a broad reach. Our crew was spent at the end of a long day of sailing, but I happened to notice that some of the larger boats ahead were starting to take down their spinnakers and managed to nag everybody into getting our own jib up on deck and ready to hoist, just in case. A few minutes later the wind clocked around some 30 degrees, and we were suddenly on a close reach, with the spinnaker thrashing like a wild animal in the gathering darkness. I hate to think how things might have gone if we hadn't been prepared. As it was, we soon had the jib up and the spinnaker down. In no time we were back in the groove and sailing toward a very satisfying podium finish.

What's the Water Doing?

Of course, flagpoles, smokestacks, and other sailboats can be few and far between along the desolate shores of, say, Patagonia. Still, there is an abundance of wind indicators to be found in nature, including some as good as or even better than those that are manmade.

Waves, for example, being the direct result of wind acting on water, are a natural for figuring out what the weather is doing. In a glassy calm, the first few puffs of a new wind will ruffle the surface with tiny ripples that will be visible as distinct dark patches from a quarter mile or even farther away. As the wind builds, gusts or puffs will be visible as cat's-paws—small, dark patches of water that stand out from larger background waves. In especially gusty conditions, these windy patches may include bits of spray as the countless tiny rivulets break over themselves like tiny whitecaps. You may also see feathery little tendrils of wind spreading out like a fan across the water, making it clear how cat's-paws get their name.

Clouds too can offer insights into what the wind may be up to in the next few minutes. You will often find some wind blowing near or under the edges of puffy, fair-weather cumulus clouds, although the breeze may be a bit light under the cloud's center. On the downside, it's nearly impossible to know the direction of this new wind. But once you've had a taste of what the wind is doing around one cloud, you can generally assume that wind behavior around other clouds in the area will be the same. Of course, if you see a big, black thunderhead coming your way or if the horizon has suddenly been blotted out by rain, that too should tell you something!

Watch Out for the Tree

When thinking about the wind and how it's going to affect your boat, also bear in mind how the wind behaves in the presence of other physical objects. Immediately to leeward of a cliff, building, tree, or another sailboat, for example, there will be a *wind shadow* of disturbed, turbulent air. This shadow can be up to ten times the height of the object itself. At its extreme tip, this shadow will comprise only a small area of slightly turbulent air. Immediately to leeward of the object, however, you will likely find the wind so effectively blocked that your boat slows almost to a standstill.

The sneaky effect of the land or some other physical object can work in reverse as well. Many is the sailor who has set out from a protected harbor, expecting an easy daysail, only to find that things are a lot more boisterous on the open water. This was driven home to me one time when I was chartering a 38-foot full-keeled Island Packet cutter out of Red Hook Harbor on St. Thomas, in the U.S. Virgin Islands. We'd spent the morning loading provisions in sweltering heat, and I fully expected to be motoring through a drifter once we cast off lines. As soon as we left the shelter of the surrounding hills, however, we found ourselves contending with a powerful 20-knot trade wind that had obviously been roiling the water of Pillsbury Sound for some time. Island Packet builds solid, seaworthy boats, to put it mildly, but we still found ourselves reefing down to keep things comfortable.

Another characteristic of fixed objects is that they can cause a shift in wind direction. Islands or headlands will cause the wind to bend as it works its way around. Similarly, if a wind is blowing at a slight angle to a shoreline, it will change direction as it approaches land to blow parallel with the shore, especially a shore marked by cliffs or bluffs. Even to windward of a cliff or steep-sided manmade object you need to be on your guard. As the wind approaches, it will often lift off the water, leaving a narrow dead zone to windward of the obstacle.

Yet another thing to be aware of is the way wind funnels through constricted areas, changing direction slightly and picking up speed in the process. A classic example of this *venturi effect* is the Columbia River Gorge in the Pacific Northwest. The steep bluffs on either side of the river accelerate cool

The land can influence wind direction in a number of ways. For example, a breeze will bend around a headland (left), and a wind nearly parallel to the land will often become even more parallel.

air descending from the mountains to a powerful 30 knots or more, making that part of the river a mecca for daredevil sailboarders. Another example is storied Cape Horn, at the southern tip of South America. Jutting into the Southern Ocean at 56° south, it bends and accelerates the already powerful west winds of the Roaring Forties and Furious Fifties.

My own most dramatic encounter with a natural wind tunnel came, oddly enough, on an otherwise benign spring day at the beginning of a Sunday daysail on Milwaukee Harbor. I had just finished restoring the *Goose*, my old 19-foot Lightning, and was taking her out with my wife, Shelly, and our dog, Lucy, on her maiden voyage. The wind was more or less out of the south at about 10 knots, gusting ever so slightly, as we started tacking out through the narrow cut that connects the basin to the main harbor. Suddenly, as we came out from behind the little isthmus, or mole, that marks one side of the cut, we were hit by a completely unexpected blast of wind that knocked the boat on its ear. In an instant, water was spilling over the leeward side into the cockpit while I tried to release the jammed mainsheet and Shelly hiked out in a desperate effort to get the boat back on its feet. Poor Lucy cowered in the cockpit, no doubt wondering what in the world she had done to deserve such a fate. For a few sick moments I was certain we were going to capsize then and there, in the middle of the channel. Needless to say, the prospect was not a happy one, especially given the close proximity of a half-dozen power cruisers, all in a hurry to get onto or off Lake Michigan.

Luckily the boat popped upright as quickly as it had gone over, and I was able to take stock and figure out what had happened. Basically, we'd been the victims of a gust that had funneled between the mole and the steep, six-foot-high breakwall that forms the other side of the channel, a mere 70 feet away. In fact, this breakwall serves as a kind of extension of the main breakwall for the outer harbor, which runs due south-southwest about a mile before coming to an end at the lighthouse marking the mouth of the Milwaukee River. Not only that, the mole, in addition to rising about 10 feet above lake level, sports a line of 30- to 40-foot trees. I can just imagine that southerly breeze running smoothly up the harbor and then getting mashed between the breakwall and the mole. In the blink of an eye, all those previously placid air molecules started fighting for room to get through, and the wind picked up speed. Before we could say "Giovanni Battista Venturi," Shelly, Lucy, and I found ourselves hanging on for dear life by our claws and fingernails.

The Sweetest Breeze

Finally, it's important to be aware of a phenomenon called the *sea breeze*. This local breeze springs up on sunny days as the land heats up and the air above it becomes less dense and begins rising. As it does so, the air over the cold water—which remains cooler and denser—flows in to take its place. The resulting wind can be surprisingly strong, especially if it's flowing in the same direction as the *gradient wind*—the wind already in place as a result of a regional weather system.

Often a sea breeze will get started in the late morning or early afternoon. When it does so, it never fails to lift my spirits, whether I'm on the water or just lazing on shore. On calm days it will first be apparent in the form of a few dark patches maybe a half mile offshore. As the breeze builds, those patches will spread out both toward and away from land. Later, as the sun goes down and the land cools off, the sea breeze will disappear, resulting in those calm, peaceful evenings that form the backdrop of so many summer memories.

Sometimes the process will reverse itself later in the night, as the land cools off faster than the nearby water. Now the warmer air over the water is muscled aloft by cooler air from the land that flows out to take its place. The resulting *land breeze*, which blows away from the shore and toward the open water, is generally not as strong as the sea breeze during the day, but it can still be significant.

Years ago, during the Hook Race from Racine, Wisconsin, to Sturgeon Bay, I was aboard a flashy 41-foot IMS racer that mistakenly chose to go straight up the middle of Lake Michigan. The first night out we logged a pathetic 10 miles. It took us more than an hour to drift close enough to a strange floating object to identify it as a blowup toy shaped like a killer whale. Weird!

Twenty-four hours later, as the fleet began to converge on the bell buoy marking the approach to "Death's Door" channel at the end of Door County peninsula, the first boat we happened upon was a 30-foot Catalina—about a mile ahead of us. By this time a new weather system had come in and we went thundering by under spinnaker. But the damage had been done. Given our respective handicap ratings, the Catalina's time allowance would put us hopelessly behind her in the standings. Later, we found out that while we had spent the previous night wallowing beyond the loom of the land, the Catalina had hugged the shore, making its way north with the help of a light but steady land breeze.

A Windy State of Mind

Now it's time to put all those wind indicators and principles of wind behavior to work as we develop a wind sense, just like the intuitive feel those old-time sailors have. Like so much in life that's worth having, all it takes is a little practice.

Luckily, wind and weather are things you can observe as easily on land as afloat. Granted, the only way you're going to learn how a particular boat responds to different winds is to get out on the water, but when it comes to studying the weather for the weather's sake, the entire world is your laboratory.

Get in the habit of looking around and noting what the wind is doing. Look for flagpoles, wind vanes, and wind socks. Study how trees behave in various weather conditions. When you're out walking the dog, note how the wind changes as you emerge from behind the lees of big and little buildings.

Another exercise I find particularly challenging is to determine the force of the wind as defined by a scale created by Admiral Sir Francis Beaufort in the early 1800s. Beaufort's scale includes a dozen categories from a Force 0 calm to a Force 12 hurricane, the latter being described as "that which no canvas could withstand." Each force level is characterized by the behaviors of flags, tree limbs, and waves. In Force 3 conditions, for example, when you have 7 to 10 knots of wind, flags will occasionally extend in the breeze, the water develops small glassy waves, and leaves and twigs are in constant motion. Observations like these are a wonderful way to train the mind, and there's nothing cooler than being able to say things like, "We had Force 5 conditions all afternoon!" at the end of a day of sailing.

If you live near the shore, get in the habit of scanning the water to see what's happening. Try to identify where the wind is and how hard it's blowing. If you have time, study the water for a while to see how conditions change. If you suspect an incipient sea breeze, try to picture the air rising up from the warming land around you as well as the cooler air over the water sliding in to take its place. If you notice a dead spot to leeward of a small island or find yourself in a lee behind some building on a windy day, try to picture how the air is flowing around the obstruction.

Like angle of sail, the wind—its strength, its direction, the way it's trending—should always be in the back of a sailor's mind.

Like angle of sail, the wind—its strength, its direction, the way it's trending—should always be in the back of a sailor's mind. Keeping tabs on what's happening, searching for wind indicators like flags, smokestacks, and other boats, and integrating this information into the big picture eventually becomes almost instinctive. Take a walk through any marina and you will see at least a couple of sailors watching the water and any boats that might be under sail out there. They may have any one of a hundred other things on their mind. They may not even be thinking about sailing. But at that moment, you can bet that at some level, they're also downloading wind data. It's something sailors do as naturally as breathing.

CATCHING THE WIND

Why Sails Are More Complex Than Airplane Wings

TO THE UNINITIATED sails are little more than great, oversized bed sheets. But sailors know nothing could be further from the truth. Sails do the things they do because they incorporate a number of carefully designed and constructed curves. The results—in appearance as well as performance—are nothing less than magical. Whether on a full-rigged ship, a schooner, a dinghy, an Arab dhow, or a racing sloop, sails are perhaps the ultimate expression of form following function.

The reason sails are curved is that *both* sides of a sail play a role in propelling a boat through the water, especially when sailing on a close reach or close-hauled. It would seem intuitively obvious that sails work because the wind pushes against them, but the reality is a good deal more complicated—and interesting.

At the heart of a sail's alchemy is something called Bernoulli's principle, named in honor of its discoverer, the eighteenth-century Swiss statistician and physicist Daniel Bernoulli. Among other things, what Bernoulli's principle says is that air pressure falls as air speed increases. At first blush this may not seem like much, but it has game-changing implications. A correctly set and trimmed sail causes air flow to speed up over its leeward surface, which creates an area of low air pressure. At the same time, air slows down over the sail's windward surface, creating a corresponding high-pressure area. Because nature abhors a vacuum, the air in the high-pressure region seeks to fill in the low-pressure side, and the resultant pressure against the sail material creates the force known as *lift* that propels a sailboat through the water.

How exactly a sail—or any other wing-shaped foil—produces this pressure differential has long been a subject of scientific research and debate. The popular simplification used to be that air accelerates over the leeward side because it has to travel a longer distance than the airflow to windward to reach the sail's trailing edge. But the reality, as clarified in the 1970s by sailor and aeronautical engineer Arvel Gentry, is far more complex.

To begin with, when air—or any fluid for that matter—begins to pass over a foil positioned at an angle to its flow, something called a *starting vortex* forms at the foil's trailing edge. This swirl of air, which results from the air on the windward side trying to curl around the trailing edge (in a sail's case, the *leech*) and onto the leeward surface, acts like a little cog, creating a so-called *circulation field* of air, in which the air seeks to flow against the prevailing flow on the windward side of the sail and with the prevailing flow to leeward.

Of course, air cannot actually move in a direction opposite the wind flowing over the sail's windward side, nor can the starting vortex avoid being blown aft. Once established, however, the circulation field *can* impede or promote the velocity of the airflow over the sail, causing it to slow down as it flows over the windward side and speed up to leeward. It also serves to push some of the air that would otherwise flow along the windward side up and around the *luff* (the leading edge) and onto the leeward side in a phenomenon known as *upwash*. The result? Air molecules

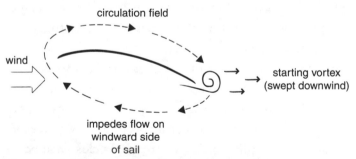

The swirl of air known as the *starting vortex* acts like a little cog, creating a circulation field around the entire foil, or sail.

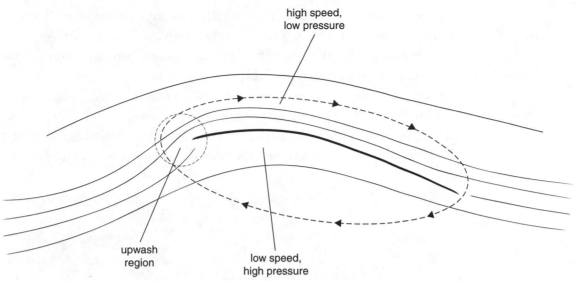

high speed,
low pressure

upwash
region

low speed,
high pressure

The circulation field causes an upwash of air to flow around the leading edge of the sail to the leeward side.

curling up and over the luff to the leeward side of the sail have to travel that much farther than their counterparts to windward and are helped along their way by the circulation field. This causes the aforementioned drop in air pressure relative to the slower-moving air molecules to windward, which have less sail area to traverse and are impeded by the circulation field. *Voila!* You get a pressure differential, with a high-pressure region to windward and a low-pressure region to leeward. Before you know it, you're on the move.

If there is a downside to this picture, it's that even in the best of cases there is a lot more lateral force pushing you sideways than there is force pushing you forward. That's where your boat's keel and rudder come in.

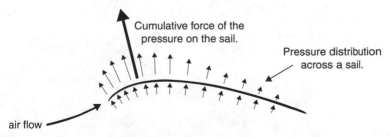

Cumulative force of the pressure on the sail.

Pressure distribution across a sail.

air flow

The small vector arrows in the diagram show the amount of force being applied at various points along the sail. The large arrow represents the cumulative effect of the smaller arrows. Even in the best cases, there is a lot more lateral force being generated by the sail than force in the direction you want to go. That's where keels and rudders come in: they oppose this lateral force, making it possible for a boat to travel to windward.

By keeping you on course and resisting that sideways motion, they allow you to make progress in the very direction from which the wind is blowing.

Of course, there's more to it than that. The theoretical basis of starting vortexes and circulation fields involves some hefty analyses assisted by computer modeling. For those interested in more detail, I recommend reading C. A. Marchaj's *Aero-Hydrodynamics of Sailing*. This big, expensive, hard-to-find tome nevertheless yields its secrets with admirable clarity to a layman willing to devote some time and effort. Another excellent place to

Next time you are out sailing, try to visualize the aerodynamic phenomenon taking place overhead. Imagine the air flow over your sail, or sails, and how it is affected by the circulation field. (Erik Skallerup and Domenic Mosqueira/YachtShots, BVI)

go is Mr. Gentry's website, www.arvelgentry.com, which includes a number of his articles on the subject. Still, the above summary covers the basics.

Note that a slight angle of sail to wind is critical. All other things being equal, the greater this *angle of attack* (as it is called), the greater the resulting windward-leeward pressure differential, and thus the more lift the sail will generate. Also note that, for a sail to generate this lift, it's vital that the air flows smoothly along its entire surface—i.e., that the flow remain attached and *laminar*. If the flow becomes turbulent and unattached, the circulation system breaks down. Unfortunately, this is exactly what happens if you overdo your angle of attack. The best tactic, then, is to find that ideal happy medium.

Finally, bear in mind that when talking about lift, we are talking about sailing close-hauled or on a close reach. When you sail on a broad reach or run, the angle of attack is such that turbulence on the sail's leeward side is a fact of life. The goal offwind, therefore, is simply to project as much sail area as possible—and Bernoulli be damned! Granted, there are still *some* lift forces at work, especially on a highly curved sail like a spinnaker, but they don't require laminar flow along the length of the sail. Sailing on a run or broad reach does not just feel fundamentally different, it truly is fundamentally different than sailing to windward.

Do You Feel a Draft?

In describing a sail's curvature, sailors will often refer to its *draft*. This term can be a bit confusing because it's used in reference to two similar but slightly different concepts. On the one hand, draft can refer to the fore-and-aft curve of the sail between its luff and leech. Imagine looking up at the mainsail from beneath the main boom. Let your eyes move back and forth across the sail. In doing so you're tracing its draft—its curve, camber, or belly. (Some sails have horizontal *draft stripes*, or sometimes just a line of stitching in a contrasting color, to make this curvature more apparent.) On the other hand, draft can refer more specifically to the perpendicular distance from the deepest part of this fore-and-aft curve to the *chord*, an imaginary straight line running from luff to leech. In this latter usage, draft is also referred to as depth.

Fortunately, it's usually pretty easy to tell from context which meaning of draft a sailor is talking about. For example, if a sailor says a particular sail needs more or less draft, he or she is likely talking about the sail's depth of curvature. If, on the other hand, someone says, "We need to do something about the draft," especially in the context of a sailboat race that isn't going well, it's safe to say that the entire sail is out of whack.

Draft depth is important to performance because, by bending the airflow, it helps create lift, or power.

Draft depth is important to performance because, by bending the airflow, it helps create lift, or power. A deeper sail is a more powerful sail. Draft is often described as a percentage of chord length. For example, a fairly full, or deep, mainsail is one with a draft depth that's 15 percent of chord length. A 10 percent draft is pretty shallow, or flat. A 12 percent draft is flat for a jib, while 20 percent is full.

While it's true that power is generally a good thing, in an especially light breeze the air becomes viscous in its behavior—like maple syrup on a frosty March morning—and can have trouble negotiating a deep curve. In a ghosting breeze, therefore, it often pays to flatten your sail (as described below) to prevent separation. A flat sail is also good when it really starts to blow, because it allows you to slough off excess power—i.e., to depower the rig—in the interest of reducing your heel angle. With this in mind, the dedicated storm sails carried by offshore racers and cruisers are made as flat as boards. In moderate conditions, on the other hand, the more power the better. A full, powerful draft can also help power a boat through a chop.

In addition to the amount of draft in a sail, another big determinant of sail performance is the fore-and-aft location of the point of maximum draft. This location is important for two reasons. First, by defining the overall shape of the sail, it dictates the cumulative direction of the lift generated

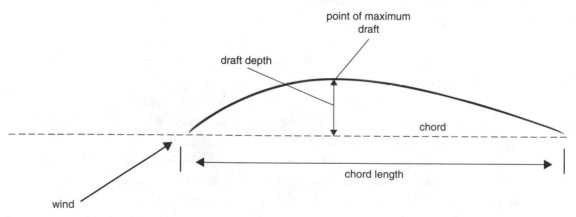

Parameters used to describe the curvature, or draft, of a sail.

by the sail. Second, the position of maximum draft affects the sail's leading edge and its pointing ability.

The first consideration is fairly straightforward. Basically, you want the point of maximum curvature well forward because this is where air speed increases most dramatically to leeward, generating the most lift force. Moving the draft forward will angle this force closer to the direction you want to go.

To understand the second aspect of draft location, imagine two sails with the same amount of draft differently distributed. One carries its maximum draft well forward, with its leading edge curving dramatically to leeward in order to create the requisite bulge. With this configuration, you will either have to sheet the sail much closer to the centerline to keep it from backwinding or sail a slightly wider angle off the wind. On the plus side, that flat run aft in the area of the leech will help keep the airflow attached, even in choppy conditions.

A sail with its draft well aft, on the other hand, has the luff forming a more acute angle with the boom, which means the sail no longer has to be pulled in quite so close to keep it from backwinding. Equally important, when the boom is pulled to the centerline—as it often is when beating—the

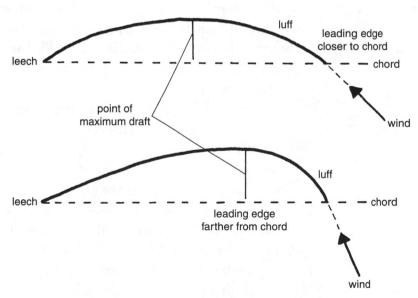

Draft location affects both the leading-edge angle and the amount of curvature in the area of the leech. Having the draft well forward provides power for punching through chop. Having the draft farther aft enhances pointing ability.

boat will be able to sail closer to the wind, which is to say that its pointing ability will be improved. On the downside, the additional curvature aft may cause airflow to separate, or stall, over the aft portion of the sail. It will also direct more of the sail's lift to leeward, where it will increase heeling angle and leeway more than forward motion.

The key, then, is a happy medium, an optimal balance between lift and pointing ability. In practice, this means positioning the point of maximum draft about 45 to 50 percent of the luff-to-leech distance aft of the leading edge in most mainsails, and 35 to 40 percent of the way aft in most jibs. Experience has shown that this compromise provides the best mix of pointing ability and lift. Aboard boats that don't have headsails—catboats, small inland scows, and high-performance dinghies, like Finns and Lasers—the mainsail draft should be about 35 to 40 percent of the way aft, the same as a jib.

Adjusting the Draft

So where does all this draft come from in the first place? The answer is that it's built into the sail by the sailmaker. The first thing a sailmaker asks any new customer is what kind of sailing he or she plans to do, in part to figure out how much curve to build into the sail. A sail for daysailing wants enough draft to provide adequate power in moderate conditions—say, 10 to 20 knots of breeze. A sail for high-level racing, on the other hand, may require a much shallower draft to provide enhanced pointing ability during the start and on a beat. Storm sails need a draft that is flatter still. The last thing you need when you're reefed down in a gale is more power!

In addition, sails come equipped with a number of control lines that can be used to optimize their shape underway. The *outhaul*, for example, can be used to control the amount of draft in the lower third of the mainsail. Tightening the outhaul pulls the *clew*—the lowest point of the leech—closer to the end of the boom. This, in turn, stretches the sailcloth along the *foot*, or lower edge of the sail, decreasing its draft.

Similarly, the *halyard*, in addition to raising and holding up a sail, can be used to adjust the fore-and-aft location of the maximum draft.

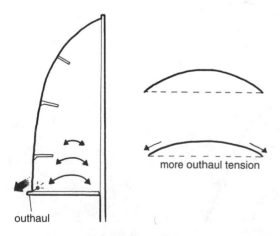

more outhaul tension

outhaul

Foot tension, which is controlled by the outhaul, flattens the lower part of the sail by increasing the tension along the foot of the sail.

Tightening the halyard stretches the sail's luff, which pulls the material immediately behind it forward to take its place, pulling the draft forward with it.

Many racing boats carry a little device called a *cunningham* so that their crews can stretch or slacken the luff without having to burn calories cranking the halyard. Named for its inventor, Briggs Swift Cunningham—who skippered the 12-meter *Columbia* to victory against the British yacht *Sceptre* in the 1958 America's Cup—it generally consists of a block and tackle attached on one end to the deck and on the other to a grommet a foot or two above the tack of the sail. Underway, the crew simply takes in on the cunningham to induce more luff tension or eases it to

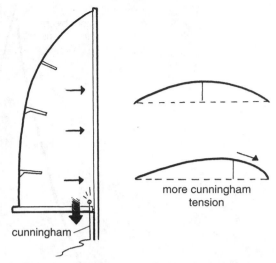

cunningham

more cunningham tension

Luff tension, which is controlled by the halyard or cunningham, pulls the draft forward by stretching, or taking out, any of the extra material in the leading edge of the sail.

relieve tension. Aboard smaller boats, the tail of the cunningham leads aft to the cockpit so that it can be trimmed without having to go forward. Aboard larger boats, the cunningham is secured to a cam cleat attached to the lower block, so that it's trimmed right there at the base of the mast. Personally, I prefer the latter. It's one more way to make those fellows in the afterguard— the tactician, helmsman, navigator, and anybody else doing all the "thinking" in the aft end of the boat—more dependent on us "deck apes" up front!

Speaking of the pointy end of the boat, you can move the draft in the jib, or foresail, forward or aft much as you do in the main—simply by adjusting halyard or cunningham tension. Adjusting draft depth, on the other hand, is a little different, because you no longer have the luxury of an outhaul. Instead, you have to manipulate the jib-lead angle. You can do this by adjusting the fore-and-aft position of the turning blocks guiding the jibsheets.

To understand how this works, imagine a jibsheet running through a turning block that's mounted well forward on the side deck. Trimming in will exert plenty of downward pull along the leech but relatively little force aft along the foot, which will let the foot bag out to leeward. The result is a lot of draft. Now imagine what happens if that turning block is positioned farther aft. Now when you pull in the sheet, there will be much less downward pull on the leech and a much stronger pull aft along the foot, making the sail much flatter.

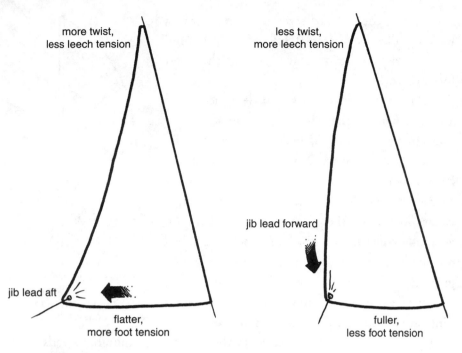

more twist,
less leech tension

less twist,
more leech tension

jib lead forward

jib lead aft

flatter,
more foot tension

fuller,
less foot tension

Adjusting the sheet lead fore and aft changes the overall shape of the headsail. With the jib lead forward, there is more downward force on the leech and less tension along the foot of the sail. The sail will have more curvature, or a greater draft, along the foot of the sail.

It's for this reason that most modern sailboats are equipped with a metal track along each side deck that makes it easy to change the turning block's position. Aboard most smaller boats this is done by hand, lifting up a spring-loaded locking pin and pushing the turning block's slide, or car, forward or aft along the track. Aboard larger boats the crew will generally have the luxury of a block and tackle to haul the car forward, while relying on a shock cord or the force of the sheet itself to force the car aft.

In either case, the tremendous forces involved in heavy air often make these adjustments impossible when the jib is sheeted in. Instead, the crew will either let the sail luff for a few moments or simply adjust the turning block on the lazy jibsheet, the one that isn't in use, so that the draft will be set correctly on the other tack.

Do the Twist

Now that we've taken care of draft, it's time to throw in a bit of a curve, both figuratively and literally—something aptly known as twist.

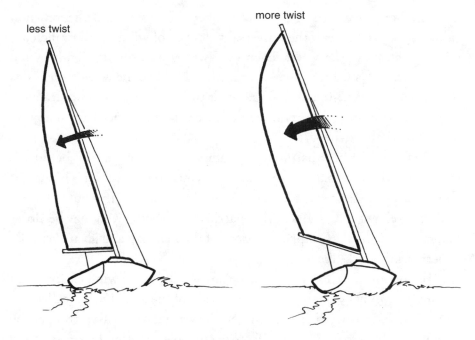

less twist

more twist

Twist refers to the degree to which the leech sags off to leeward. When the angle of the sail's trailing edge is cupped to windward, there is less twist. When the leech is allowed to curve off to leeward, there is more twist.

In discussing jib-lead position we talked about varying the amount of draft in the foot of the sail, but what about changing the shape of the leech? By moving the jib car forward, we not only put more draft in the sail, we also pull the leech downward into a fairly tight—perhaps even cupped— trailing edge. Similarly, when we move the car aft we not only stretch out the foot of the sail, we also substantially reduce the downward force of the jibsheet. When this happens, the aftermost third or so of the sail will relax, flattening out, and the leech will sag to leeward, especially in the area of the uppermost battens. This combination of sagging and flattening is what is referred to as *twist*.

By flattening the upper part of the sail, twist reduces the power generated there. Remember, more curvature equals more power. In a blow, all that power at the upper end of the mast can create some pretty intimidating heeling forces. Adding more twist depowers the sail dramatically, allowing the boat to sail on a much more even keel. Conversely, in light air, reducing twist—bringing the upper leech closer to the boat's centerline—adds power aloft and helps keep the boat moving.

Another reason twist is important is because of a natural phenomenon called the *wind gradient*, the universal tendency of wind speed to increase with height above the water. Even on a windy day, the friction between air and water is such that the air immediately above the water's surface is barely moving. Within a foot or so of altitude the air speeds up dramatically, but it doesn't reach its maximum free-stream velocity until a good 30 feet or so above the water.

This wind gradient has important implications for sail trim because it means that the wind's direction relative to your boat moves aft with height above the deck. Let's say, for example, you're sailing in 15 knots of wind at deck level, with 20 knots at the masthead. Although you may be close-hauled at deck level, the upper portions of the mainsail and jib are actually experiencing a close reach.

The reason for this is that the *apparent wind*—the wind experienced aboard your moving boat—is a combination of the actual wind (called the *true wind*) and the wind created by your forward motion. The stronger the true wind, the less important a factor your boat's motion becomes. Near the top of your mast, therefore, the apparent wind angle will be farther from your bow than it is on deck.

As a result, if your sails are set so that they have a uniform angle of attack from head to foot, it's inevitable that they will be largely out of trim. Shape and trim the lower part of a sail to perfection, and the upper portion will be sheeted too tightly. Trim the upper part of the sail correctly and the lower part won't be sheeted in adequately.

Luckily, thanks to twist, the higher you go, the more the chord of the sail naturally falls off to leeward, creating a changing angle of attack that conveniently matches the wind gradient. Although it might seem a bit obsessive to get worked up about the precise trim of that pointy sliver of sail aloft, it can make a big difference in boat speed. Wind pressure increases with the square of wind speed, because you are not only being affected by air molecules traveling at higher velocities, but a greater number of these high-velocity molecules are passing over your sails. Therefore, if you have 10 knots at deck level and 15 knots at the top batten, you have 50 percent more wind speed, but you have more than *twice* as much wind pressure aloft.

On most jibs, twist is controlled using sheet tension and jib-lead angle. With the mainsail, on the other hand, twist is controlled using the vang and mainsheet. The *vang* is basically a powerful block and tackle (or its hydraulic ram equivalent) running from the base of the mast to a point on the boom a few feet aft of the gooseneck fitting. Tightening the vang pulls the boom down, which tightens the leech and takes out twist. Easing the vang lets the boom rise a little, which loosens the leech and puts twist back into the sail. Similarly, trimming the mainsheet when the boom is close to the boat's centerline—which is the case on a beat or close reach—puts a downward force on the boom, while easing the sheet lets it rise.

In fact, on racing boats and performance cruisers, the mainsheet is regarded primarily as a device for controlling twist, not angle of attack. The latter is controlled by the *main traveler*—an athwartships track with a slide that secures the lower block of the mainsheet tackle. By moving this slide to windward or leeward you move the boom in or out. Only when the boom begins to angle out over the leeward side of the boat on a beam reach does the mainsheet become the sole means of controlling angle of attack. At this point the vang becomes the primary means of controlling

When sailing to windward on racing boats and performance cruisers, the mainsheet is regarded primarily as a device for controlling twist, and the main traveler is used to control angle of attack. (Erik Skallerup and Domenic Mosqueira/YachtShots, BVI)

leech tension. This becomes especially important on a run or broad reach, when pressure in the sailcloth tends to lift the boom skyward. By cranking down on the vang, you pull the boom back down, maximizing boat speed by maximizing the sail area you're projecting to the wind.

All Together Now

We've talked about how a single sail generates lift on a beat or close reach. Now let's talk about what happens when two sails—a jib and a main—work together.

This interaction is another subject about which the sailing community—myself included—formerly held a number of misconceptions. Historically, it was believed that the space, or *slot*, between the jib and main somehow squeezed the air flowing between the two sails, speeding it up and creating an area of low air pressure. This extra-low pressure allowed the two sails to create more lift together than they could independently—the whole, it was thought, was greater than the sum of its parts. Alas, while it's true that the jib-main interaction enhances both speed and pointing ability, we now know, thanks to Mr. Gentry, that this theoretical construct is completely wrong.

The real reason the jib and main create more lift has to do with the meshing of their circulation fields. Together these fields actually slow down the air in the slot rather than speed it up. This works to a sailor's advantage,

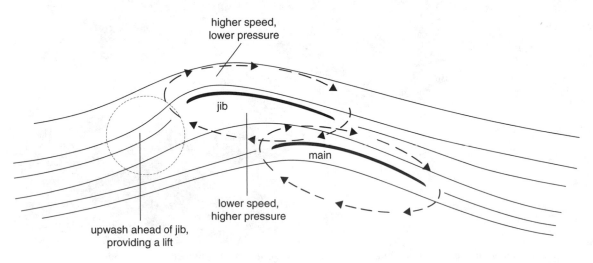

The combined circulation fields of the jib and main allow the jib to point higher and provide more power than it would on its own.

because this slower air and the upwash curling around the leading edge of the main—the mast, basically—serve to increase the upwash effect at the leading edge of the jib. This means you have that much more air speeding up as it curls around the jib luff, which means that much more lift. In addition, this upwash creates a slight change in the direction of the flow in the form of a lift, which means you're able to point higher than you would otherwise. Finally, the air coming off the leech of the jib flows into a high-velocity zone created by the circulation field surrounding the main. This serves to boost the air velocity along the entire leeward side of the headsail, increasing its overall efficiency and power.

More lift and better pointing ability . . . I say, give me a jib and main any day.

5

STEERING WITH YOUR SAILS

And How the Keel and Rudder Lift You to Windward

AMONG MY FONDEST memories afloat is the time my buddy Bob "Overboard" Oberbrunner and I delivered the 33-foot Tartan Ten *Helldiver* to Milwaukee from Sturgeon Bay, Wisconsin, after the 197-mile Hook Race. We were utterly exhausted, and *Helldiver*, being fitted out strictly for racing, was without an autopilot. Luckily, we had great weather—moderate seas and a steady wind out of the west-southwest. Within minutes of clearing the lighthouse at the end of the ship canal, we trimmed sails for a close reach and lashed the tiller. After that we were able to kick back and relax, barely touching a line much of the rest of the day.

The reason we could do this is that a well-designed sailboat will remain on a more-or-less constant heading when its sails and hull are in balance. Not only that, the boat sails better that way—faster and with much less effort from the person at the helm. Old-time square-riggers didn't carry all those triangular staysails, jibs, and flying jibs on their bowsprits simply to create more sail area. They did so because hoisting or dousing those relatively small sails way up front allowed them

The bark rig. (Christine Erikson)

to fine-tune their balance. The same was true of the spanker and other small fore-and-aft sails carried way aft on the mizzenmast. In fact, controlling the caravels, frigates, full-rigged ships, barks, pinks, and snows of old—with their relatively minuscule and inefficient rudders—would have been difficult or even impossible without the little sails in their ends.

Conversely, when a rig and hull are out of balance the rudder can be rendered useless, especially in heavy weather. Alas, I remember another time aboard a Tartan Ten—no, it wasn't *Helldiver*—when the wind was blowing absolute stink and we were trying to figure out the best route through a crowded mark rounding. It was the first race of the season, and the crew was still working out the kinks after a long, cold winter. Without warning the skipper announced that he wanted to "flop over onto port tack" and duck behind a competitor just a couple of boat lengths to windward. With that the helm went down and we began spinning around. Unfortunately, the mainsail trimmer kept the sail strapped in on the new tack instead of easing it out. Instantly the boat was on its ear, making it impossible for the skipper to steer astern of our now *very* close competition. Before anyone could react, we T-boned the other boat just aft of its portside shrouds. Luckily we hadn't yet picked up much speed, so the physical damage was minimal. Our wounded pride was another matter entirely.

Getting Centered

The key to balancing a boat lies in understanding the related concepts of center of effort and center of lateral resistance.

The *center of effort* (CE) is the focal point of the lift and sideways forces generated by a boat's sails, especially when sailing on a beat. Again, it's important to remember that on this angle of sail, the sideways pressure of the rig trying to force the hull to leeward is far greater than the rig's forward thrust.

Pinpointing exact centers of effort is a job for naval architects and sailmakers. Using a sail plan, however, it's possible to approximate a mainsail's CE by drawing one line from the clew to the middle of the luff and another from the tack to the middle of the leech (ignoring the *roach*, the curved portion of the sail outside an imaginary straight line from head to clew, which is supported by battens and gives the sail additional area). The point where these lines intersect represents the geometric center of the mainsail triangle and serves as a close approximation of CE.

The CE of a jib can be found in the same fashion using the *foretriangle*—the area bounded by the mast, the headstay, and a line from the base of the mast to the jib's tack fitting in the bow. First draw a line from the tack to a point midway between the base of the mast and the spot where the mast attaches to the headstay. Then draw another line from the base of the mast to a point midway up the leading edge of the jib. The intersection of these two lines represents the jib's CE. To find the combined center of effort of a main and jib, draw a line connecting their individual CEs and divide this line into two segments based on the ratio of the areas of the mainsail and foretriangle. If, for example, the mainsail represents 60 percent of the total area, the combined CE will be 60 percent of the way aft on this line.

To find the approximate center of effort (CE) for each sail, draw a line from the clew to the middle of the luff and from the tack to the middle of the leech. The intersection of those lines is the geometric center of the sail—a near approximation of the CE.

Of course, this traditional method, while simple, is not as accurate as an in-depth calculation of the true aerodynamic CE of the two sails. In fact, the true aerodynamic CE will be a bit aft of the geometric center. Further, the geometric center fails to take into account the large headboards and roaches that characterize an increasing number of mainsails. It also fails to take into account the additional sail area in larger overlapping headsails, like genoas. Nonetheless, it gives you a good approximation.

It may seem incredible that the lifting forces being generated by a set of sails can be boiled down to a single point. But this is in fact the case, as is evident in the "free-sailing" method of tank testing scaled-down models of new sailboat designs. In the more widespread captive towing method, the model is firmly attached to an overhead gantry by a sturdy mechanical linkage, which then drags it through the water. The free-sailing method, however, mimics actual sail forces by placing a "mast" in the model at the point of the rig's CE. The model is then "sailed" down the length of the tank by pulling on a single line set at an angle that reproduces the aerodynamic forces at work when beating. The result is a hull that moves in one direction even as it's pulled in another. "Even with a firm knowledge of the theory of the forces at work in sailing, it's still rather amazing to watch a scale-model yacht heeled over and traveling straight down the tank, pulled by a single string leading well off to one side," says Canadian naval architect, veteran tank tester, and author Steve Killing of this phenomenon.

Gettin' So Much Resistance

On the other side of the balance equation is the *center of lateral resistance* (CLR), which refers to the aggregate resistance to sideslip created by a boat's keel (or centerboard), rudder, and hull. Determining this point is critical to the success of a new boat design because it has a direct effect on performance. It's far more difficult to approximate CLR than the CE, especially on a boat with a full keel, in which the hull's forefoot sweeps down into the keel and then back to the rudder in a single elegant curve. The CLR of a modern fin-keel boat is a little easier to approximate because it will be somewhere near the middle of the fin.

In practice the center of lateral resistance functions as a pivot point around which the entire boat turns like an oversized wind vane. For example, if the CE is located aft of the CLR, the bow will want to turn into the wind, a condition known as *weather helm*. If the CE is located forward of the CLR, the bow will want to turn away from the wind, a condition known as *lee helm*. If the CE and CLR are perfectly aligned, the boat will sail in a straight line and the helm will be neutral.

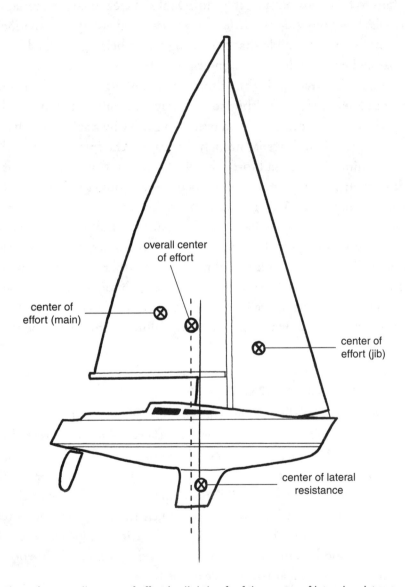

overall center
of effort

center of
effort (main)

center of
effort (jib)

center of lateral
resistance

Note how the overall center of effort is slightly aft of the center of lateral resistance when the sails are sheeted in, so that this performance cruiser will have a tendency to want to turn up into the wind. A little of this weather helm is good because it gives the helmsman a feel for the water passing over the rudder.

Although neutral helm might seem the obvious ideal, a little weather helm when sailing to windward is preferable for a couple of reasons. First, because the rudder has to be kept slightly off center to counter the weather helm, there will always be a little pressure on the wheel or tiller. This slight pressure gives the person at the helm a feel for how the hull is interacting with the water. A perfectly neutral helm feels mushy, or slack, leaving the helmsman blind to what is happening below the waterline.

Second, a slight weather helm allows the rudder to generate lift, further reducing leeway, as the hull moves through the water. To understand why, picture a rudder blade with its trailing edge angled a few degrees to leeward to keep the bow down. This creates an angle of attack analogous to that of the sails overhead, with the water passing over the rudder establishing a circulation field like the one that creates lift in the sails. There is a critical difference, however, in that the rudder presents its leeward surface—not its windward surface—to the flow. Thus, water molecules slow down on the leeward side of the blade and speed up to windward—the opposite of what happens to airflow over the sails. Cue Bernoulli's principle: The two contrasting water flows create a pressure differential across the rudder, which causes a lift to windward.

Speaking of lift, these same forces are also at work over modern keels. A keel's angle of attack results from the fact that a boat always experiences a little sideslip, or *leeway*, when sailing to windward. The resultant course-made-good

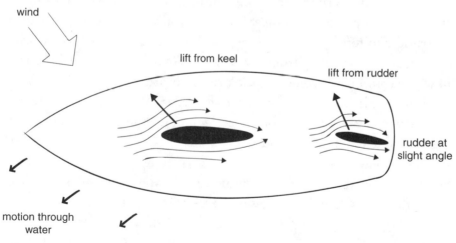

A fish's-eye view of how the keel and rudder produce lift. Because a sailboat travels through the water at a slight angle, especially when sailing to windward, the water hits the keel and rudder at an angle. This causes the water on the windward side of the two appendages to travel farther and faster than the water on the leeward side. This results in a force to windward—lift.

may only be 2 or 3 degrees to leeward of the course steered, but that's enough to cause the flow of water past the hull to impinge more directly on the keel's leeward surface. This sets up circulation around the keel and causes the water to flow a little faster over the windward surface, creating lift. In other words, modern keels aren't just passively resisting leeway, they're creating a dynamic force driving the hull to windward. What could possibly be cooler?

It's for this reason that yacht designers put so much time and effort into a sailboat's underwater appendages. Modern keels and rudders are far more than flat planks. They're carefully designed foils—like airplane wings with symmetrical curves on each side—deliberately tailored to maximize lift under a wide range of sailing conditions. Thickness, size, depth, curvature—everything is carefully studied to maximize efficiency.

Bear in mind that we're not talking about big angles of attack here. As in the sail plan, too great an angle of attack creates a separation of flow—in other words, turbulence—which destroys efficiency. Weather helm, in particular, should be limited so that you don't have to use too much rudder to keep the boat on course. The ideal rudder angle is between 3 and 10 degrees. Any more than that causes the flow to start separating, turning the rudder into a brake.

Finally, what about lee helm? Since a little weather helm is beneficial when sailing to windward, does it follow that a little lee helm will actually be harmful? Absolutely! Think about it. How exactly does a rudder work? It pivots the hull around the center of lateral resistance by pushing the stern in the opposite direction from where you want to go. If you're using the rudder to force your stern to leeward to counteract the bow, which is also trying to turn away from the wind, you're hardly creating a situation in which your boat is going to rocket to windward.

Not only that, there is the small matter of safety. When a boat with weather helm is overpowered by a gust or its steering gear malfunctions, it will immediately round up, spilling the wind from its sails. A boat with lee helm, however, will fall *off* onto a lower course, presenting its entire rig to the gust beam-on and thereby making the situation immeasurably worse. Fortunately, lee helm is rare these days thanks to strides in the science of naval architecture.

Steering Without a Rudder

By this point you probably have a fair inkling of how to steer a boat using its sails—simply adjust the fore-and-aft location of the CE relative to the CLR. Aboard many boats it is also possible to manipulate the CLR. Small-boat sailors, for example, will often raise or lower their centerboards to move the CLR aft or forward. The CE is generally far more malleable, however.

Remember how we determined the combined center of effort when sailing with a jib and main? Now imagine what happens if instead of sheeting in the main all the way we let it luff a little. Immediately its contribution to the rig's total lateral force declines, causing the combined CE to move forward. As soon as the CE is forward of the CLR, it creates a lever arm that will pivot the bow to leeward.

Now imagine sheeting in the main and letting out the jib. This time the main makes a disproportionate contribution to the total lateral force and moves the CE aft of the CLR, pivoting the stern to leeward and the bow into the wind.

That's pretty much it.

Of course, theory is one thing, application another. Nonetheless, learning to steer with your sails is a great way to improve your seamanship.

A windsurfer shifts his weight and position along the boom to alter the CE and CLR of the boat. (Daniel Forster)

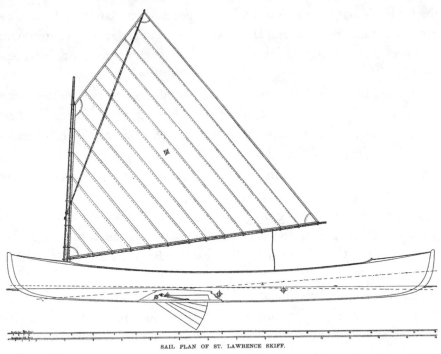

SAIL PLAN OF ST. LAWRENCE SKIFF.

This sail plan from a St. Lawrence skiff shows the CE location on the sail, and three CLRs marked on the hull depending on crew weight and location. (Courtesy of the Adirondack Museum)

Many high school and collegiate sailors practice this skill as part of their training regimens. Over time, some are said to become good enough that they can sail away from the dock, tack, jibe, and return home without ever touching the tiller. Not that this is the point of the exercise. The reason they do this is that knowing how to steer with your sails makes you much faster and more nimble when you're steering with the rudder.

Let's say you're sailing around a buoy or the end of a breakwall and need to bear off from a beat to a broad reach. The first thing many beginning sailors do in this situation is give the boat plenty of rudder—often substantially more than originally intended. The reason is that with the main strapped in for a beat, the weather helm that has been so helpful in gaining ground to windward isn't going to turn itself off just because you've decided to change direction. Remember the collision I referred to at the beginning of the chapter? (I certainly haven't forgotten!) The Tartan Ten has a large main and a small jib, and when that big main is strapped in, falling off in a blow isn't an option. Even if you *are* able to muscle the boat down to a lower course, you will have the rudder so far off centerline that it will be doing as much braking as turning.

A much better approach is to help the boat turn by using its sails. In this case, that means easing out the main to move the CE forward, creating a helm that's neutral or even nudging the bow to leeward. Now the jib is doing the grunt work while the rudder simply helps guide the hull around. There is no dramatic yanking on the wheel or tiller, no dramatic rush of water under the stern as you force the boat to go where it doesn't want to. Everything is smooth as silk—and fast. As the boat begins turning, with the main already well out, the crew on the jibsheet begins easing for maximum speed on your new course, and away you go!

You can also use your sails to ease a course change from a reach to a beat. This time the key is to sheet in the main before the jib, thereby pulling the CE aft. This will create weather helm, swinging the boat up to the desired course with only minimal rudder action.

In this same vein, oversheeting the mainsail to windward with the help of the main traveler will help turn the bow through a tack in choppy seas. In fact, according to Chicago-based sailor Rich Stearns, who helped design and trim the mainsail for the *Heart of America* America's Cup campaign in 1986, the main trimmer on a 12-meter or International America's Cup racer can throw the boat into a tack all by himself, whether the skipper wants him to or not!

Speaking of tacking, one of the most dramatic examples of steering with sails is the laborious process that old-time sailors (and modern sail-training cadets) had to go through when tacking a square-rigger. First, they would oversheet the spanker on the mizzenmast and ease the staysail and jibs up in the bow, thus moving the center of effort aft and inducing some turning moment to help the helm. Then, as the ship began turning through the eye of the wind, they would ease the spanker and shift around the yards of the mainmast—"Mainsail haul!" the command would ring out. At the same time they would leave the yards on the foremast braced around so that those sails would backwind, moving the CE well forward to help pivot the bow through the wind. At this point, the ship would usually be dead in the water or even drifting backward, rendering the rudder nearly useless—it could take five or ten minutes in good conditions to bring a full-rigged ship or bark around—so it was nearly all up to the sails. Only when the ship was safely on its new course would the captain call out, "Let go and haul!", at which point the crew would swing the foremast yards to the new tack.

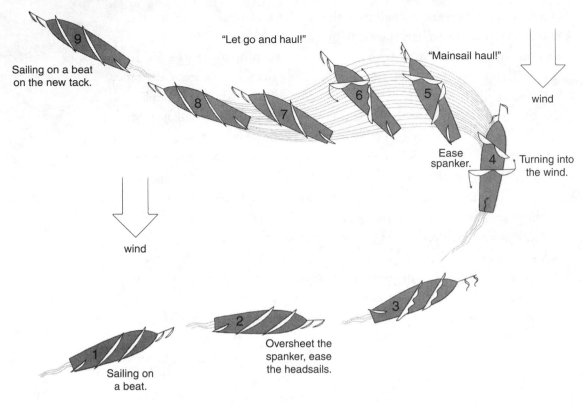

"Let go and haul!"

"Mainsail haul!"

wind

Sailing on a beat
on the new tack.

9

8

7

6

5

Ease
spanker.

4

Turning into
the wind.

wind

1

Sailing on
a beat.

2

Oversheet the
spanker, ease
the headsails.

3

To successfully tack a three-masted bark it's necessary to adjust the rig's center of effort by selectively backing (4, 5, and 6) and filling (6, where the main is beginning to fill, and 7) the sails.

This kind of creative sail trim can come in handy aboard modern sailboats as well. When a boat gets stuck in irons midway through a tack, for example, the best way to force its bow off the wind—often back to the original tack—is by backwinding the jib. Similarly, knowing which sail to trim or raise first when leaving a dock can make the difference between a smooth departure and chaos.

Let's say you're sitting in a 16-foot daysailer alongside a small pier with the wind blowing from straight ahead. When you first push your bow away you will barely have steerage and may even be drifting backward. In this situation, sheeting in the main too quickly could result in the bow swinging back into the wind and your boat immediately getting into irons—not a good situation, especially if there are other boats tied up along the pier in your immediate vicinity. Sheeting in the jib, on the other hand, will move the CE forward, pulling the bow off to leeward, away from the dock and out into the open where you can sheet in and start using your rudder.

Balance and Heel

Finally, when thinking of balance, it's important to be aware of heel, which can generate overwhelming amounts of helm in two ways.

First, as the boat heels, the rig leans farther over the water, causing the CE to move to leeward and outboard as well. When this happens, the forward component of the lifting force will start trying to pivot the hull to windward around the CLR, which is still inboard with the hull and keel. Note that it's now the *forward* vector doing the spinning, as opposed to the lateral vectors we've been dealing with to this point. Nonetheless, the effect is the same.

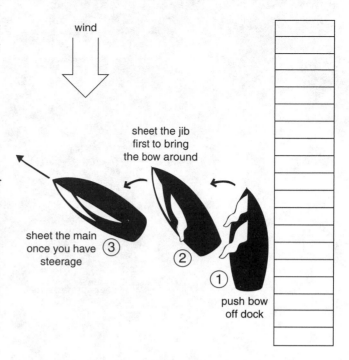

Using sails to help steer away from a dock.

An outboard CE also comes into play when sailing on a run or broad reach. As you ease out your sails—especially the main—the CE will move off centerline, creating a weather-vane effect around the inboard CLR. In moderate conditions this doesn't constitute much of a problem. The loads on the rig are substantially less than when beating. When the wind pipes up and the seas start building, however, look out! If there's already a fair amount of pressure in the sails and a big roller heels you to leeward—or worse yet, to windward—that CE hanging well out over the water may suddenly start exerting more leverage on your helm than you can handle.

Alas, this situation is often made even worse as a result of the other way angle of heel affects helm, which is through hull shape. Specifically, when a hull begins to heel, its immersed shape is no longer symmetrical about the fore-and-aft centerline, as it is when at rest. This in turn affects its tracking ability. Aboard seakindly boats with relatively narrow beams and full bows and sterns, the distortion is minor, and such boats maintain a fairly balanced helm even when hard pressed. Aboard boats

When the center of effort gets far outboard, it will want to pivot the boat around the hull and keel's center of lateral resistance, which is still inboard. In the case of the boat farthest astern, the rig rolled dramatically to leeward under the force of the wind and waves, and then pivoted the boat around to windward. Because of the boat's extreme heel angle, the rudder is almost completely out of the water, rendering it useless. The boat is now pinned on its side, nearly motionless with the wind coming from slightly forward of abeam. (Onne van der Wal)

with excessive beam and narrow bows and sterns, however, the story can be entirely different. As these boats heel, the immersed shape becomes increasingly unbalanced, with the leeward side developing a dramatic bulge amidships as it is pressed deeper into the water. This asymmetry causes the boat to want to turn into the wind. In some cases this is a good thing; dinghy racers will often use their body weight to induce

course sailed

either windward or leeward heel to help them maneuver through a jibe or a tack. In heavy weather, however, excessive heel simply makes a boat difficult to steer.

Worse yet, a beamy boat can start lifting its rudder out of the water when heel angles reach 20 degrees or more and the bow starts digging in, compromising performance even further. Even when still partially immersed the rudder can be rendered nearly useless as air is sucked down along its sides in a phenomenon known as *ventilation*. Couple this with a powerful rig well out to leeward—for example, when a racing boat is carrying a spinnaker on a heavy-air broad reach—and an asymmetrical

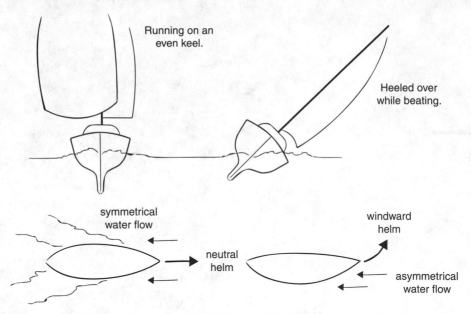

Running on an
even keel.

Heeled over
while beating.

symmetrical
water flow

neutral
helm

windward
helm

asymmetrical
water flow

When heeling hard over, the hull presents an asymmetrical shape to the water, creating additional windward helm.

immersed shape, and in a flash you may find your boat rounding up into the wind—and there ain't nuthin' you can do about it. Suddenly, what was an exhilarating sleigh ride deteriorates into a maelstrom of foaming water and flapping sailcloth. Welcome to the celebrated world of the broach.

THE ANATOMY OF A KNOT

6

*The Role of Friction and Knowing
When to Let Go*

O NE OF HUMANKIND'S most admirable traits is our never-ceasing search for the world's irreducible elements and principles. In the fifth century B.C., the Greek philosopher Empedocles posited four root elements—earth, water, air, and fire—which were moved together and apart by the forces of love and strife. More than 1,300 years later, Albert Einstein's theory of relativity reduced the known universe still further, to a mishmash of interchangeable mass and energy. When it comes to marlinspike seamanship, we can go even Albert one better. For all the complexity of rope, knots, and splices, marlinspike seamanship is about friction.

Think about it. After making a knot, what's the last thing you do to ensure it will stay put? You give it a sharp tug. Fair enough, but why does a tug keep a knot from unraveling?

The answer is friction, something scientists say results when *two or more surfaces are in contact with one another and creating a force, or potential force, that is opposing any attempt to move them.* Friction can be also described using the equation $F_f = \mu N$, in which the amount of friction (F_f) is equal to the coefficient of friction (μ, basically a "stickiness factor") multiplied by the force with which two surfaces are being pressed together, referred to as the normal force (N). In layman's terms, by giving a knot a quick tug you are squeezing the parts of the knot together, which bumps up the normal force. This, in turn, cranks up the friction wherever the rope is in contact with itself, so that the knot won't slip apart again.

Of course, friction can be a double-edged sword. It's the greatest thing in the world when your boat is tied to the dock, but how about when it's time to cast off? When I was working on dive boats in the Gulf of Mexico, we used to call our knives "rope wrenches," and for good reason. It really is incredible how firmly some types of rope—or *line*, as rope is called once it's taken aboard a sailboat—can bind up on themselves after they've been under load.

It was with this Gordian-knot complex in mind that many of the most useful sailing knots were created with a release mechanism—a lever, if you will. The idea is that knots should be as easy to take apart as they are to tie in the first place, no matter how hard or how long they've been at work. The ubiquitous bowline—that bane of junior sailors the world over—is useful not just because it knows how to hold on, but because, like a good parent, it knows when to let go.

Let's Twist Again!

Before delving into the intricacies of the bowline, though, let's take a quick look at the stuff it's made from—namely rope, one of the most ingenious and useful tools ever invented by man.

When most people think of rope, they think of that salty-looking stuff twisted into a spiral, a type of rope known as three-strand, twisted, or *laid*. This kind of rope has been around for hundreds of years and was developed to overcome rope makers' dependence on fibers found in nature. Manila, for example, long renowned for its durability, is made from the fibers of the banana-like abacá plant, a native of the Philippines. Hemp comes from a hardy but dreaded little weed that also goes by the name of marijuana. Cheap and light coir is made from the fiber found in coconut shells. Sisal, also used in cheaper line, is made from agave.

Because none of these fibers can ever be any longer than the stems, leaves, or nuts from which they were made, they need to be twisted into

Three-strand, or Z-laid, Rope

In laid rope, the fibers that make up the yarns are twisted in one direction, the yarns that make up the strands are twisted in the other direction, and the strands that make up the rope are twisted in the same direction as the fibers. No matter which direction you twist the finished rope, either the strands or the yarns will get tighter, cranking up the friction that holds the rope together. (New England Ropes)

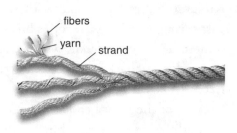

fibers

yarn

strand

"yarns" in order to acquire any kind of useful length. The yarns are then twisted into "strands," which are then twisted in groups of three to form three-strand rope.

The real genius of this process lies in the exact way these elements are twisted together. The fibers that make up each yarn, for example, are twisted in the opposite direction from the yarns that are twisted into each strand. That way, no matter which direction you twist an individual strand, either the yarn or the fibers will tighten. The three strands that will make the rope are then twisted in the opposite direction from their constituent yarns, so that any attempt to untwist the finished rope has the same tightening effect. Twist the rope in one direction and the strands may want to come apart, but the rope itself and the fibers that make up the yarns will bind even tighter. Twist the rope the other way and the rope and fibers may want to unravel, but the strands will lock things tight. In either case, all that twisting and binding produces friction—between the fibers, between the yarns, and between the strands. Stagger the countless fibers that make up the yarns, crank up the normal force with some tight twisting, and suddenly a material no longer than your average pot plant can hoist the mainsail of a frigate. (It's estimated that the famed frigate USS *Constitution* had about eight miles of hemp line on board!)

The vast majority of three-strand rope today is *right-laid*—in other words, when you hold the rope vertically, each strand angles upward from left to right. Right-laid rope is also called Z-laid because the angle made by the seam between the strands looks like the diagonal stroke of the letter *Z*. Left-laid rope is sometimes called S-laid because the seam between the strands looks like the diagonal portion of the letter *S*.

Because it's constructed with a built-in twist, right-laid three-strand rope should always be coiled clockwise to avoid putting kinks in the line. Kinks are not just a nuisance—they can damage the fibers that make up the yarns, compromising the rope's breaking, or *tensile*, strength. Worse still is something called a *hockle*, which happens when the strands separate and make a kind of back turn, becoming tightly twisted against their natural lay. Excessive twisting or the sudden release of a heavy load can cause hockling. Because of the tight bends that result, a hockle can reduce a rope's tensile strength by more than a third—in which case you may very well need to replace it.

One of the great benefits of three-strand rope is that it stretches—the reason many sailors use it for anchor rodes and mooring lines. A little "give" helps reduce shock loads on cleats and anchor bitts. Three-strand rope is also simple to splice. Whether it be an eye-splice to create a permanent loop, a short splice to join two separate ropes, or a back splice to create a fray-proof end, the splicing process is the same. Simply tease apart a few strands and then weave them up and under the strands that are still twisted together in the area of the splice. Once the strands are cozy and snug, our old friend friction takes over, especially when the splice is made in a rope created from natural fibers, with their sticky μ values.

Good Chemistry

The downside of using organic fibers is that they rot, especially when stowed wet—a treatment the avoidance of which, on a sailboat, is problematic to say the least. Organic fibers can also be difficult and time-consuming to harvest in large quantities—one of the main reasons researchers figured out ways to create inexpensive, effective, synthetic substitutes in the early twentieth century.

The first of these, nylon, was discovered in 1935 by American chemist Wallace Hume Carothers, who worked for DuPont. Nylon is strong, abrasion-resistant, and impervious to rot. It's also stretchy, which makes it an especially good material for anchor rodes and mooring lines. In fact, most of the three-strand line manufactured today is made of nylon, specifically for these two purposes. Under load, nylon can safely stretch up to 20 percent of its length—which goes a long way toward lessening the shock loads on a vessel's foredeck cleat when it's tugging at its dock lines in a blow. On the downside, nylon can absorb up to 6 percent of its weight in water, causing the loss of about 10 percent of its tensile strength.

Polyester—or Dacron as it's often called—provides approximately the same tensile strength as nylon, but without all that stretch. It's also abrasion-resistant and absorbs very little water. For decades, polyester has been an almost-universal workhorse within the sailing community, where it's used for everything from halyards to sheets and smaller control lines.

Polypropylene, like nylon, is stretchy, but it's only half as strong. Worse yet, it's hard on hands and degrades over time when exposed to ultraviolet light, making it unsuitable for use aboard a sailboat. One advantage it does have is that it floats—making it a useful material for water skiing towropes. It is also sometimes used as a towrope for dinghies, because it is less likely than a sinking line to get caught in a towboat's propeller should it ever go slack.

In addition to the advantages of strength and durability they offer, synthetic fibers can be made in unlimited lengths. Unlike sisal, which can be no longer than a single leaf—albeit a fairly long one—a single polyester or nylon fiber can stretch the entire length of even the longest halyard. This means you no longer have to twist together countless little fibers to create a rope of useful length for a sailboat. Instead, you can simply braid the fibers into a rope that's loose, soft, and easy to handle.

Of course, braids are nothing new in the world of sailing craft. For centuries, sailors used lightly braided sail ties, or *gaskets*, to furl sails snug against the yardarms aboard old-time square-riggers. The difference now is that braids are both strong and stretch resistant in a way that would have been unimaginable prior to the twentieth century. A $1/4$-inch-thick line of three-strand hemp, for example, has a breaking strength of about four hundred pounds, and a $1/4$-inch manila line has a breaking strength of more than five hundred pounds. A $1/4$-inch line of *braided* polyester, on the other hand, has a breaking strength of just under a ton.

As with laid line, the first step in creating a braided line is to twist the yarns into thin strands. But in contrast to laid line—in which all the yarns are twisted in one direction—half the yarns in braided line are twisted in one direction, while the remainder of the yarn is twisted in the other. The strands are then loosely braided—often in pairs or groups of three—by large, complex, cool-looking braiding machines that turn them into rope. Because there's no need for any severe twisting to keep a bunch of short vegetable fibers in close contact with one another, the resulting matrix remains loose and flexible. This opens up a whole new world of possibilities, like *double-braid line*, in which one braided line is entirely enclosed within another. In this configuration, the inside rope—or inner core—usually takes on most of the load, while the outer sheath both protects the inner core from abuse and makes the rope easier to handle. A typical polyester $1/4$-inch double-braid line has a breaking strength of about two thousand pounds—a significant improvement over three-strand hemp.

sleeve   core

Double-braid rope. (New England Ropes)

Another possibility is something called *parallel-core rope*, in which a braided outer sheath encloses a core comprised of fibers simply running parallel to one another—no braiding or twisting required—thereby producing a rope with that much less stretch.

In many cases both the sheath and the core of these two-part ropes are made of polyester, although rope makers often mix and match various exotics to maximize a particular rope's performance. In the interest of weight they can also remove the outer sheath from a portion of the rope that doesn't especially need it. The spinnaker sheets on many modern racing boats, for example, are double-braid with the braided cover stripped off near the sheet's attachment to the clew. That way the crew in the cockpit benefits from having the outside braid for easy gripping, but the sail doesn't have to support the weight of that extra layer of material out where it's rarely used anyway.

In addition to nylon, polyester, and polypropylene, there are several "miracle" materials on the market today, whose strengths and weaknesses are worth reviewing. Kevlar, for example, is substantially stronger than nylon and polyester. It also provides minimal stretch. On the downside, it tends to absorb water and is susceptible to damage from ultraviolet light—a problem for those who like to go sailing during the day! Kevlar also tends to break down when subjected to repeated bending—a problem given all those pesky blocks and cleats on a sailboat. For these reasons, rope makers rarely use Kevlar anymore, although it's still used in some high-performance sails.

Ultrahigh molecular weight polyethylene (UHMWPE)—which goes by a number of names, including high-modulus polyethylene, Dyneema, and Spectra—is also extremely strong and stretch resistant. Single-braid $1/4$-inch Dyneema line, for example, has a breaking strength of nearly four tons! Ropes made from this material are more workable than Kevlar, don't absorb water, and are less vulnerable to ultraviolet radiation. On the downside, UHMWPE has a low μ factor, which makes it slippery, with poor knot-holding ability. It's also subject to *creep*—it slowly elongates over time under a heavy load and then stays that way.

Technora is strong, low-stretch, and unaffected by creep. Like Kevlar, however, it doesn't take well to bending and is sensitive to ultraviolet light. Technora is often encased in a polyester sheath and blended with other fibers (such as Spectra) to minimize its weaknesses, allowing rope makers to take advantage of its strength.

Vectran produces ropes that are strong, extremely low-stretch, water and UV resistant, durable, and unaffected by creep. A $1/4$-inch single braid fabricated from this stuff has a breaking strength of around seventy-five hundred pounds. Nice! Not surprisingly, Vectran is becoming increasingly popular among grand prix racers. The only downside—the price tag!

Personally, I have a heck of a time remembering which of these miracle materials is which. But then again, I don't plan on being in the market for the highest of high-tech ropes in the near future anyway. Ultimately,

Modern Synthetic Fibers

Nylon
Pros: Strong and stretchy, making it useful for dock lines and anchor rodes
Cons: Absorbs water; loses some strength when wet

Polyester
Pros: Strong, low-stretch, abrasion resistant, and water resistant
Cons: There really aren't any. There's a reason Dacron line is ubiquitous

Polypropylene
Pros: Its one outstanding quality is that it floats
Cons: Relatively weak and stretchy; breaks down over time in sunlight; is hard on the hands

Kevlar
Pros: Very strong with minimal stretch
Cons: Absorbs water and breaks down in sunlight; breaks down after repeated bending

Ultrahigh molecular weight polyethylene (also known as high-modulus polyethylene, Dyneema, and Spectra)
Pros: Extremely strong and stretch resistant; doesn't absorb water; does well even in direct sunlight
Cons: Susceptible to creep

Technora
Pros: Very strong, low-stretch, and unaffected by creep
Cons: Sensitive to sunlight; doesn't take repeated bending well

Vectran
Pros: Extremely strong and stretch resistant; durable and unaffected by water or sun
Cons: The price tag!

polyester and nylon are more than adequate for the vast majority of applications afloat. They may not be the latest miracle fibers on the dock, but they're miracles of modern chemistry nonetheless. If you ever reach a point in your sailing where you need to spend an arm and a leg on the latest miracle rope, you'll know it. In the meantime, take pride in your nylon dock lines and polyester double-braid sheets, and be glad you got 'em!

A Different Kind of Life Preserver

Now that we've looked at how rope is made, let's go a step further and see how it functions in knots—starting with one of the most important in seamanship: the bowline.

When I was taught as a kid how to tie a bowline, I was pretty unimpressed. The thing was so asymmetrical, so random-looking—all it did was create a temporary loop at the end of a piece of line. It had none of the grace and complexity of, say, an eye splice. What's the big deal?

Years later I volunteered to do some work on the floating docks at the Center for Wooden Boats on the south end of Seattle's Lake Union. A big part of the job consisted of checking and sometimes replacing a number of large plastic drums that were lashed underneath the docks to increase their buoyancy. Dropping into the water with a mask and wet suit on, I found myself confronting a snarled rat's nest of weedy line lashing a couple of barrels to an old ringbolt set into one of the dock's timbers. How in the world was I going to get this thing apart?, I wondered. I had my trusty diver's knife, of course, but where was I to begin cutting?

Luckily, upon closer inspection, I realized that all I was looking at was a bunch of bowlines—and things started to make sense. Better still, they all functioned exactly the way they were supposed to, coming apart with remarkable ease despite being encased in a layer of slime. I've had nothing but good things to say about the knot ever since.

The key to the bowline is the overhand loop, or "rabbit's hole," and the way it interacts with that bight of rope going around the standing part— called the "life preserver," in reference to the hideous orange life jackets with the pillow-like collars that were once all the marine world had to offer by way of personal flotation devices. The rabbit's hole is the heart of the knot, because it is the mechanism that actually holds the loop together. Imagine you're using a bowline to lift a hook attached to a heavy weight.

Tying and Untying a Bowline

To make a bowline, first loop the rope in a counterclockwise direction laying the bitter end across the standing part of the line. Next, thread the bitter end up through the overhand loop you just created (a step often described as the "rabbit" coming out of its hole), making sure there's enough line in the loop you're creating to serve the knot's purpose. Then pass the bitter end behind the standing part of the line (the rabbit running around the tree) and down through the overhand loop again (the rabbit going back down the hole), and snug things tight.

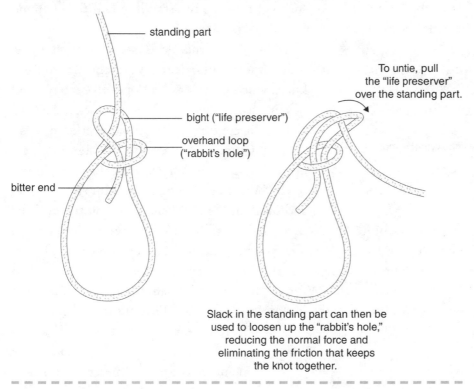

standing part

To untie, pull the "life preserver" over the standing part.

bight ("life preserver")

overhand loop ("rabbit's hole")

bitter end

Slack in the standing part can then be used to loosen up the "rabbit's hole," reducing the normal force and eliminating the friction that keeps the knot together.

As the hook pulls down on the loop you've created, the rabbit's hole gets tighter and tighter, which in turn cranks up the friction on the bitter end of the rope, keeping the loop from pulling apart—the heavier the load, the greater the normal force, the greater the friction.

The life preserver, on the other hand, plays a vital supporting role by keeping the rabbit's hole from untwisting. It also serves as the "release lever" when you want to take the knot apart. To do so, simply push the standing end through the bight in the direction of the loop, at the same time pushing up on the bight, kind of like pulling a life jacket over your head. The moment you start pushing the standing end through, you also cause the rabbit's hole to get bigger. Instantly the normal force goes down, the friction that was holding the knot together disappears, and the knot comes apart.

The beauty of the bowline is that, while the bight making up the life preserver plays a critical role in stabilizing the knot, it does almost nothing to support the load. In other words, it is never subject to an inordinate amount of normal force or friction. Therefore, no matter how hard or how long the knot has been working, pushing the standing end through and taking the knot apart is inevitably a breeze.

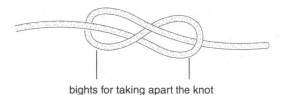

bights for taking apart the knot

The figure-eight knot.

A similar dynamic is at work with many other knots sailors use. Take the figure-eight knot, which is used as a stopper to keep the end of a line from running through a block or halyard clutch. In contrast to a simple overhand knot, the bight that curves around the standing part of the line provides a release mechanism similar to the bowline's life preserver: pull the bight up and over the standing end, and you turn off the friction machine. Try taking apart an overhand knot after it's been given a good tug, and you'll soon find yourself reaching for your rope wrench.

It's the same thing with the square knot. In this case you have two bights to work with. Granted, there isn't the same magical release that comes with breaking the life preserver on a bowline, but it works. It's certainly better than a "granny knot," which looks similar but lacks the square knot's symmetry and has a tendency to bind up after being under load—rope-wrench city!

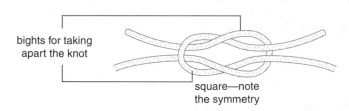

bights for taking apart the knot

square—note the symmetry

The square knot.

Note that the square knot—or reef knot as it is also called due to fact that it is an excellent knot for tying together sail ties when shortening sail—is only supposed to serve as a temporary knot and is not especially secure. Therefore it should never be relied on for either joining ropes that will be under heavy load or joining two ropes of different diameters. The correct knot for these tasks is the sheet bend, a close cousin of the bowline—in fact, the basic structure of the two knots is identical.

To tie a sheet bend, create a counterclockwise loop in one of the two ropes, then run the bitter end of the second rope up through the hole, around the "tree," and then back down through the hole—that's it! Give it a quick tug to crank up the friction so the knot won't unravel, and you've got a connection almost as strong as the rope from which it is made. To take the knot apart, simply push the standing end of the first rope through the life preserver.

Some day when you have some spare time, throw together a few knots and study them for a while—especially the bowline. It really is a marvel of utility. The same is true of the others. There's absolutely nothing in any of them that is without purpose. You can neither add to nor subtract from these simple inventions without diminishing them. Like mousetraps, they can't be improved.

As for the bowline, it's been around for centuries—the seventeenth-century English sailor John Smith of Pocahontas fame mentions the bowline in his book *Seaman's Grammar*— so I doubt it's going anywhere soon, much as it may irk all those junior sailors. The term is derived from *bow line*, which refers to its task of holding the leading edge of a square sail toward the bow when a square-rigged ship was sailing close to the wind. The bowline remains to this day a vital means of trimming sails on countless boats, and it's a marvel of basic engineering. A callow youth no more, I now regard the bowline as pure genius.

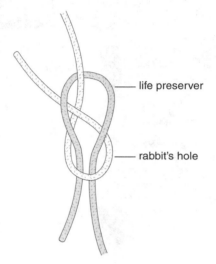

— life preserver

— rabbit's hole

The sheet bend. Note that the overhand loop and "life preserver" are identical to those in a bowline.

DOCKING UNDER SAIL AND POWER

The Two Are More Similar Than You Might Think

THERE ARE TWO ways of docking a sailboat—under power and under sail—and oddly enough, the two are not that different. No matter what makes a sailboat move through the water, it still turns the same way—the rudder still needs to have water passing over it to create the lifting force the boat needs to change direction. Remember, rudders are foils, just like sails, and without a flow of water they can't create lift any more than the wing of an idling airplane—no lift, no steerage. Sailboats also don't have brakes. Granted, you can throw your inboard into reverse to slow yourself down, but it's hardly the same as applying the brakes of your car.

With this in mind, it just makes sense to approach a dock from downwind, whether you're under power or under sail. That way the wind will work with you to bring your boat to a stop, as opposed to scooting you along that much faster. You also allow yourself the luxury of a second chance; being to leeward of a solid object takes a lot of the pressure off. Let's say you're coming in under power and the auxiliary suddenly conks out.

(It really *has* been known to happen on occasion!) If you're to leeward and motoring into the wind, the first thing your boat will want to do is slow down. Maybe you'll have enough momentum to reach a piling where you can throw a bow line around and take stock of the situation. Maybe you can throw a line to a friend. In the worst-case scenario, you'll come to a gradual halt a few feet short of your goal and start drifting to leeward. Unless it's blowing a hurricane, you should still have plenty of time to figure out what to do next—drift gently downwind to another dock, restart the engine, bleed the fuel line, drop anchor—whatever.

Now imagine what would happen if you were motoring down on that same dock with the wind at your back. Not only will the wind want to keep you moving along at a steady clip, you may even start accelerating. This is not good—docks and speed make a bad combination.

Even if your engine doesn't actually conk out, coming up on the leeward side of a dock makes it easier to stop and reconsider what you're doing in the event things start looking a little dicey. You say you don't like the way things are lining up as you try squeezing into a spot between a couple of close-parked cabin cruisers? No problem—just shift into reverse and let the wind help push you clear. Coming in a little too fast under sail? No sweat—just jibe around and get yourself in position to start over again. What's the rush? Never feel pressured to make a dock on your first attempt. Trying to force a questionable situation is a sure way to create painful memories!

Rudders are foils, just like sails, and without a flow of water they can't create lift any more than the wing of an idling airplane— no lift, no steerage.

Docking Under Sail

I honestly wonder whether it isn't sometimes easier to dock a boat under sail than under power. I personally feel much more in tune with what a boat is up to when it's functioning as intended, as opposed to simply being shoved around by a propeller. Of course, I'm talking smaller boats here; it's a gutsy sailor, indeed, who will attempt to sail a 50-footer into a tight slip at the far end of the pier. Then again, I may just be psychologically scarred from the dozens of times the outboard engine died while I was docking our family's trusty old Ensign. Whatever the case, docking a boat

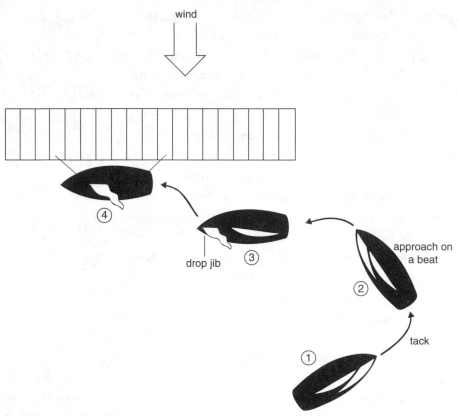

Docking when the wind is coming off the dock.

under sail is surprisingly straightforward. The actual execution can be a bit tricky on occasion, but it's a skill well worth learning.

Let's say, for example, that the wind is blowing straight off the dock. Just beat up until you're a boat length off, and then reach along, luffing your sails to kill speed until you're just maintaining steerage. When you reach your chosen spot, simply let the main fly and head up a little.

Note that when I suggest letting the sheets fly during a docking maneuver, I mean let 'em fly! The main, in particular, can cause real problems if it starts filling with air. Having it sheeted in even a little too tight can leave you clinging with all your strength to a dock cleat to keep your boat from running up some other guy's transom.

It's also a good idea, at some point, to drop the jib. In some cases it may be necessary to keep it up to help you maneuver as you're tacking back and forth on your approach. Otherwise it's generally best to do without it—the fewer sails you have to worry about, the better. In addition, unlike mainsails, which will flap like a flag when you point the bow into the wind, jibs tend to get caught on things like foredeck cleats and shrouds, creating a belly that will try to push your boat around when you least expect or want it. The jib also creates a blind spot in the worst possible place when docking—just ahead of your boat.

Another convenient docking scenario is one in which the wind is blowing parallel with the dock. This is not as unusual as it might seem. Imagine a simple pier that has three sides to which you can tie up. The chances are good that at any given moment, the wind direction will be roughly parallel with at least one of them. Then again, in a typical harbor basin, it's not at all unusual to find multiple seawalls offering multiple angles relative to the wind. The key is to figure out well ahead of time the most advantageous side for docking, given the number of boats already tied up and the conditions—yet another example of how "wind sense" and an ability to play the angles is invaluable to a sailor.

No matter what docking situation you face, make sure all your fenders and lines are ready well in advance. Give your sheets and halyards a once-over to be sure they'll run free. More often than not, when you want to drop a sail during a docking maneuver you want it to come down *now*. Sort out your

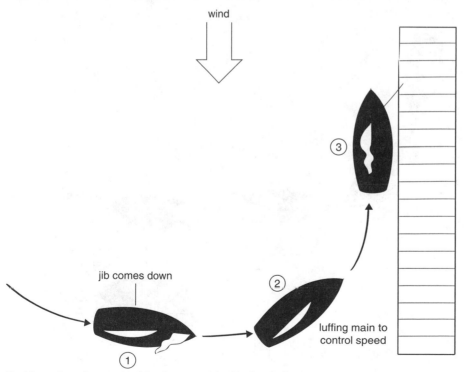

Docking when the wind is blowing parallel with the dock.

dock lines well in advance, and make sure they're correctly coiled. While you're at it, double-check to make sure they're running fair and won't get caught on any stanchions when it comes time to tie up. The last thing you want is to have to untangle a snarl or re-run a bunch of lines at the same time you're barreling down on a pier like the *Titanic*.

As you approach the dock, watch for anything that may cause you to alter your original plans. Thanks to all those buildings and trees on shore and all those other boats on the water, marinas are notorious for their unreliable winds. One moment you could be drifting along in a near calm, and the next you could emerge from a wind shadow created by a boat shed and find yourself with all kinds of pressure on your sails again.

Of course, every now and then you'll be in a situation in which you have no choice but to sail in to a dock that's downwind of you. The good news is that actually getting there won't be a problem. The bad news is that getting there without putting on a show for the rest of the folks milling about the marina sometimes is.

Ultimately, the best way to come alongside a dock that's downwind is to bring your boat to a stop directly to windward of your chosen spot—preferably not too far to windward—and then drift down gently

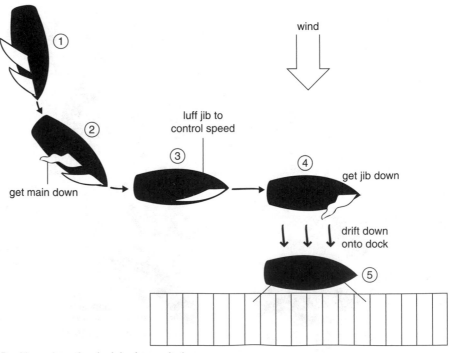

Docking when the dock is downwind.

to your goal. In this case, it's generally a good idea to come in under jib alone, dropping the main as much ahead of time as possible. There's no way to spill air out of the main when you're on a run or broad reach. You may be able to keep the main up in very light air—but be warned, just one stray zephyr can transform this gamble into a "memorable occasion."

One time I—or rather, a friend of mine—decided to come in under full sail aboard a spritely little 14-foot Rhodes Bantam. All was well until the last moment, when Murphy's Law kicked in—with a vengeance. Just as the hull was kissing the dock—it really was a beautiful bit of seamanship—the boom bumped against a piling, which pushed the boom inboard at the very moment a small gust started filling the sails. The next thing I—I mean my *friend*—knew, he was clawing at anything he could reach as his trusty little 14-footer began surging inexorably toward an inflatable dinghy with a shiny new outboard. Unfortunately, the kicker in a situation like this is that, with the boat surging ahead, you've suddenly got your hands full at the same moment you really need to do something with the sail. Let go of the dock to pull down the main, and in the blink of an eye the boat could dial itself up to "ramming speed." Hang on to the dock, and the boat could get walloped by another gust.

The 125 square feet of sail on a Rhodes Bantam may not seem like much, but just wait until you find yourself opposing its force with nothing more than your fingernails!

Docking Under Power

In many ways the biggest difference between docking under power and docking under sail is expectations. Even with its engine running, the typical sailboat isn't good at coming to a dead stop, and even under power it presents a lot of above-the-waterline surface area, or *windage*, for the wind to push around when you're maneuvering at slow speeds. Granted, tacking a 50-footer directly to windward to reach a slip in the far corner of one of today's tightly packed marinas is pretty much out of the question—but then again, that's precisely why they are such a recent phenomenon. Before the advent of reliable auxiliary power, today's tract-housing-style marinas would have been nearly useless, because it would have been pretty much impossible for anybody to use them. The "iron genny" does provide two big advantages: it allows you to go backward and gives you at least *some* degree of braking ability—although these are things many sailboats still do only marginally, if at all.

Backing up, for example, has long been the bane of sailors. To understand why, first imagine what happens when a sailboat is powering ahead. The helmsman pushes the throttle forward, the propeller starts spinning, and a blast of water shoots aft, passing over the rudder positioned directly astern. Thanks to all this manufactured water flow, the helmsman gains a fair amount of steerage, even if the boat itself is barely moving.

When you put the transmission in reverse, however, the propeller sends a blast of water *forward*, so it passes over the keel. Granted, the prop is sucking water in from astern—but it's doing so over a relatively wide area, so that at any given point the water flow is pretty minimal. The result: when you first start powering in reverse, you have no steerage!

The situation is further complicated by a phenomenon known as *prop walk*. As the propeller spins, it grabs the water in much the same way a rotating gear grabs the toothed track in a rack-and-pinion arrangement. As a result, the propeller doesn't just push your boat forward or backward, it also tries to force the stern sideways. The vast majority of sailboat propellers are right-handed—when viewed from astern, they turn clockwise to move the boat forward. In operation, as a right-handed propeller pushes the hull forward, it also tries to kick the stern out to starboard. In reverse, it spins counterclockwise and tries to kick the stern to port.

stern swings to port

A standard right-handed propeller will turn counterclockwise in reverse, pulling the stern to port.

Happily, prop walk is generally of little or no consequence when a boat is powering along under a full head of steam. You have plenty of water flowing over the hull, keel, and rudder, and the prop walk forces pale in comparison. Maneuvering at slow speeds, however, is another story—especially when you're trying to go backward. Pop the transmission into reverse when your boat is at a standstill, and the first thing it wants to do is swing its fanny off to port—and with minimal water passing over the rudder, there ain't a whole heck of a lot you can do about it! Aboard some older, heavier boats that have full keels and older, less efficient props, going in reverse may be virtually impossible.

Unfortunately, even after you're moving in reverse, you still need to be on your guard. When the hull is moving forward, the rudderpost—which is also the rudder's pivot point—is up near the rudder's leading edge. Therefore the water passing over the rudder naturally wants to push it back toward the boat's centerline. When you're in reverse, however, everything is, well, reversed—which puts the pivot post at the rudder's *trailing* edge. Now the moving water wants to push the rudder *away* from the centerline—and you need to stay alert to keep the rudder from slamming off to one side.

I remember one time testing a fine little French-built sloop for *Sailing* magazine. I was doing my best to play the nonchalant professional—and doing a pretty good job of it—until we got back to the marina.

"Before we go in, I want to see how she does under power," I said, after we took down the sails.

"No problem," the sales rep said, giving me the helm. "Be my guest."

The boat was a nimble 30-footer with a fine diesel and highly efficient propeller—perhaps too efficient. Things went well until I decided to see how she performed in reverse. I had barely put the throttle down before the boat started surging astern—what a nice little barky, thinks I. Then—bang!—the wheel went spinning out of my hands as the rudder slammed to starboard. So much for my nonchalant professional act! From that point on, I kept a firm grip on the wheel and was sure to execute only *small* rudder movements.

Finally, when maneuvering at slow speeds, always be aware of windage. With the sails up, you have no choice but to consider how the wind may be affecting your ability to stay on a particular heading. Under power, however, it's possible to remain blissfully unaware of how the wind will impact your ability to maneuver until it's too late. Executing a turn when motoring downwind can be particularly problematic, because the wind will start pushing against your bow as soon as you begin your turn. Once again, think of your boat as an oversize wind vane. Suddenly, the bow *wants* to point downwind, and you may find yourself covering a lot of ground to leeward before you can force it around.

wind

When head-to-wind, the bow comes around with ease.

wind

When going downwind the wind will resist your efforts to turn.

When you're motoring at slow speed, the wind can impact your ability to maneuver.

For the same reason, when motoring with the wind abeam, it's much easier to turn downwind than in the other direction.

If, on the other hand, you're motoring directly into the wind, turning to either side will be that much easier. Be prepared, however, to begin using some helm to slow the turn well in advance of its completion—otherwise, with the wind pushing its bow, the boat may try to shift to a heading much lower than you actually want.

The Power and the Glory

Given all these caveats, what's a poor sailor to do? Well, by reading this chapter you've already done the most important thing: you've made yourself aware of the caveats. Be on the alert for these glitches as you start making your way into the

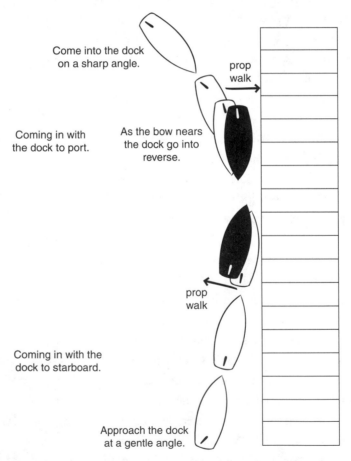

When you dock under power, get prop walk working for you (top) rather than against you (bottom) if possible.

marina. Is there a stiff breeze coming from astern? Will you be making a turn into the wind as you enter the channel that leads to the dock or your slip? No worries—just be sure to prepare yourself mentally for the possibility that your boat won't answer its helm as quickly as it normally would. Are you head-to-wind and preparing to turn 90 degrees to starboard to enter the slip? Great! Just be sure to start straightening out the helm *before* you're lined up with the entrance so you don't accidentally head toward the leeward piling.

When you must overcome prop walk, a quick burst of forward propeller with the rudder hard outboard may bring the stern in.

Assuming there isn't a strong current running and there's only a moderate amount of wind, it's best to position yourself so that the dock is to port as you sidle up against it. This will allow you to come in at a moderate angle and speed, and when it's time to stop the boat with a little reverse thrust, any prop walk you experience will pull your stern into the dock.

If you simply must make your approach starboard-side to, do your best to come in at a shallow angle and use as little reverse as possible—a burst of reverse prop will likely kick your stern away from the dock. If your stern is still hanging out a little after you've come to a stop, try giving a quick burst of forward propeller with the rudder hard to port. With luck the prop wash against the rudder will pop your fanny in without creating undue forward motion. You'll also have the forward prop walk on your side. If you can, get a crewmember onto the dock to secure a couple of lines forward and aft, and use these to crank yourself in the rest of the way.

If you're docking in a current, a strong wind, or both, contending with the elements takes precedence over whether the dock is to port or starboard. Dock in such a way that your bow is pointing into or as close to the wind or current as possible. If the wind and current are in opposition, let the current dictate your approach—water pushing against the hull will pack a far greater force than wind pushing against your boat's topsides and rig.

Happily—although it may be intimidating at first—a bit of wind or current can actually be your friend. Not only will it help you stop after you bring your boat alongside, it can improve your maneuverability. Having to use a little extra throttle to keep your boat on the move translates into extra prop thrust washing over the rudder—and more flow means more lift when you angle the rudder to port or starboard. When docking into a slight current in particular, you may be able to "crab" from one side to the other with ease,

Braking with Dock Lines

There's nothing wrong with using dock lines to help you stop—as long as you do so with care. Unless your boat is very light and moving very slowly, it's best not to just cleat a line with the idea that it will bring the boat to a stop when you run out of slack. At the very least, you run the risk of giving everyone on board a jolt when the boat suddenly screeches to a halt. At the worst, it could wrench the cleat out of the deck.

A far better approach is to have someone put a single wrap around a handy cleat, bollard, or piling, and then work the tail end, creating just enough resistance to gradually ease the boat to a standstill. You should never use a bow line for this, as doing so would cause the bow to shear into the dock and the stern to swing out into the channel. Better to brake the boat with a line you've cleated at or slightly aft of amidships. This will force the entire boat into the dock, giving you much better control.

Stopping your forward motion with a line cleated amidships will bring the entire boat in.

Stopping with a bow line will swing the stern away from the dock.

thanks to the fact that you're moving relative to the water, even if your progress relative to a fixed object such as the dock is minimal. The downside to powering into a wind or current on your approach is that you don't want to miss getting those dock lines over! First and foremost, get that bow line secure. The wind or current will then naturally push you toward the dock.

If a stiff wind is blowing off the dock, it may be necessary to come in at a fairly sharp angle, ideally with the dock on your port side, to prevent the bow from blowing downwind. It may also be necessary to come in fairly hot. At the last possible instant, put the helm over hard to turn the bow off and bring in the rest of the hull. Then pop the throttle in reverse to stop your forward motion and get a little beneficial prop walk going. Oh, and get those lines over!

As much as possible, avoid docking on a leeward dock face, especially in a stiff breeze. In this situation, the best you can do is position yourself parallel to and a little to windward of the dock and then drift down onto your selected spot. This maneuver is fraught with potential hazard because you're at the mercy of the wind and waves.

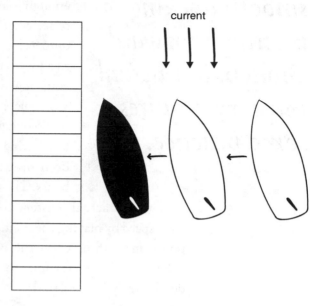

Crabbing sideways against a current.

One way to gain a certain measure of control is to drop an anchor to windward of where you want to tie up—but that's a radical course of action best reserved for compelling need in an exotic port of call. A more reasonable approach might be to try rafting up with somebody on a more sheltered face of the dock. Then again, is it really so vital that you tie up at the dock in the first place? If there is a good stiff breeze coming in, it's also going to be kicking up waves. These will likely cause your boat to surge up and down, possibly damaging your topsides. Ask yourself if it might not be better to anchor out or grab a mooring. You can always use your dinghy to conduct whatever business awaits you ashore.

Practice, Practice, Practice

Like so much of sailing, when it comes to docking, there's nothing like a little practice. Next time you're out tootling around, practice a few slow-speed maneuvers on the open water before you hoist your sails. Try stopping as quickly as possible at various speeds. Try backing up, slowly at first, and then a little faster. Throw in a few turns and note how your boat responds to the helm at various wind angles.

The theory of smooth docking is straightforward enough, but actual mastery requires some practice.

- - - - - - - - - - - - - - - - - - -

While you're at it, do the same thing under sail. Practice slow-speed sailing, with the sails drawing just enough to maintain steerage. Throw in some tight turns to see what happens, and don't sheet in as you harden up onto a close reach or a beat. If there's a buoy you can use as a target or reference point, so much the better. Point your bow directly into the wind and practice coming to a complete stop—then once you're stopped, pay attention to what it takes to get moving again. There's nothing like having the ability to make your mistakes where you don't have to worry about bumping into other people's boats. The theory of smooth docking is straightforward enough, but actual mastery requires some practice. Being able to regulate your speed by playing the main, knowing how quickly your boat turns under power in a stiff breeze—these are things that can only be learned through experience. When it comes to docking and maneuvering in tight places, the devil is truly in the details.

SAIL PLANS AND LINES DRAWINGS

How Sheer Lines, Bows, and Sterns Affect Sailing Performance

THE INSCRIPTION on the masthead of my old alma mater *Sailing* magazine reads, "The Beauty of Sail," and nowhere is this better illustrated than in a naval architect's rendering of a sailboat's hull and rig. Granted, there's a certain elegance in the most prosaic of mechanical or architectural drawings, but really, what compares with the lines of even the doughtiest catboat or dinghy? There's magic in the curves and balance of a sail plan or lines drawing, a dramatic tension that knows no equal.

And yet, for all that we admire about these maritime technical drawings, who among us can truly claim to know what we're looking at? Sure, pretty much anyone can tell at a glance that there's a world of difference between, say, an America's Cup boat and an old wooden cruising ketch—it's as obvious as the contrast between a minivan and a Ferrari. But how many sailors can explain *why* these boats are designed so differently? Who can explain exactly what it is that enables a given boat type to do the things it does so well?

The clues are there, in even the most basic drawings, and it pays to spend some time learning how to

49'-6" ABO'

P=39'-0"

TOTAL
800 S.F

10

3

STAYSAI
132 S.F.

read them. Understanding a naval architect's rendering not only broadens your understanding of how boats work, it can dramatically improve your sailing ability. Just as a little sail theory can make you a better trimmer, knowing how a particular hull shape interacts with the water can make you a better helmsman.

Knowing such things also adds another new dimension to the pleasure of sailing. When I'm out on the water, I love to kick back and think about the forces at work around me. I love to hike out as far as I can when a boat is on its ear and glance down over the windward topsides to watch the keel or centerboard slice through the water. In my mind's eye, I see flow lines curving along the foil's sides and a vortex swirling off its tip. I imagine the boat's hull shape and how it's interacting with the water. In the process, I get more in touch with the experience of sailing.

Far from making a boat seem like a purely mechanical object, a naval architect's drawings help us appreciate a boat's inner beauty for what it truly is.

How We Got Here

Although sailboats have been around since time immemorial, the naval architect's profession is a fairly modern invention. Until the late 1800s, the craftsmen who built boats also designed them, often based on little more than a hunch, tradition, personal prejudice, and a healthy number of misconceptions. My favorite is the old belief that *skin friction*—the resistance created by water passing over the hull surface—increases with depth. If this were true, the lower portion of a fin keel would have a harder time passing through the water than the part closer to the waterline, and the deeper a submarine went, the harder it would have to work to keep moving!

In his book *Yacht and Boat Sailing*, published in 1878, pioneering naval architect Dixon Kemp observed, "A curious feature in connection with yacht construction is that naval architecture should have had so little to do with the designing of yachts. . . . It is, therefore, satisfactory to note that yacht designing is gradually gaining recognition as a profession." In a sign of the times, it would take almost another 20 years before Lloyd's Register of Yachts began including both builders *and* designers in its entries.

Not surprisingly—given the nature of the sea—the rule-of-thumb approach resulted in numerous disasters. Perhaps the most famous of these was the 1,200-ton Swedish warship *Vasa*, which capsized and sank in Stockholm Harbor in 1628—a whopping one mile into her maiden voyage. Another, more recent example was the 146-foot racing schooner *Mohawk*. One of the most spectacular yachts of its day, this beauty was capsized by a gust in July 1876 while at anchor off the New York Yacht Club station on Staten Island. Five people were killed, including the owner and his wife. Yet another mishap was the loss of the cutter *Oona* in heavy weather off the Irish coast in 1886, which took the lives of her designer, William Evans Paton, her captain, and two crewmembers.

As the job of designing sailboats fell more and more to specialists with a background in naval science, early standouts included William Fife III, one of a whole line of famous Fifes, and Edward Burgess, an early catboat racer who designed the sloops *Puritan* and *Mayflower* of America's Cup fame. Another formidable pair was England's George Lenox Watson—the designer of the royal yacht *Britannia* and Sir Thomas Lipton's America's Cup challenger *Shamrock II*—and the legendary Nathanael Greene Herreshoff of Bristol, Rhode Island, who first made a name for himself as an inventor of powerboats and steam engines.

Sumurun, a William Fife ketch, in the Fox Islands Thorofare, Penobscot Bay, Maine. (Molly Mulhern)

Lines Drawings and the Sail Plan

Central to the new profession of yacht design was the use of standardized *lines drawings* as a substitute for three-dimensional models carved from wood (although Herreshoff, for one, continued to carve wooden models to his dying day). A modern lines drawing is actually comprised of three separate drawings—the plan view, the profile drawing, and the body plan—which together illustrate four different views of the hull. The *plan view* is a fish's-eye perspective showing the hull as it would look from beneath; the *profile drawing* shows the hull from the side; and the *body plan* provides a split view of the boat from the bow and the stern, with the stern view occupying the left side of the illustration and the bow view, the right.

Although they look dramatically different, the three perspectives are all derived from the same three sets of lines created by "slicing" the hull in three different planes that intersect one another at 90 degrees. The *waterlines* are created by slicing the hull horizontally, as in the layers of a

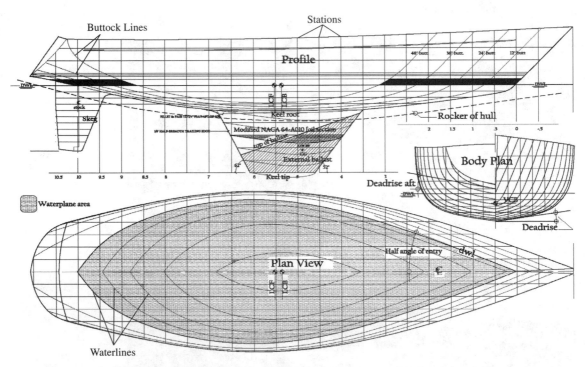

The Nordic 44, designed by Robert Perry, has a skeg-hung rudder, a low-aspect keel, moderate bilges, a length-to-beam ratio of 3.39, and a displacement-to-length ratio of 241—all indicating a moderate design that emphasizes comfort and "seakindliness" over top-end speed, as we'll see in the next few chapters. (Reprinted with permission from *Yacht Design According to Perry*, by Robert Perry)

wedding cake or the contour lines on a topographic map—imagine tracing lines along the waterline as a hull settles deeper into the water. *Stations* are derived by slicing the hull vertically, perpendicular to its fore-and-aft centerline, as if it were a loaf of bread. Typically, naval architects will employ ten stations, starting with station 0 where the hull meets the waterline at the bow and counting aft to station 10 where the hull exits the waterline at the stern. Finally, *buttock lines* are derived by slicing the hull vertically and parallel with the fore-and-aft centerline.

In addition to the three illustrations that comprise the lines drawing, there is the *sail plan*, a rendering that shows the rig in profile along with the hull. Sometimes the sail plan will show just the portion of the hull

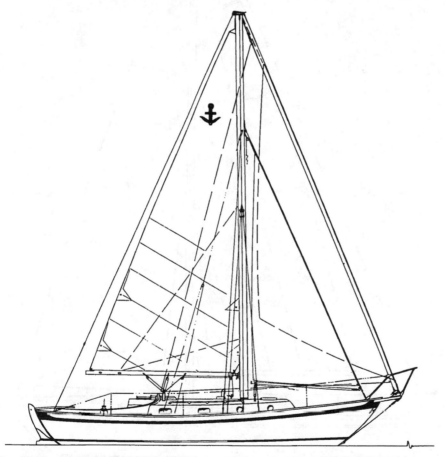

The sail plan of the Southern Cross 31 shows a boat meant for voyaging. Note the inner forestay for a heavy-weather jib and the dashed outline of a trysail to be flown in a storm in place of the mainsail. This is a small, full-keel cruiser that will cross oceans safely and comfortably, albeit somewhat slowly.

visible above the waterline, and sometimes it will include the rudder and keel.

Finally, there may be detail drawings to highlight some finer construction detail such as a *taffrail*—a railing around the stern of a traditionally influenced design—or a bit of scrollwork up on the bow.

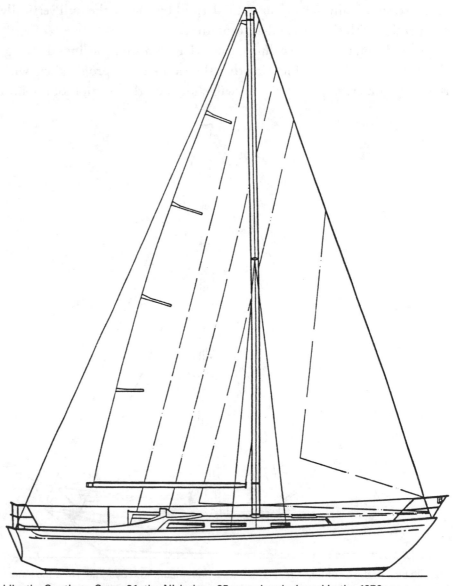

Like the Southern Cross 31, the Nicholson 35 was also designed in the 1970s as a seaworthy cruiser. Though not a speedster, the boat features a fin keel, which helps make it faster and better at sailing to windward than the Southern Cross 31.

Bows and Sheerlines

When it comes to the various features and shapes that make up a hull, you would be hard-pressed to find even the tiniest curve or angle that doesn't have a name. Whether it's the product of a racing rule or a basic principle of hydrodynamics, you can bet someone, somewhere, at some time has named it.

Looking at the profile drawing, for example, one of the most dramatic characteristics of any hull is the *sheer*, or *sheerline*, formed where the deck meets the hull or along the top of the bulwarks. Traditionally, this line creates a concave shape that's higher at both ends. The sheer can also be dead straight or even slightly convex, in which case the boat is said to have

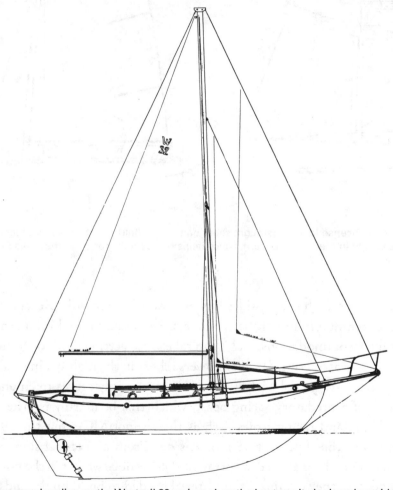

The concave sheerline on the Westsail 32 cruiser gives the boat a salty look and provides plenty of reserve buoyancy in the bow and stern to lift the hull over the waves in heavy seas.

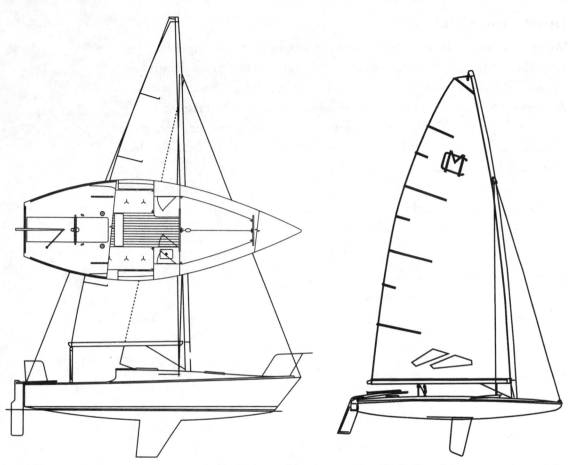

In addition to creating a racy, no-nonsense look, the straight sheer on the J/24 (left) and the reverse sheer of the MC-scow (right) minimize the weight in the bow and stern, which helps reduce hull motion as the boats rides up and down through the waves.

a *reverse sheer*, with the topsides highest toward the middle. Reverse sheer is more common in motorboats, where it creates additional volume amidships for accommodations, and it can take some getting used to. Nonetheless, it can be attractive. The bit of reverse sheer in the high-octane and—in my opinion—*very* cool Melges 32, for example, only serves to emphasize the look of a predatory racing beast, which this boat truly is. The same is true of inland racing scows such as the 16-foot MC-scow, the 28-foot E-scow, and the super-fast 38-foot A-scow. From a practical standpoint, both a reverse sheer and a dead-straight sheer reduce weight in the bow and stern because they eliminate the material needed to build up the ends into that graceful concave shape. The weight savings can yield big performance gains, because weight at the extreme ends of a boat accentuates how much the boat will "hobby horse" as it rides up and down waves.

In addition to being aesthetically pleasing, a traditional sheer is eminently practical. By elevating and enlarging the topsides forward, you create a strong shape for slicing through waves. Because these raised bow sections contain mostly air—much like the rest of the hull—you also create a lot of *reserve buoyancy*, which helps lift the bow over waves, as opposed to simply burrowing into them like a submarine. The same goes for the stern. By elevating the hull profile aft, you protect the cockpit and help the stern rise above an overtaking wave. By keeping the topsides low amidships, you reduce hull weight and windage and make it possible for any water that comes over the bow to drain overboard before it reaches the cockpit. Aboard old-time workboats, lower topsides amidships also made it easier to do things like launch boats, take on cargo, or haul in fishing nets.

The buoyancy and seaworthiness of a particular sheer can be further augmented by the shape of the bow and stern. A traditional spoon bow, for example, encloses a substantial amount of air, dramatically increasing the

The spoon bows that helped fishing schooners muscle their way through rough seas were retained for schooner yachts like this one. This boat's angle of heel obscures its traditional sheer, but reveals its elegant counter stern. (Molly Mulhern)

immersed volume as the bow digs into a sea. The slightly convex shape it gives to a boat's topsides forward also provides extra strength. That's why spoon bows were so common on those tough old Grand Banks schooners in the nineteenth and early-twentieth centuries, including the famous Canadian schooner *Bluenose*. Those boats needed to be able to muscle their way through pretty much anything if they were to successfully navigate to their fishing grounds in the stormy North Atlantic.

The same is true, albeit to a slightly lesser degree, of the straight overhanging bows that are common on racing boats and cruisers built in the 1970s and 1980s. Although finer than spoon bows because of their relatively straight sides, these bows projecting out over the water still offer a fair amount of reserve buoyancy to help lift a boat over a chop.

By contrast, take a look at the "classic" clipper bow. In the early 1800s, opium smugglers in Southeast Asia developed these forms for the purpose of outwitting both the authorities and the contrary monsoon winds of the China Sea. In contrast to the bulbous, convex "bluff" bows that preceded them—think warships like the USS *Constitution*—these bows were highly concave, creating a narrow angle of entry in the interest of hydrodynamic efficiency. In doing so, however, they also dramatically reduced the amount of buoyancy—not to mention the amount of physical structure—available for bashing through waves. It is for this reason that the clipper ships of the mid-nineteenth century—now considered by many to be the ultimate sailing machines—were widely condemned by their contemporaries as being inherently unsafe.

Another bow type lacking in buoyancy is the straight or "plumb" bow, in which the leading edge—or *stem*—is perfectly vertical. This shape is interesting in that it satisfies two different but related demands. First, like *tumblehome bows*—in which the stem curves aft just a touch—vertical bows were once used to maximize the amount of hull volume for carrying cargoes. Why bother building a pointy little bow on a Thames River sailing barge if you can't load a worthwhile amount of freight into it? Second, a vertical bow

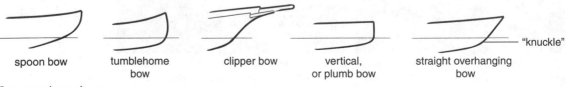

| spoon bow | tumblehome bow | clipper bow | vertical, or plumb bow | straight overhanging bow |

"knuckle"

Common bow shapes.

helps maximum the waterline length for a particular length on deck. All other things being equal, a boat with a greater *load waterline length* (LWL) will be faster than a boat with a shorter LWL. Therefore, if a racing class is defined by its *length overall* (LOA), it makes little sense to leave a part of that LOA projecting out over the water, where it isn't contributing to speed.

Take the 18-foot skiffs that regularly race in Sydney Harbor, Australia. These boats—which sport ridiculous amounts of sail, more than 1,200 square feet downwind!—were traditionally governed by a single design rule, LOA. As a result, both the bow and stern are perfectly vertical, so that the LOA and the LWL are essentially identical. The same is true of the various "Open Class" boats that are raced across oceans and even around the world, often by solo sailors. These boats include the Open 60 class, the Open 40, and the Mini Transat 650, which can be no more than 6.5 meters, or approximately 21 feet long. Again, one of the main design parameters is LOA, creating boats with vertical bows and sterns.

If you are shaking your head at the folly of modern racing fanatics, remember that competitive folly is nothing new. In particular, the plumb bow and the LWL game have been around since the dawn of competitive sailing. Back in the 1870s and 1880s, some of the most cutthroat racing in the world took place among the "sandbagger" fleets of New York Harbor and Long Island Sound. Named for the piles of sandbags their sailors used as moveable ballast to keep their huge rigs from tipping over in a stiff breeze, these boats were rated strictly according to LOA. The result? That's right, plumb bows. It's the same story for that paragon of traditional boating, the catboat. Originally designed for inland fishing and hauling freight, these boats were also the focus of a lot of competitive sailing in the late nineteenth century—often for cash prizes. Again, the boats were rated almost exclusively according to length, which resulted in plumb bows and even bows with a little tumblehome. In other words, the salty, traditional-looking plumb bows of modern catboats were first developed as rule beaters!

A Few Thoughts about Sterns

Questions of strength and buoyancy also come into play with regard to stern design, although not quite to the same degree as the bow. Granted, there are times when the stern will take a beating—for example, when sailing in heavy conditions on a run or broad reach. Nonetheless, when the going gets rough, a sailor's first instinct is to turn around, heaving-to so the sharper, more durable bow takes the brunt of the seas.

There are a number of reasons for this, including the valid urge to protect the rudder and steering gear. In addition, the crew in an aft cockpit is vulnerable to the impact of any waves breaking over the stern, and the cockpit itself is susceptible to filling with water. A water-laden cockpit is not only uncomfortable, it is also heavy (a 6-foot-long, 3-foot-wide, 2-foot-deep cockpit well carries 2,300 pounds of seawater when full), and all that extra weight will make the boat that much more vulnerable to the elements. Finally, sailing into heavy seas is less hazardous than sailing with them, because a cresting wave from astern can easily throw a boat over on its side and broadside to the seas in a broach. (Running off before storm seas has proved a legitimate tactic for sailboats encountering storms on the open ocean with plenty of sea room to leeward. But a boat running off like this will likely have to trail a drogue from its stern to prevent a broach.)

The traditional transom, which rakes aft from its lowest point to its crown, offers a number of advantages. In following seas it provides a measure of reserve buoyancy to help lift the stern and avoid being pooped. By extending the deck farther aft, it also allows the cockpit to be moved aft, providing more room for the cabin trunk. Finally, it allows you to lead the backstay as far aft as possible so it won't catch the mainsail leech during tacks and jibes.

Traditional transoms come in a number of shapes and sizes. Some are little more than rectangles or ovals when viewed from astern, while others are bowl-shaped and still others have a wineglass shape that's nearly irresistible to traditional-boat fans. Some transoms are large and others are downright tiny. In some cases there will be a substantial *counter*—an upward slope of the hull profile from the aft end of the waterline to the transom, so that the transom actually begins somewhere in midair. The advantage of a compact, curvaceous transom sitting atop a counter is that it is better able to withstand the assault of a following sea. On the other hand, a boxy transom close to the waterline provides a lot of internal volume for an aft cabin and cockpit storage lockers, as well as a broad external surface for a boarding ladder.

Alas, large or small, the downside of a raked-aft transom is weight—and we're not talking about any old weight, but weight where you least want it, out

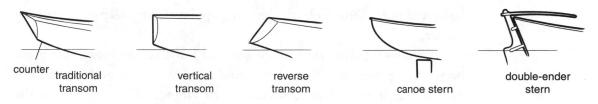

counter   traditional
transom

vertical
transom

reverse
transom

canoe stern

double-ender
stern

Common stern shapes.

at the end of the hull. To solve this problem, race-boat designers have created the *reverse transom*, which angles forward instead of aft from the end of the LWL, eliminating a big "triangle" of material in the process. First developed in the 1960s for use aboard America's Cup boats, the reverse transom represents the very essence of speed—or at least its appearance—for sailors like me who came to the sport in the 1970s. So popular was the reverse transom that it was adopted for use on cruisers. The speed advantage may have been minimal, but the "cool" factor was huge. Designers also figured out that cutting a step or two into a reverse transom created a handy platform for boarding from a dinghy. This "sugar scoop" transom shape has become ubiquitous aboard cruisers large and small.

The failing of a reverse transom is the cockpit space and interior volume it sacrifices. Lounging and interior amenities aboard a race boat are a secondary concern, however, and the reverse transoms on cruising boats feature only moderate rake so they can look fast yet still retain a decent cockpit—the maritime equivalent of having your cake and eating it too. Another option is a no-nonsense, straight up and down plumb transom like that of the ubiquitous J/24. This approach gives you a little more cockpit space and allows you to run the backstay a little farther aft, which helps prevent the battens of the mainsail from getting snagged when you tack in light air.

Finally, there are so-called *double-ended boats*, boats that lack a transom altogether. These sterns can be sleek and narrow—like those on racing canoes or the venerable 30-foot 210 sloop designed by C. Raymond Hunt—or they can be the stocky sterns of cruisers such as the fabled Westsail 32, designed by Colin Archer, or the Pacific Seacraft line designed by Bill Crealock. Derived either directly or indirectly from the sterns of double-ended rescue boats, lifeboats, and pilot boats—vessels that have to go out in pretty much any weather or sea—these sterns are both sturdy and buoyant and can withstand the force of a big overtaking sea.

Salty and purposeful looking, they are popular among deepwater cruising sailors.

Having said that, there is no ironclad law that double-enders make better voyagers than their wider-fannied brethren. None other than naval architect Bob Perry, the creator of such famous double-enders as the Valiant 40 and Baba 30, has called into question the idea that double-enders make better blue-water cruisers. "Nobody loves double-enders more than I do, but even I can't convince myself that [they] make the best sea boats," Perry wrote in a design review of Bill Crealock's Pacific Seacraft 40 for the August 1995 issue of *Sailing* magazine. "Certainly a moderate approach to volume in the ends and an effort to create near-symmetrical waterlines fore and aft can result in a well-mannered boat. But not all double-enders are well mannered, and not all transom-sterned boats are bears offshore."

9

KEELS, RUDDERS, AND OTHER HULL FEATURES

Different Shapes for Speed, Comfort, and Durability

NEXT AMONG a hull's features are its rudder and keel—its "underwater appendages," or *foils*. A stroll through any boatyard will show you a dizzying array of sizes and shapes. Today the majority of rudders reside more or less on their own near the stern, while the keel takes the form of a separate fin farther forward. Nonetheless, there are still plenty of boats on which the rudder is attached to the aft edge of the keel. The contrast in these two configurations is startling, yet they share pretty much the same objective: an optimum balance of performance and safety.

Over the past 150 years, keels and rudders have evolved dramatically, thanks to a better understanding of hydrodynamics coupled with vast improvements in materials and boatbuilding technology. In fact, before the late nineteenth century, the fin keels that are now so common would have been physically impossible to build.

Until the late 1800s, ships and boats alike carried their ballast in the form of stones, bricks, or iron or lead ingots stowed as deeply as possible in their bilges. They were also equipped with a *full keel*, basically a smooth

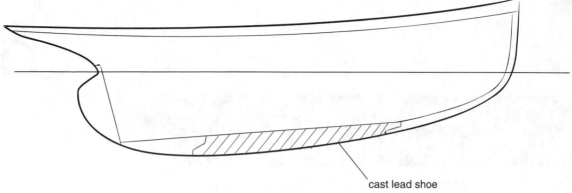

cast lead shoe

A full-keel cutter hull from the 1880s with outside ballast.

continuation of the bow profile curve into the keel and then aft to the rudder. Toward the end of the century, boatbuilders began making yachts with *outside ballast* in the form of a cast lead or iron "shoe" bolted to the bottom of the keel. The modern fin keel, in which a portion of the ballast is sometimes contained in a torpedo-like bulb at the very tip of the keel, is a continuation of the trend that began then. The advantages of outside ballast are twofold: First, the weight of the ballast is located as low as possible, providing a better righting moment, or lever, for keeping the boat upright under sail. Second, you don't have to worry about a bunch of loose ballast flying around the cabin in the event of a rollover or severe knockdown.

"Never will I go to sea with inside ballast again," the famed English yacht designer Uffa Fox once wrote, reflecting on a stormy Atlantic crossing during which the boat he was sailing turned completely upside down in a gale. "That ballast might easily have dropped out through the deck house, and had it done so *Typhoon* would have gone to the bottom and no more would have been heard of her. She must have come within a hair's breadth of it as it was."

root chord length

keel span

keel tip

tip chord length

trailing edge   leading edge

The anatomy of a fin keel: This slight top-down view shows how the keel has been carefully shaped as a foil.

The Shape of Speed

Modern keels are built as precision foils that provide lift when sailing to windward, as opposed to just passively resisting leeway with their bulk.

This is true even of heavy cruisers. The full-length keels of the hugely successful Island Packet line, for example, may look like just another big chunk of fiberglass, but they are in fact carefully designed to create maximum lift for their surface area—just like the keel of the hottest racing boat.

When looking at keels, it's important to be aware that the lift forces they generate under sail increase exponentially with velocity—in other words, hydrodynamic lift increases much faster than boat speed. If, for example, you increase boat speed by a factor of two, the lift force will increase by a factor of four. That means an inherently faster boat generally requires a smaller keel area to generate the same amount of lift for a given set of conditions. This is one of the main reasons racing boats have much narrower keels than cruisers.

Another reason racers like deep, slender keels is that a *high-aspect foil*—a foil that's long and skinny, with a short *chord length* and long *span*—generates more lift and less water resistance for a given surface area than a foil that's short and wide. This is because water, air, or any other fluid passing over the surface of a solid does so in a smooth, laminar fashion at first, but then inevitably breaks up into turbulent eddies. On most keels, these eddies begin to form a couple of feet back from the keel's leading edge and become progressively worse as the water flows aft. Because keels—like sails—work best when the flow is laminar, the farther aft the water flows along a wide, shallow keel, the less lift it will generate per square foot. A deep, high-aspect keel, on the other hand, enjoys smooth laminar flow along most of its fore-and-aft width, making it that much more efficient for its total area.

High-aspect foils also help reduce the effect of the pressure loss that occurs at the tip of a keel. As a keel passes through the water, some of the high-pressure water on its leeward side inevitably leaks around the

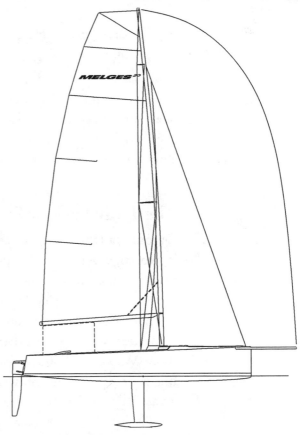

The high-aspect keels on racing boats, like this Audi Melges 20, provide lots of lift and righting moment, which in turn provide sparkling, high-speed performance when sailing to windward. (Melges Performance Sailboats)

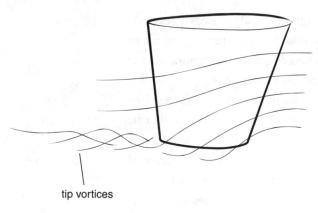

tip vortices

As a keel passes through the water, some of the high-pressure water on the leeward side will inevitably do an end run around the bottom of the keel instead of flowing aft along the foil to develop lift.

bottom of the keel instead of flowing aft to develop lift. Such leakage not only reduces the amount of lift the keel generates, it also forms tip vortices that impede the keel's motion through the water. Designers like to put in a little extra span to help compensate for this loss in efficiency.

It was in part to minimize this tip problem that designer Ben Lexcen created his famous winged keel for the 1983 America's Cup winner *Australia II*. By placing a pair of small horizontal wings on the tip of the keel he was able to reduce the amount of water going where it shouldn't. This *endplate effect* also comes into play when a keel is equipped with a bulb.

Finally, a deep keel—no matter what its aspect ratio—helps lower a boat's center of gravity, which in turn produces a more powerful righting force, or moment, that works to keep the boat upright when it starts to heel. A high-aspect keel also has less wetted surface area than a low-aspect keel of the same depth. Therefore, it will generate less resistance as it passes through the water, whether you are sailing into the wind or on a run.

The Drawback of Draft

Of course, all this performance comes at a price. First and foremost, a deep keel is great when you've got plenty of water, but what about when it's time to return to the marina, or you want to go cruising in the notoriously shallow Bahamas, or you feel like exploring a muddy little estuary off the Chesapeake?

My wife, Shelly, and I once went for a cruise off Mobile, Alabama, where the water was only 12 feet deep in the middle of the bay, a couple of miles offshore. We were sailing a 35-foot shoal-draft sloop that only drew about 4 feet. But as we explored the Intracoastal Waterway to Pensacola, Florida, I suspect we actually touched the murky bottom in at least a couple of anchorages.

I'll also never forget coming in a little after dark at the end of the 230-mile Port Huron-Mac race aboard *Mainstreet*, a 48-foot, deep-draft J/145 owned by *Sailing* magazine publisher Bill Schanen. We were tired, hungry, and ready to drink some beer, but I'll be damned if we could get our 9-foot-deep selves tied up at the marina on Mackinac Island. Apparently, the ferries that regularly thunder their way back and forth from the mainland have a tendency to kick up sand into little ridges along the edge of the marina. Again and again we tried to motor our way through, only to come to a halt with a gentle thump. Eventually, with the help of two or three dozen sailors shouting directions between sips of beer, we managed to thread our way in—by following the trenches carved in the bottom by faster competitors. I swear there were moments I wondered whether we would be stuck out there forever, like some kind of modern-day *Flying Dutchman* doomed never to set foot ashore again.

Of course, what we're talking about here is just a gentle tap. Imagine hitting bottom with some authority. A full-keel cruiser with a gently angled leading edge can hit a sizable rock at speed and suffer little more than a scratch. Hit that same rock with a high-aspect fin, though, and you run the risk of damaging not only your keel, but the entire hull. All that force concentrated on a narrow attachment point can do some serious damage. I know of a 70-foot racing boat that hit a reef in Northern Lake Huron at full speed. Not only was the keel nearly pulled out, the better part of the hull had to be largely rebuilt.

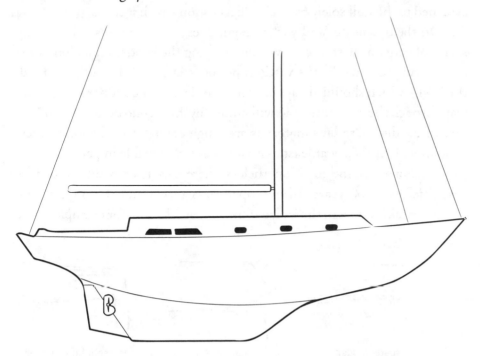

A full-keel cruiser with a gently angled leading edge can hit a solid rock at speed and suffer no serious damage.

Finally, while it's true that high-aspect fins work well for racers, a lower-aspect keel will track much better at lower velocities, which means much less work for whoever—or whatever, in the case of an autopilot—is at the helm. When considering a sailboat, always remember that performance varies depending on the kind of sailing you plan to do. It makes no sense to stick a thin, "go-fast" appendage on the bottom of a cruising hull that will rarely if ever take advantage of it.

Rudders

Not surprisingly, many of the same issues are at work in rudder design. Back in the good old days, as mentioned above, rudders were almost universally attached to the trailing edge of the keel. This was true even in racing boats. Boat design in the years following the Second World War, however, saw the rudder and keel moving apart in the interest of maneuverability. Separating them creates a longer lever arm for turning the hull and also allows the rudder's foil shape to help generate lift to windward. This increasing separation ultimately produced the modern *spade rudder*, a high-aspect fin that's attached to the hull solely by the rudderpost on which it turns.

On the downside (and yacht design does sometimes resemble a long series of bargains with the downside) hanging the rudder on its lonesome leaves it unprotected by the vastly superior strength of the keel. Granted, the keel—which should always be at least as deep as the rudder—carves its way through the water first and will bump anything solid before the rudder does. In addition, today's materials are tough enough that a good rudderpost should, in theory at least, withstand any reasonable impact and even the occasional grounding. Nonetheless, there have been plenty of rudder casualties over the years. Beamy open-class racers and the high-octane machines taking part in the Volvo round-the-world race, for example, carry

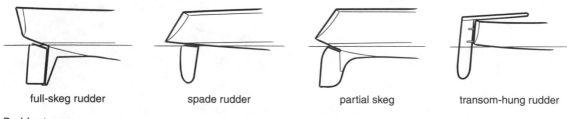

full-skeg rudder   spade rudder   partial skeg   transom-hung rudder

Rudder types.

twin rudders—one on either side of the transom where they're completely unprotected. Numerous tales tell of these poor foils colliding with a variety of underwater objects, including oblivious whales. (Poor foils? Heck, poor whales!) In plenty of other cases, water penetrating the blade of a poorly constructed rudder has corroded the rudderstock and caused the rudder simply to fall off.

To solve these problems, many builders mount their rudders behind a *skeg*, a kind of mini keel that helps keep the rudder safe and can also enhance the boat's *tracking ability*—its tendency to sail in a straight line. Many hardy cruisers employ a full skeg, with a sturdy heel bearing connecting the bottom of the skeg to the bottom of the rudder. Not only does this configuration provide maximum security if and when a boat grounds, it also prevents stray fishing lines and other junk from getting tangled in the narrow seam between the rudder and skeg. On occasion this arrangement includes an aperture for the propeller, so that the prop will be protected as well.

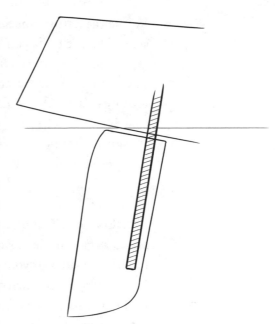

A balanced rudder with the rudder shaft set about 15 percent of the chord length aft of the leading edge.

For sailors unwilling to give up entirely on the performance of a spade rudder, there is the option of a partial skeg, which might be as much as three-quarters the length of the rudder or merely a small *skeglet* to prevent lines from getting caught in the gap between the hull and the spade.

Another advantage of free-standing spade rudders or rudders with only partial skegs is they can be balanced. In this configuration a small portion of the rudder blade—maybe 15 percent of its chord length—is forward of the rudder shaft, where it serves as "power steering," helping to deflect the rudder off centerline as the helmsman moves the tiller or wheel.

A Question of Curves

We've talked about sheerlines, bows, sterns, keels, and rudders, but there's still a lot more hull that needs to be pushed through the water. What follows is a partial list of the various curves and features found in and on most sailboat hulls, as well as how they affect performance under sail.

While the definitions are fairly brief, they're more than sufficient to make sense of most hulls you'll encounter when strolling through the boatyard.

If you're interested in learning about hull shape in greater detail, check out the bibliography at the end of this book. A real standout is Steve Killing's *Yacht Design Explained*, one of those rare, highly technical books that is nevertheless a joy to read. Another good one is Bob Perry's *Yacht Design According to Perry*, which discusses the principles of yacht design and performance as well as the design process—i.e., the interplay of art, science, imagination, client guidance, and cost that shapes a new boat.

TURN OF THE BILGE. When a boat sitting on jackstands is viewed from ahead or astern, the *turn of the bilge* is where the hull bottom curves upward into the topsides. If you're looking at design drawings, look at the body plan. Every section has a turn of the bilge, and though the turn is likely to be gentler in the bow sections and harder amidships and in the quarters, you'll also see that one boat has, overall, a gentler turn of the bilge than another. When this curve is smooth and gentle, naval architects say the hull has *slack bilges*. If the curve is tightly radiused, the boat is said to have *hard bilges*.

The turn of the bilge plays an important role in a boat's stability, especially when the boat first starts to heel. On a boat with hard bilges, a substantial amount of hull volume immerses quickly as that tight turn and the topsides above it dip into the water. The result is a powerful righting force that counters the heeling force of the wind against the sails, so hard bilges create a *stiff* boat that likes to sail upright. On a boat with slack bilges, however, significantly less hull volume immerses as the boat goes over, so it has a greater tendency to heel. Naval architects use the term *tender* to describe a hull exhibiting this kind of performance.

DEADRISE. Closely linked to a boat's turn of the bilge is its *deadrise*, the degree to which the bottom of the boat is angled above the horizontal when viewed in section. More deadrise generally means more displacement, but not always. A modern fin-keel boat with flat sections and minimum deadrise is generally pretty light, displacing a minimum of water. The sections of a heavy full-keel boat, on the other hand, are generally angled more steeply upward from the keel to the turn of the bilge, creating substantial deadrise.

That said, freighters and old-time sailing barges generally employ a dead-flat bottom to maximize cargo-carrying capacity for a given depth.

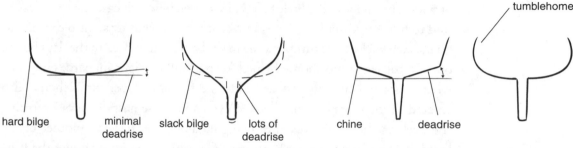

Turn of the bilge and deadrise.

Chines and tumblehome.

The thousand-foot ore freighter *George A. Stinson* that I worked aboard back in my mid-20s had a bottom that was flat as a pancake, but with its belly full of some 56,000 tons of taconite it could hardly be called a skimming dish!

In terms of performance, less deadrise enhances a boat's planing ability, while more deadrise imparts a smoother motion in a seaway because deeper-angled sections are less likely to pound in the waves. Deadrise aboard a cruising boat also creates additional storage space down low for heavy things such as water, fuel, and anchor chains. In addition, it provides a low point for water to collect in the bilge. Boats with minimal deadrise often have a small *sump*, or low point, carved out of the stub where the hull attaches to the keel, but you can still end up with bilge water slopping over the floorboards of the cabin sole when the boat is sailing on its ear.

CHINES. In some boats, a distinct angle, or corner—as opposed to a curve—forms the transition from the bottom of the hull to the topsides. This angle, as it runs the length of the hull, is called a *chine*. Like a hard bilge, chines usually impart initial stability, and they're often employed because they're less difficult to build than a complex curve. They work well if you plan to build a plywood, steel, or aluminum boat, because these materials come in large sheets that are difficult to shape into complex curves. This is not to say that chined boats are inferior to their more curvaceous cousins—some of the most celebrated boats in the world have been built with hard chines, including Stars, Lightnings, and the old "sharpies" that once plied the waters of Long Island Sound.

TUMBLEHOME. Viewed in cross section, a boat's topsides might be more or less vertical, or they might flare out a little between the waterline and the deck. Or they might curve outboard and then back inboard, with the point of widest beam located a little below deck level, in which case the topsides are said to have some *tumblehome*. A few boat types, including some old-time catboats, even have a little tumblehome in the bow profile. Back in the days before outside ballast, tumblehome helped keep a hull's weight inboard, especially when it started heeling. Aboard old-time fighting ships, tumblehome also created a little more distance between you and those nasty fellows swarming the deck on the enemy vessel drawing up alongside. It's also another of the loopholes that helped racing boats get a favorable speed rating under the IOR rule in the 1970s and 1980s.

Tumblehome has become increasingly rare of late, however, because it makes popping a fiberglass hull out of a mold somewhat problematic. Flare, on the other hand, directs spray outward when you're crashing through waves, as opposed to letting it slop onto the deck as tumblehome can. In addition, if a boat has a little flare, the crew can sit that much farther to windward to help keep the boat sailing flat in heavy air.

FREEBOARD. The height of the deck above the waterline, called *freeboard*, is a little like draft—the more the better, until it starts causing problems. On the plus side, freeboard provides room for storage and inside accommodations. On the downside, it creates windage, which means decreased efficiency to windward and greater vulnerability in heavy weather. More freeboard also means a higher center of gravity, which increases the tendency to heel.

Worse yet, excessive freeboard is downright ugly, making an otherwise fine boat look awkward and ungainly. Naval architects use a number of tricks to minimize the effects of excessive freeboard—including *cove stripes*, which are thin lines carved into or painted on the hull a few inches below the deck edge—but nothing can make freeboard disappear.

The tendency toward excessive freeboard becomes especially acute in cruising boats with LOAs below 30 feet, as designers and builders strive for that all-important commodity called "standing headroom." (Oddly enough, headroom is rarely an issue aboard a 70-footer.) Personally, I think standing headroom—generally considered to be a little more than 6 feet—is highly overrated, and I'm 6 foot 2 inches. These are sailboats we're talking about here, not floating condominiums. As L. Francis Herreshoff (Captain Nat Herreshoff's equally accomplished son) once said, "If you want standing headroom, go into the cockpit."

10

WHY SAILBOATS DON'T (USUALLY) TIP OVER

And How Best to Leverage Your Center of Buoyancy

UNDERSTANDING sailboat stability is a little like understanding the sun's apparent motion across the sky. Over the millennia, human beings came up with all kinds of weird and wacky explanations for why the sun rises in the east and sets in the west, but it took astronomers and mathematicians like Nicholas Copernicus and Isaac Newton to finally get to the heart of the matter—and in the process they discovered gravity and invented calculus. Understand why the sun does what it does, and you can't help but gain a much better understanding of the universe in general. Understand why sailboats don't (usually) tip over, and you can't help but gain a more profound understanding of how their rigs interact with air and their hulls with water. The key concepts here are center of buoyancy and righting moment.

First, a question: How does ballast work? Answer: When a sailboat heels, the ballast pulls down on the keel until the boat returns to vertical. Excellent! Now, another question: What exactly is the ballast working

Understand why sailboats don't (usually) tip over, and you can't help but gain a more profound understanding of how their rigs interact with air and their hulls with water.

against as it levers, or pivots, the hull and mast back upright? If you guessed the hull, you're right—partially. More precisely, what the ballast works against is something called the *center of buoyancy* (CB)—the geometric center of the hull's underwater portion, what can be thought of as the focal point through which the collective force of all the water molecules pressing upward against the outside of the hull is acting. In essence, the center of buoyancy is the fulcrum against which the ballast works (in concert with the rest of the boat's weight) to lever the hull and rig back up to vertical.

Momentous Stuff

The neat thing about the center of buoyancy is that it doesn't just stay in one place. On the contrary, it's continually moving around, especially to port and to starboard, creating something called *form stability*. Imagine, for example, a sailboat at rest and perfectly vertical. Gazing up at it from the bottom of the harbor (presumably through a face mask), we see that the hull is symmetrical about the keel. This, in turn, means that the force with which the water is pushing up against what is essentially a wood- or fiberglass-encased hole in the water is the same on both sides. Thus the center of buoyancy is right on the centerline, immediately above the keel.

Now imagine what happens when the wind starts blowing the rig off to one side, causing the boat to heel. Immediately, the windward side begins lifting out of the water, while a progressively larger volume of the leeward side submerges. Now if you happened to look up from below you would see a dramatic change in the immersed shape, with a whole lot more hull submerged to leeward of the keel than to windward. Of course, as the leeward part of the hull is driven over, it also displaces a lot of water. This water is heavy stuff and wants nothing more than to push that enclosed volume of air back up into the atmosphere where it belongs. Suddenly, the center of buoyancy is well to leeward, as opposed to directly over the keel—form stability in action.

Better still, even as all those water molecules are focusing their combined upward push on that offset center of buoyancy, the combined weight of the hull—the keel in particular—is pushing down at another point, the *center of gravity* (CG), forming a lever of sorts called a *righting arm*. A force (weight) pushing on the end of a lever creates a *moment*, the magnitude of which is the force times the distance (i.e., the length of the lever arm), and it is this *righting moment* that keeps a sailboat from tipping over. The pivot point around which the sailboat revolves during this process—and which is always directly above the center of buoyancy—is called the *metacenter*.

It should now be apparent why a wide hull with a hard turn of bilge provides more form stability—because the CB moves more rapidly outboard with each increment of heel, and the righting arm is longer than it will be for a narrow, slack-bilged boat.

The effect of ballast is a bit harder to describe. The center of gravity is on the boat's centerline, usually near the waterline, and unlike the CB, the CG doesn't move when the boat heels. So how does ballast increase righting moment? It does so by increasing the weight of the boat (which increases the force in the force x distance calculation of right-ing moment) while lowering the center of gravity—the lower the CG, the longer the righting arm for any given location of CB in the heeled boat.

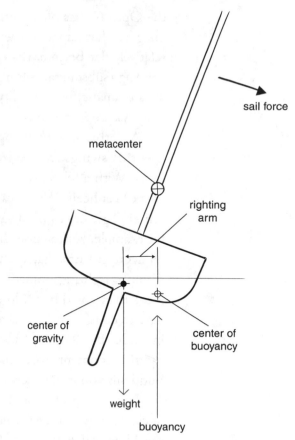

The heeling and righting forces acting on a sailboat underway.

Righting Moments in Action

Knowing how the center of buoyancy, center of gravity, and righting moment work allows you to dig beneath the surface and understand why sailboats—and naval architects—do the things they do. High-powered Open 60 open-water racers, for example, displace very little water for their size, but still carry tremendous amounts of sail. How is this possible? To find the answer, follow the center of buoyancy.

When you view an Open 60 from astern, its hull is wide and shallow, like the wide, shallow scows raced on many inland lakes in the Midwest. In fact, the Open 60 has often been described as an oversized racing dinghy. Now, imagine what happens when an Open 60 starts to heel. Because of its wide, relatively flat bottom, the center of buoyancy immediately races outboard, creating a substantial righting arm even if the boat is only heeling a few degrees. This dramatic form stability is further amplified by the boat's low center of gravity, a product of its deep, skinny keel, often with a lead bulb at the bottom.

As if that weren't enough, many Open 60s are equipped with a canting keel that swings from side to side with the help of a system of hydraulic rams. With a fixed keel, the location of the center of gravity remains fixed as the boat heels. With a canting keel, however, it is possible to shift a boat's center of gravity to windward or leeward depending on the conditions. Say, for example, you're under sail, the wind pipes up, and the boat heels maybe 15 degrees. Immediately the center of buoyancy shoots to leeward, but the resulting righting moment isn't enough to keep the boat from heeling a little more than you'd like. No problem: to keep the boat on her lines, all you have to do is cant the keel a bit to windward. Moving the CG to windward increases the length of the righting arm, and thus the magnitude of the righting moment, to counter the heeling force of the wind in the sails. Suddenly you've got a lever arm on steroids! Who needs displacement?

For a comparison let's look at an old-time 12-meter boat, one of a series of classes built to the prewar International Rule. Like its U.S. counterpart, the Universal Rule—which produced the spectacular J-class yachts used in America's Cup competition in the 1930s—the International Rule was

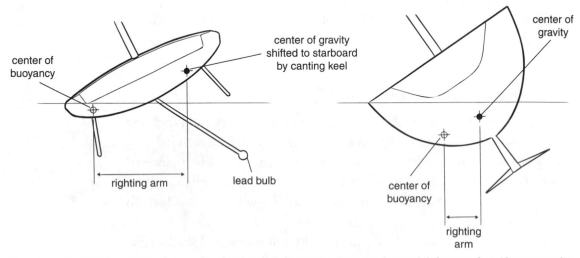

The dramatic righting arm in a beamy Open 60 racer (left) and the more moderate righting arm in a 12-meter yacht.

expressly designed back in 1907 to compel boatbuilders to create moderately proportioned boats that sailors could use both for racing and cruising. To this end, old-time 12-meters in particular are long and narrow, with slack bilges, plenty of deadrise, and even a little tumblehome. Their draft is also specifically limited.

When a boat like that gets hit by a puff and starts to heel, the center of buoyancy moves to leeward, but nowhere near as dramatically as in an Open 60. The result: the boat keeps right on heeling—until the two centers are far enough apart to create sufficient leverage to counter the wind acting against the rig. Even then, you'll likely need significant ballast if you're planning on flying any kind of sail. It's no accident that, even in their heyday, 12-meters were often derided as "lead mines" because of all the ballast they had to carry.

These skinny boats with lots of displacement become stiff as churches at around 20 degrees of heel, but before that they can be quite tender—which can be disconcerting to a sailor accustomed to beamy hulls and deep fin keels. The first time I went sailing on a Star boat I was shocked at the way it behaved, even in what felt like the lightest of zephyrs. Despite being some 23 feet long and carrying a hefty 285 square feet of sail, the boat has a beam of just 5 feet 8 inches. Compare that to the famed Catalina 22, which has an LOA of 21 feet 6 inches and two more feet of beam—7 feet 8 inches to be exact. No wonder Star crews are always hiking so far to windward it looks like they're barely hanging on by their ankles!

The Physics of Dinghies and Cats

The same righting principles apply to unballasted vessels such as catamarans and dinghies, the difference being that the center of gravity is often as much a function of crew weight as it is the weight of the boat and rig. Basically, whenever you hike out you're moving the center of gravity to windward of the unballasted hull's center of buoyancy. By doing this you create a powerful righting moment to counteract the heeling moment caused by the wind pressing against the sails.

Once again, hull shape makes a big difference. Some boats, like the fast and light 505 dinghy, have narrow, rounded bottoms that can get pretty tippy because of their minimal form stability. Others, like the Wayfarer 16 or the boxy Optimist dinghy, have broad bottoms with firm bilges or chines (the Optimist has one chine per side and the Wayfarer

righting arm

buoyancy   weight

Crew weight in a dinghy serves the same function as ballast in a keel boat. In this instance, the crew is suspended over the water on a trapeze. (Erik Skallerup and Domenic Mosqueira/YachtShots, BVI)

has two) that make the boats much more stable and remarkably forgiving for their size.

Many high-performance dinghies are built with flaring topsides to help get crew weight that much farther outboard. Some, like the 505, the 420, and the Flying Dutchman, are also equipped with trapezes—wires that run from the mast to a harness on the crew. A trapeze makes it possible to suspend your entire body out over the water, with only the soles of your feet touching the edge of the deck, thereby maximizing the righting moment.

The ultimate is when a boat is equipped with both a trapeze and racks, or wings. The world-famous 18-foot racing skiffs of Sydney, Australia, for example, have a beam of just 6 feet, but racks to port and starboard extend the platform width from which the crew can hike to 14 feet. A 6-foot crew-member on a trapeze can thus extend nearly 13 feet from the boat's center-line. Talk about moving around your center of gravity!

Equally dramatic is the interaction between center of gravity and center of buoyancy aboard a small multihull. At rest, the center of buoyancy is on centerline, just as it is for a monohull, but that changes quickly as the wind applies a heeling moment to the mast, driving the leeward hull deeper into the water and lifting the windward hull into the air. In a flash, the center of buoyancy shoots to leeward as the leeward hull supports more and more of the boat's weight. At the same time, the center of gravity races in the other direction as the crew positions itself to windward.

The famed Hobie 16 has a beam of nearly 8 feet, in addition to a trapeze. Put a 6-foot surfer-dude out on that wire and you've got a heck of a lot of leverage to play around with. The 20-foot Tornado catamaran, designed for Olympic competition, measures 9 feet 11 inches from hull to hull and also has a trapeze.

The same physics is at work on larger cruising multihulls. The Maine Cat 30, for example, has an 18-foot beam, while the 31-foot 10-inch Corsair 31 trimaran has a total beam—from one outboard hull, or ama, to the other—of 22 feet 5 inches. Compare that to the Catalina 310 monohull

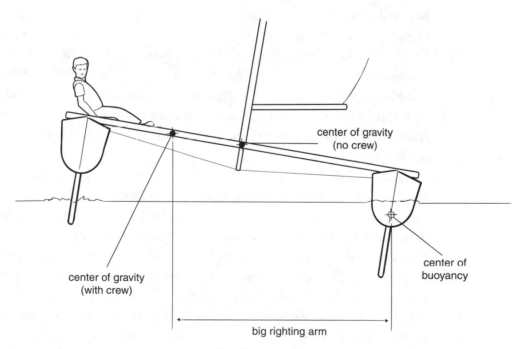

A catamaran's widely separated hulls create a tremendous amount of righting moment under sail.

cruiser, which has an LOA of about 31 feet and a beam of a little over 11 feet—and the Catalina is considered wide for a monohull.

So effective is the righting moment of multihulls that they need no ballast—the lighter the better. By comparison, the Catalina 310 needs to carry 4,000 pounds of lead in its keel to keep it on its feet. Not surprisingly, a multihull's weight saving can make for some serious speed.

Point of No Return

So far we've been talking about stability and righting moment under "normal" sailing conditions. Now let's take a look at what happens in extreme conditions, when the wind and waves can knock a boat on its beam ends—90 degrees or more of heel—and it's uncertain whether the boat will pivot upright again.

This question received a lot of attention after the 1979 Fastnet Race—a 600-mile race from Cowes, England, to Fastnet Rock off the southwestern tip of Ireland, then back to Plymouth, England. During the race a sudden gale disabled or sank more than two dozen boats and killed fifteen sailors. Despite the hurricane-force winds and steep seas, many sailors believed a number of the boats rolled too easily or turned turtle because of design characteristics resulting from the International Offshore Rule (IOR), then in its heyday. Specifically, it was believed that the boats' generous beams and narrow, or *pinched*, bows and sterns had seriously compromised their seaworthiness in sharp, breaking waves. In response, the sailing community jettisoned the IOR and adopted a whole new set of rules—the International Measurement System—in order to create a "healthier" class of racers.

Alas, stability and righting moment in extreme conditions came to the fore yet again in the late 1990s. During the 1996–97 Vendée Globe solo, round-the-world race, three boats capsized in the stormy Southern Ocean. (One sailor, Canadian Gerry Roufs, disappeared.) Not only did the combined forces of wind and waves flip boats upside down, the boats stayed that way. A number of photographs taken at the time show the rolled boats in storm conditions, keels and rudders sticking up in the air, pretty as you please.

The concept at work in cases like these is something called the *limit of positive stability* (LPS), also known as the *angle of vanishing stability*. To understand how this operates, imagine what happens to the center of buoyancy and center of gravity as a monohull of moderate dimensions heels from 20 to 45 to 90 to 110 degrees—the angle that can result from broaching or being struck by a large breaking wave. As the boat heels through 20 and 45 degrees, the center of buoyancy moves farther from the center of gravity, and the righting moment increases—eventually reaching a point known as the *angle of maximum stability*, or "peak" of stability. After this, though, as the boat heels farther still, the center of buoyancy reverses direction and moves back toward the center of gravity, and as it does so the righting moment becomes progressively less. Eventually you reach a point of *zero righting moment*, and your fate literally hangs in the balance. The center of buoyancy is directly beneath the center of gravity, and the righting arm has disappeared. It's left to the wind or waves to push you one way or the other. The point of zero righting moment is also called the *limit of positive stability*, because beyond that point the boat's

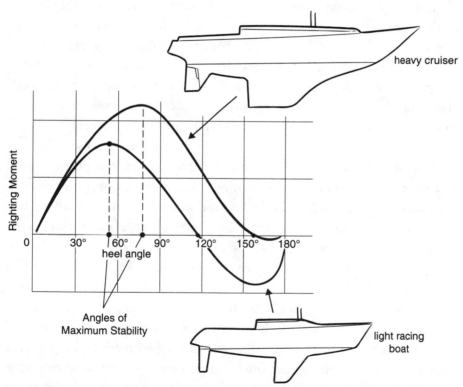

The stability curves for a heavy cruiser and a lightweight racing boat. Notice how much farther the cruiser can heel before it reaches the point of zero righting moment—which is over 150 degrees for the cruiser versus about 115 degrees for the racing boat. Also note how little of the cruiser's stability curve is below the zero point. In the event it does capsize, it will re-right itself that much faster.

center of gravity will actually start pulling the hull the rest of the way over, as opposed to trying to pull it upright again.

Unfortunately, once a boat reaches this point, you can soon find yourself in very big trouble indeed—thanks to that same form stability that keeps your boat upright when things aren't so crazy. The portion of a stability curve that's located below the point of zero righting moment represents the angles of heel at which the form stability of the inverted hull will work to *keep* the boat upside down—even with the weight of the keel pointing at the sky. In fact, it will do so indefinitely, barring any outside force such as a wave. The deeper the negative curve, the harder it will be to pop the boat back upright.

If you're aboard a relatively narrow boat with plenty of ballast, a low center of gravity, and moderate form stability, the chances are pretty good that the next wave set—together with the ballast that's now sticking up in the air—will pull you back onto your feet. If, however, you happen to be aboard a light, beamy Open 60, all that beam and form stability can be problematic to say the least. Worse yet is if you're aboard a catamaran or trimaran that lacks any kind of ballast and is stabilized in its inverted position by all the buoyancy in those widely separated hulls. Your chances of popping back up again are pretty much zero. The history of extreme, offshore multihull racing is replete with examples of otherwise magnificent sailing vessels coming to an untimely end in just this fashion.

Note that a boat's topside volume, as well as the height and volume of deck structures such as cabin trunks and pilothouses, can play a critical role in recovering from a knockdown and in promoting positive stability in extreme conditions. As long as they remain watertight, structures like these can provide a tremendous amount of buoyancy to help a boat in distress get back up on its feet. Better still, submerging them in an extreme knockdown can move the center of buoyancy just far enough to leeward to avoid turning turtle altogether.

Some bluewater cruisers have a limit of positive stability of as much as 140 degrees. In other words, the mast can be pointing almost 50 degrees *below* horizontal and there is still some righting moment trying to lift it back up. In a safe, sedate boatshow environment, the beefed-up hardware aboard some heavy-duty cruisers may seem somewhat absurd. But those portlights and hatchways are built tough for a reason!

11

THE NUTS AND BOLTS OF DESIGN RATIOS

Comparing Apples and Oranges in the Sailing World

TO SAY THAT sailboats come in a variety of shapes and sizes would be to make the understatement of the year. How, then, is it possible to make objective comparisons between two sailboats? Unless the boats happen to be fairly similar to begin with—say, a pair of heavy-duty, full-keel cruisers or a pair of lightweight racers—it would seem that sailors are forever doomed to compare apples with oranges.

Fortunately, much as chemists can perform a nutritional analysis of two foods to see which is healthier, naval architects have learned how to use *design ratios* to objectively compare even the most strikingly different sailboats. Design ratios highlight the relationships between multiple design parameters, and in the process provide a glimpse into the underlying performance potential of a particular boat.

The process is similar to the way investors use ratios to evaluate the health of various companies in the stock market. To say, for example, that a company is thirty million dollars in debt says nothing. Thirty million

Simply knowing a sailboat's beam means little. Knowing both the beam and the length, on the other hand, tells you quite a bit about the kind of boat you're dealing with.

could be the beginning of the end for some firms, while to huge corporations like General Motors it's less than a drop in the bucket. A company's debt-to-equity ratio, on the other hand, compares the amount owed to the total amount of shareholder equity—a far more telling indication of whether a particular company's stock deserves its market valuation.

It's the same thing with design ratios. Simply knowing a sailboat's beam, for example, means little. Knowing both the beam and the length, on the other hand, tells you quite a bit about the kind of boat you're dealing with.

Hull Volume and Displacement

When most people see a sailboat, the first thing they want to know is its length. "How big is it?" they inevitably ask. But plain old length, more formally called *length overall* (LOA), can be deceiving. In fact, displacement is a far more telling measurement. Displacement is akin to volume: it's the volume of water displaced, or moved aside, when the boat is afloat and at rest. Volume, in turn, means room for things like bunks, the galley, stoves, storage, showers, and Jacuzzis. It also means having to overcome that much more resistance from the water when under sail.

When thinking about "size," it's important to be aware that volume increases at a much faster rate than length. Imagine the difference in volume between a 1-inch cube and a 2-inch cube. Whereas the volume of the first cube is 1 cubic inch—$1 \times 1 \times 1$—the larger cube is 8 cubic inches—$2 \times 2 \times 2$. Similarly, the total surface area increases from 6 inches to 24. (For a more complete discussion of this phenomenon, I recommend David Gerr's *The Nature of Boats*.) No naval architect would ever simply double the dimensions of a boat to make it bigger, as we did with the cubes. Among other things, as boats get larger, stability increases at an even greater rate than volume—which is why dinghies are so much wider for their length than clipper ships. In addition, hulls are longer and thinner than cubes, so the size-to-volume ratio is less extreme. Nevertheless, the basic idea that volume increases faster than length holds true, as do hull loads, rig loads—and prices. A Pacific Seacraft 44 cruiser, for example, is about 30 percent longer than a Pacific Seacraft 34, but at 27,500 pounds—compared to the 34's 13,500 pounds—it displaces twice as much. Similarly, a 39-foot Dehler performance cruiser displaces two-and-a-half times as much as Dehler's equally sporty 29-footer.

Bear in mind that there's volume and then there's *volume*. Some boats are definitely heavier and more voluminous for their LOA than others. Take the case of two fiberglass classics from the early 1970s: the Catalina 30 and the Tartan 30. They have exactly the same LOA—29 feet 11 inches—but the Catalina displaces 10,200 pounds while the Tartan displaces just 8,750. The J/30, big brother to the ubiquitous J/24, has a similar LOA of 29 feet 10 inches, but displaces even less—just 7,000 pounds. Finally, although slightly longer than the other three, with an LOA of 31 feet 10 inches, the Melges 32 displaces a mere 3,900 pounds not counting crew weight—nearly two-and-a-half tons less than the Tartan. Can you guess which of these three boats is the racer, or which has the most comfortable sleeping accommodations?

Crunching the Displacement Numbers

To compare the relative displacements of boats of various configurations and lengths, naval architects look at the *displacement-to-length ratio* (D/L)—derived by dividing the displacement in *long tons*, or metric tons, by 1 percent of the LWL cubed. A long ton is 2,240 pounds, so if you want to find the number of long tons, simply divide the displacement in pounds by 2,240. Note that we're using waterline length here, not LOA. LOA can include overhangs on the bow and stern, but unless the boat is well heeled (see next chapter) these add nothing to *sailing length*—the part of the hull involved in wave making and wetted surface area. Waterline length, on the other hand, delineates the part of the hull that's in direct contact with the water.

When calculating D/Ls it's important to use decimals as opposed to inches. For example, 4 inches is 0.33 feet; 6 inches is 0.5 feet; 8 inches is 0.67 feet; and so on. The mathematical formula for D/L is

$$\frac{\text{Displacement in long tons}}{[(0.01)(\text{LWL})]^3}$$

So let's figure out the D/Ls for three boats I mentioned earlier—the Catalina 30, the J/30, and the Melges 32—which happen to represent three of today's most popular sailboat types. We'll start with the Catalina.

First we calculate the number of long tons the Catalina measures, by dividing the boat's displacement by 2,240.

$$\frac{10,200 \text{ pounds}}{2,240} = 4.55 \text{ long tons}$$

Next we take 1% of the boat's LWL and then raise that to the third power.

$$25 \text{ feet} \times 0.01 = 0.25$$
$$0.25^3 = 0.0156$$

Finally we divide the number of long tons by 0.0156 to arrive at the Catalina's D/L:

$$\text{D/L} = \frac{4.55 \text{ long tons}}{0.0156} = 291$$

Simple. Now let's compare this to the J/30.

$$\frac{7,000 \text{ pounds}}{2,240} = 3.13 \text{ long tons}$$

$$26 \text{ feet} \times 0.01 = 0.26$$
$$0.26^3 = 0.0176$$

$$\text{D/L} = \frac{3.13 \text{ long tons}}{0.0176} = 177$$

Here we find that the J/30 has a D/L of 177, substantially less than the Catalina. Not surprisingly, the Melges 32 comes in lower still, with a D/L of 75. Yikes! Here's the math.

$$\frac{3,900 \text{ pounds}}{2,240} = 1.74 \text{ long tons}$$

$$28.5 \text{ feet} \times 0.01 = 0.285$$
$$0.285^3 = 0.023$$

$$\text{D/L} = \frac{1.74 \text{ long tons}}{0.023} = 75$$

Actually, this D/L for the Melges 32 is a bit deceptive because it fails to take into account the weight of the crew. Plunk down a typical racing crew of seven or eight burly sailors aboard such a light boat and things start to look different. Assuming a total crew weight of 1,400 pounds, the numbers for the Melges are as follows:

$$\frac{5,300 \text{ pounds}}{2,240} = 2.36 \text{ long tons}$$

$$\text{D/L} = \frac{2.36 \text{ long tons}}{0.023} = 103$$

That's a little more like it. Accounting for crew weight would increase the D/L's of the J/30 and Catalina 30 as well, of course, though not by as much.

Generally, high-octane racers have D/Ls of around 100 or less. Performance cruisers, or cruiser-racers as they're also known, have D/Ls of around 150 to 200. Cruisers will generally have D/Ls higher than 200, while heavy-duty cruisers will have D/Ls of 300 or more.

Bear in mind that none of these ranges is absolute. We're talking about a spectrum here. In addition, trends and categories change over the years. Today's boats, for example, are becoming lighter and lighter thanks to advances in building methods and materials.

Also bear in mind that it often pays to take publicized boat dimensions—and especially displacement—with a grain of salt. Manufacturers often employ unrealistically low numbers to make their cruising boats, in particular, appear lighter and faster than they truly are. Even if a boat does weigh what's advertised, the displacement value often doesn't account for the weight of equipment and supplies you need to take on board before sailing. Food, water, anchor chain, dodgers, fuel, foul-weather gear, electronics, extra sails, extra anchors, spare parts—these all can add hundreds or even thousands of pounds. Many sailors make a point of differentiating between light-ship weight and *half-load displacement*—the total displacement of a boat after the crew has worked its way through half the stores on passage.

In the excellent *Nigel Calder's Cruising Handbook*, veteran cruiser and sailing journalist Nigel Calder estimates that, for a typical coastal cruiser, you should add a minimum of 2,500 pounds to the boat's published weight to ballpark its half-load displacement. Add about 3,700 pounds to offshore cruisers. Calder claims these are *conservative* numbers, and that many sailors will carry far more stuff. If these figures seem high, consider that just 30 gallons of water weigh nearly 260 pounds, 30 gallons of diesel weigh more than 200 pounds, and $^5/_{16}$-inch chain weighs about a pound per foot. Do a weight study of all the items on your boat, and you might be surprised at what you find.

How Much Sail?

After hull size, the next most common question people ask is how big the rig is. On the plus side, sail area translates into speed, like the cylinder volume of an internal combustion engine. On the downside, sail area means work—bending on canvas, raising and lowering sails, and reefing in ugly weather. To compare rig sizes, naval architects have created a formula that divides the sail area by the displacement of the hull in cubic feet raised to the two-thirds power. The resulting *sail area to displacement ratio* (SA/D) allows them to determine not just the "size" of the rig, but its size compared to the displacement of the hull. The mathematical formula is

$$\frac{\text{sail area in square feet}}{(\text{displacement in pounds} \div 64)^{2/3}}$$

For decades, naval architects have determined sail area by using a number of design dimensions derived from the size of the hull and the spars that make up the rig. The most widely employed dimensions include the *foretriangle base*—measured from the jib's tack to the mast and designated as *J*; the *foretriangle height*—measured from the mast base upward to where the forestay attaches to the mast and designated as either *I* or *IG*; the mainsail foot length, designated as *E*; and the mainsail luff length, or *hoist*, designated as *P*. Given these dimensions, figuring sail area is a simple matter of multiplying E × P and J × I, and then dividing each product by 2. To derive the total rig area, simply add the results of each calculation.

Obviously, as was the case when estimating centers of effort, this approach yields a very conservative number. It doesn't account for the overlap that results when the clew of a headsail extends aft of the mast, nor does it include the curved portion of the mainsail leech, known as the *roach*, that extends beyond the simple triangle defined by E and P. Nonetheless, for years this approach was sufficient. Before the advent of modern, flexible

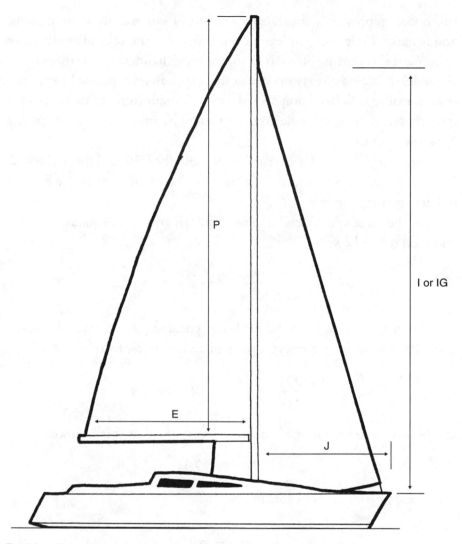

Traditionally, sail areas have been calculated using a few simple rig dimensions.

battens, roaches were generally kept to a minimum. So were overlapping jibs—at least until a German-born yachtsman by the name of Dr. Manfred Curry used a radical new overlapping jib to wipe out a fleet of 6-meters during a regatta in Genoa, Italy, back in the 1930s.

Today, of course, genoa jibs are commonplace even on cruisers, and the roaches on many mainsails have become downright huge. As a result, many designers and manufacturers measure actual sail area, as opposed to using I, J, E, and P. This new approach makes some sense—a dramatic roach does represent a substantial amount of sail area in many designs, and it makes little sense to leave it out simply for the sake of tradition or convenience. Including jib overlap, on the other hand, is a little more questionable, and doing so may make a sailboat appear, on paper, to be speedier than it really is. When comparing boats, the main thing to be aware of is how their sail areas were derived, so you aren't inadvertently comparing apples with oranges.

Let's figure the SA/Ds for the Catalina 30, the J/30, and the Melges 32. We'll use published figures for the boats' working sail area in the interest of keeping things simple.

For the Catalina, which has a working sail area of 444 square feet, the equation is as follows:

$$SA/D = \frac{446 \text{ square feet}}{(10,200 \text{ pounds} \div 64)^{2/3}} = 15.2$$

The first step in solving this fairly complicated equation is to divide the displacement by 64 to convert it from pounds to cubic feet.

$$\frac{10,200 \text{ pounds}}{64} = 159.4 \text{ cubic feet}$$

Next we raise the number of cubic feet to the two-thirds power.

$$159.4^{2/3} = 29.4$$

Finally, divide the sail area by 29.4

$$SA/D = \frac{446}{29.4} = 15.2$$

For the J/30 the equation is as follows:

$$SA/D = \frac{444 \text{ square feet}}{(7,000 \text{ pounds} \div 64)^{2/3}} = 19.4$$

Breaking this down into steps, first divide the displacement by 64 to convert from pounds to cubic feet.

$$\frac{7,000 \text{ pounds}}{64} = 109.4 \text{ cubic feet}$$

Next, raise the number of cubic feet to the two-thirds power.

$$109.4^{2/3} = 22.9$$

Finally, divide the sail area by 22.9.

$$SA/D = \frac{444 \text{ square feet}}{22.9} = 19.4$$

Finally, the equation for the Melges 32 is as follows. Once again, we are going to use a figure that adds in about 1,400 pounds of crew weight. I'll let you work through the math yourself this time.

$$SA/D = \frac{699 \text{ square feet}}{(5,300 \text{ pounds}/64)^{2/3}} = 36.8$$

As with D/Ls, SA/Ds can be broken down into three categories: heavy cruisers will generally have a conservative SA/D of 15 or less; performance cruisers and racer-cruisers will typically have a moderate SA/D of 15 to 20; over 20 and you're getting into true racing territory. Greater than 30—well, let's just say you and your crew had better know what you're doing. Because they don't require ballast to stay upright, multihulls tend to have much greater SA/Ds than monohulls. Even heavier cruising cats will often have SA/Ds in the 20s. The late Steve Fossett's 105-foot racing catamaran *PlayStation* has an SA/D of 102!

Be aware that when computing SA/Ds we're only looking at a boat's *working sails*—the main and jib—not spinnakers, reachers, drifters, gennikers, or any of the other myriad downwind sails that have been developed over the years. These sails vary tremendously in area, irrespective of foretriangle size or spar length, and are therefore no real reflection of the basic power provided by a particular sailboat's rig.

How Wide Is She?

Generally, a skinny hull will travel through the water more easily than a wide one, because it has less water to shoulder out of the way. Given the additional stability that comes with beam, however, a wider boat may be able to compensate for this greater resistance by means of its better form stability and subsequent sail-carrying ability. Wider, and especially flatter, stern sections may also help a lighter boat skim across the surface in the high-speed phenomenon known as *planing* (which we'll return to in the next chapter), while a wider boat will certainly provide more interior volume.

The easiest way to compare the widths of two boats is to determine their *length-to-beam ratios* (L/B) by dividing their lengths by their beams. Generally, this is done using the LOA and maximum beam, for the simple reason that beam waterline numbers are often not readily available. Obviously, this means your L/B will not be able to account for things like flaring topside sections or bow and stern overhangs, but it still serves as a good approximation. Generally, a boat that has an L/B of 3.2 or less is considered to be on the wide side, while a boat that has an L/B of 3.4 is deemed moderate. A boat that has an L/B of 4 or more is considered narrow.

These numbers are most applicable to boats in the 25- to 40-foot range—the range in which the battle to cram in accommodations requires the most delicate compromises. Because stability increases dramatically with size, boats smaller than 25 feet will often be proportionately wider,

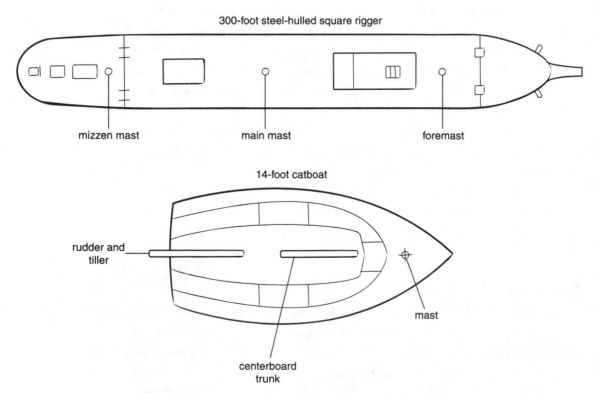

Stability increases dramatically with hull size, which is why bigger boats need so much less beam relative to their length to carry sail.

while boats longer than 40 feet will often be much narrower for their length. The old square-rigged windjammers of the late 1800s, for example, would often have L/Bs of as much as 8, and the modern, square-rigged 289-foot super-yacht *Maltese Falcon* has an L/B of about 7.

The definition of "fat" and "skinny" boats also tends to change over time, a fact worth bearing in mind when considering L/B. When it first came on the market in the mid-1970s, the Catalina 30—which has an LOA of 29 feet 11 inches and a beam of 10 feet 10 inches, yielding a 2.78 L/B—was considered radically beamy and voluminous. However, it was produced in an era when sailors were accustomed to boats like the Alberg 30, which has an L/B of 3.46. Today, after years in which French companies such as Beneteau and Jenneau have stretched the upper limits of beam and accommodations, it's the Catalina that looks "normal," while the Alberg 30 looks a little strange.

Also, as was the case with volume, there's beam and then there's *beam*, especially toward the stern. In recent years, as part of the never-ending quest for greater accommodations, beam near the transom of some cruising boats has become almost as great as the point of maximum beam just aft of amidships. There's nothing "wrong" with this kind of design—indeed, generations of boatbuilders used this same approach to maximize the freight-carrying ability of the sailing barges that once plied Holland's canals and the Thames River. But there's no denying that you pay a performance penalty when the boat starts to heel and that wide corner begins digging into the water—creating all kinds of unwanted resistance.

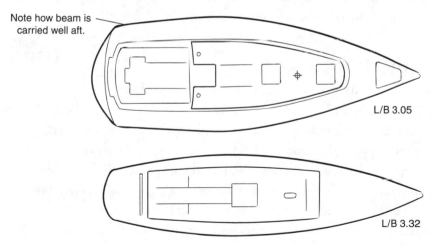

Today's sailboats are not only much beamier than in the past but carry their beam much farther aft, often in the interest of maximizing accommodations below.

Is She Stiff?

Finally, when comparing boats, note how much ballast they're carrying. Generally speaking, the more ballast, the lower the boat's center of gravity (only a crazy person would put the ballast up on the cabin trunk or on the side decks!), which translates into more righting moment and a stiffer boat with better sail-carrying ability. To determine "how much" ballast a boat is carrying, calculate its *ballast-to-displacement ratio* (B/D): divide the weight of the ballast by the boat's total displacement, and then multiply that result by 100 to obtain a percentage. Generally, the higher the number, the stiffer the boat. The 12-meters of old had B/Ds of 80 percent, while cruising boats generally have B/Ds in the 30s and 40s, not counting all their extra cruising gear.

Be aware that when thinking about ballast you also have to consider the location of all that ballast weight. In other words, you can't just blindly follow the numbers. A shallow-draft boat with a heavy keel and lots of ballast, for example, isn't generating the same righting moment pound for pound as a lightweight, deep-draft boat with a narrow keel—especially if the deep-draft boat's ballast is concentrated in some kind of bulb, moving the boat's center of gravity even deeper. The highly competitive 40-foot 8-inch Farr 40 sloop, for example, has a displacement of 10,902 pounds and a B/D of 45 percent—which might not sound that impressive until you consider that it has a draft of more than 8 feet. Compare this to the full-keel Island Packet 40 cruiser, which displaces 22,800 pounds and has a B/D of 44, but only draws 4.5 feet—and that's with the "deep-draft" keel option. The Island Packet 40, now out of production, was also available in a shoal-draft version drawing just 3 feet 10 inches!

Putting It All Together

So where do all these numbers and ratios leave us? Ultimately, what you need to do is look at the big picture, keeping in mind that boats are often designed for very different kinds of sailing. Let's take a look at a couple of cruisers: the Alerion Express 38, built until a few years ago by Newport R&D Inc. of Portsmouth, Rhode Island; and the Island Packet 37, now out of production, but formerly built by Island Packet Yachts of Largo, Florida. Both boats have LOAs of 38 feet 5 inches, but there the resemblance pretty much ends—and I'm not just referring to the Alerion's yawl rig versus the Island Packet's cutter.

The Alerion features a fin keel swept aft and a balanced spade rudder with a tiller. The Island Packet has a full-keel underwater profile, with a rudder securely fastened at the heel. The Island Packet also has 12 feet 2 inches of beam, whereas the Alerion's beam measures 10 feet 9 inches. Although the basic layouts are similar, everything is bigger and roomier in the Island Packet. Look, for example, at the quarter berths back in the stern, to port of the companionway. The Island Packet has a true stateroom with a separate seat, a hanging locker, and a door for privacy. Chances are the quarter berths in the Alerion are used as much for storing sea bags as for sleeping.

Now look at the two galleys, both on the starboard side of the companionway. Once again, there's no comparison—just look at the size of the counters on the Island Packet. A cursory look would seem to indicate that the Island Packet is all about comfort and roomy accommodations afloat, while the Alerion places more emphasis on handling and boat speed. To get an idea of just how much these two boats differ, let's run the numbers.

First the D/L: the Island Packet displaces a healthy 18,500 pounds and has an LWL of 31 feet, which gives it a D/L of 277. The Alerion, on the other hand, displaces 10,400 pounds and has an LWL of 30 feet, 1 inch, giving it a D/L of 170. Wow! No wonder the Island Packet's galley has more counter space. It's a much bigger boat! In fact, the Alerion falls right in the middle of the cruiser-racer category, while the Island Packet can be safely

The Island Packet 37. (Island Packet Yachts)

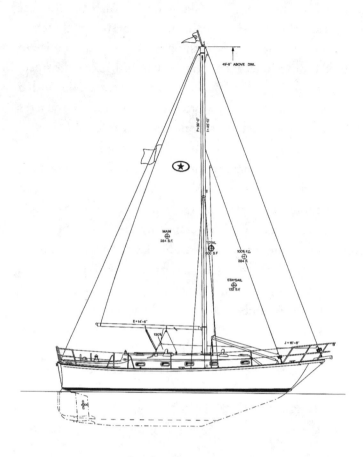

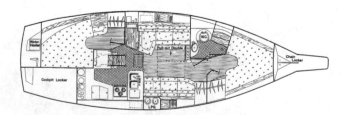

With its full keel, heavy displacement, and roomy accommodations, the Island Packet 37 is clearly designed to provide safety and comfort afloat.

With its fin keel, spade rudder, and narrow hull, the Alerion Express 38 is designed to provide nimble performance under sail.

classified as a heavy cruiser. Meshing very nicely with these numbers are the two L/Bs—the Island Packet rates a stocky 3.0, while the Alerion comes in at a svelte 3.57. Clearly, the Alerion will be easier to get moving in a drifter.

Speaking of which, how do the two boats rate in terms of sail area? According to the literature, the Island Packet carries 668 square feet of working sail—not including the staysail, which would be a good deal more than you would get simply using I, J, E, and P figures. The result is an SA/D of 15.3. In contrast, the Alerion carries around 645 square feet of sail, not counting the mizzen, which gives it an SA/D of 21.76. (This is not as unfair as it sounds—the mizzen doesn't add much driving force when sailing to windward, because it's inevitably backwinded by the main.) It should by now be apparent that there is simply no competition between the two in terms of boat speed. I can't think of any reasonable conditions in which the Alerion wouldn't come out the winner.

Interestingly, the Island Packet has a B/D of 44 percent, while the Alerion has a B/D of 40. Remember, though, that B/Ds are especially slippery numbers because of the role ballast location plays. The Island Packet, for example, has a standard draft of 4 feet 6 inches and an optional shoal draft of just 3 feet 8 inches. The Alerion's fin, on the other hand, draws 5 feet 10 inches and includes a bulb containing a big chunk of lead. Having said that, the Alerion's narrow beam won't offer as much initial form stability as the Island Packet—in other words, it will be a bit more tender, although once you get a few degrees of heel, the righting moment that results from all the ballast in the fin and the Alerion's lower center of gravity should keep her nice and steady. The Island Packet, on the other hand, will not only be stable in moderate conditions—thanks to all that beam—she will also stand up to a blow—thanks to all that ballast.

In the end, the numbers pretty much confirm our initial impression. While these boats are both "cruisers," they go about their cruising in very different ways. Specifically, the Alerion Express 38 is better suited to inshore work and shorter weekend jaunts, while doubling as a sprightly, super-comfortable daysailer.

The Island Packet, on the other hand, is all about comfort, safety, and accommodations for longer voyages. You can take the Island Packet daysailing, but expect to see a lot of other boats showing you their transoms, especially in lighter conditions. In fact, in light-air regions in particular, expect to do a lot of motoring. This is not to say the Island Packet is a less desirable boat—on the contrary, in my experience, Island Packets are wonderful at doing what they're designed to do. It's just that the Alerion and the Island Packet do different things well.

BOAT SPEED

12

Drag, Waves, Bustles, and Theoretical Limits

A **S WITH STABILITY** and righting moment, nothing could be simpler than boat speed—at least at first glance. Look at any sailboat on the move and the first thing you'll notice is the bow wave, created as the bow shoves water aside faster than it can get out of the way without piling up on itself. Meanwhile, back at the stern, there is another wave crest, caused when the water parted by the bow and hull comes together again, followed by an area of disturbed water called the wake.

These waves, however, are just part of the picture. In fact, as the pioneering English naval architect William Froude discovered in the nineteenth century, displacement hulls are subject to not one but two major types of resistance as they pass through the water: *frictional drag* and *form drag*—also called *normal pressure drag*.

Frictional drag results from the turbulence created by the skin of the hull as it passes through the water. The amount of frictional drag is directly proportional to the *wetted surface area* of the hull—i.e., the surface area of the hull below the waterline. In a nutshell, more surface area produces more resistance while less surface area produces less resistance. At speeds of 3 knots or less, frictional drag makes up the bulk of the resistance a boat encounters as it passes through the water, and it increases linearly when plotted on a graph against speed. Narrow boats with small appendages have less wetted surface area for a given displacement—and will experience less frictional resistance—than boats that displace the same volume but are wide and flat or have keels and rudders with larger surface areas.

At its most basic, form drag—the resistance a sailboat hull encounters as it shoulders water aside while making its way forward—is a function of hull shape and displacement (the latter, as we have seen, being the all-up weight of a sailboat and its attendant hardware and gear, or the amount of water it displaces as it floats at rest). Basically, the more water a boat needs to shove out of the way, the greater the form resistance it encounters. The shape of the bow is also a factor: a sharp bow shoves water aside more gradually than a blunt one. Similarly, a stern with a fair, or smooth, *run* will allow the water to flow past the transom without having to make sharp turns, further enhancing speed by minimizing turbulence. Form drag also includes the turbulence that eddies from the tip of a fin keel or rudder when sailing to windward, the drag of a propeller, and other such things.

Unlike frictional drag, form drag is negligible at low speeds, as is evident in the minimal bow wave and wake. However, it quickly begins to assert itself at around 3 knots—especially the wave-making component— as the water starts piling up on itself, creating a bow wave followed by a trough and the first crest of a series of waves radiating astern—a kind of mini wave system. Form resistance then increases dramatically as the boat goes faster and faster, until it becomes the main force opposing the boat's forward motion. In fact, so great is wave-making drag that it eventually forms a kind of insurmountable speed barrier known as a boat's *theoretical hull speed*, or its *hull speed* for short.

This theoretical limit is the result of a very real relationship between wavelength and wave speed, as described by the equation $S = \sqrt{WL} \times 1.34$—in which S is speed in knots and WL is the *wavelength*, or the distance between two successive wave crests. Basically this equation says that wave speed and wavelength are proportional. The faster the wave, the longer the wavelength, and the longer the wavelength, the faster the wave.

Let's say you have a series of waves measuring 4 feet between crests. The square root of 4 is 2, and 2 times 1.34 is 2.68, so the waves must be

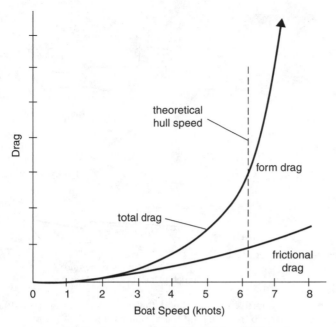

The drag components of a displacement hull with a 21-foot LWL underway.

traveling at 2.68 knots. A series of waves measuring 9 feet between crests would travel at 4.01 knots. (I'll let you do the math on this one.) Keep in mind that the speed/wavelength relationship is independent of wave *height*, or the vertical distance between the trough of a wave and its peak.

Now imagine you're on a boat traveling at 4.01 knots. Big or small, the boat is creating a bow wave that's moving through the water at the same speed as the boat. Because speed and wavelength are inexorably linked, the length of the wave from the peak at the bow to the peak of the next crest back is 9 feet. Increase your boat speed to 5 knots and you get a 14-foot wavelength.

Fair enough. Now let's say you're reaching along at 7.33 knots aboard a boat with a 30-foot LWL. It just so happens that the wavelength of a wave traveling at 7.33 knots is 30 feet. Pretty cool. But wait—the moment your 30-footer tries to go any faster, the wavelength stretches until it's longer than your boat's LWL. Suddenly the aftermost point of your boat is suspended over the trough of the bow wave, the stern squats down to fill the void, and your boat finds itself sailing up the backside of its own bow wave. This, of course, requires a whole lot more power than just throwing up a bow wave, and before you know it, you've stopped accelerating. Your

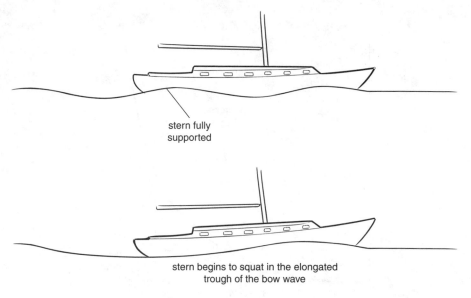

stern fully
supported

stern begins to squat in the elongated
trough of the bow wave

As a displacement hull approaches hull speed, the stern begins to squat in the trough of
the elongated bow wave, so that the boat finds itself having to sail "uphill."

dreams of going much faster remain just that—dreams. Bummer—your boat has hit its hull speed.

Ways to Boost Speed

Luckily, as upper limits go, hull speed is a pretty flexible one, and over the years naval architects have come up with various ways to get around it—at least a little.

Back in the late 1800s, for example, boatbuilders figured out how to create bow and stern overhangs that angled gently over the water in such a way that they became immersed as the boat heeled. These overhangs lengthened the heeled LWL beyond what it was when the boat was upright, thus increasing the boat's speed potential. Nathanael Herreshoff's boat *Gloriana*, built in 1891, is an early example of this phenomenon. Measuring 70 feet overall, she had an LWL of just 45 feet 4 inches on the level, but this LWL lengthened appreciably as she dug in. This was unpenalized gold back in the day when racing boats were rated according to LWL, with no mention of LOA. The long, tapered overhangs that today's sailors associate with "traditional" old-time yachts may look like naturally occurring forms dictated by nature—but they were, in fact, developed as rule beaters, pure and simple.

The long overhanging bows and sterns of yachting's "Golden Age" served to increase hull speed for a given LOA. The two photos here, of the Q-Boat *Hayday* (under sail in the Eggemoggin Reach Regatta and on the hard), illustrate how the bow and stern become immersed when heeling, increasing the waterline length and hence the boat speed. (Molly Mulhern)

Another way to boost hull speed is by incorporating flat, broad stern sections with minimum deadrise into the aftermost portion of the hull, which increases volume and buoyancy. Alternatively you can employ a *bustle*, essentially a swelling of the hull located just forward of the rudder that, like a broad stern, increases volume and buoyancy aft and thus prevents squatting at hull speed. Famed designer Olin Stephens of the Sparkman & Stephens design firm first used bustles—named for the voluminous stern sections of Victorian-era dresses—in the 1967 America's Cup 12-meter *Intrepid*. They were also one of the many design quirks that marked the IOR era, but have since fallen out of fashion.

Today many lightweight, generously rigged sailboats have the ability to generate enough power and speed to lift their hulls over the bow wave and skim across the water like high-speed motorboats. When they're *planing* like this, they're no longer functioning as displacement hulls—hulls that displace a volume of water equal to their own weight. Instead they're riding on top of the water, using the dynamic lift forces that result from higher speeds to help support the weight of the rig and hull and escape the confines of simple buoyancy.

To facilitate this kind of performance, planing boats are built with wide, flat sections amidships and aft. Lightweight dinghies like the 470, Sydney 18-footers, 49ers, and International 14-footers are made this way, and some larger centerboard boats like Lightnings and Thistles are capable of getting up on a plane as well. The 11-foot Moth class—a truly cutting-edge experimental class in which pretty much anything goes—has taken planing performance to a whole new level by using hydroplanes. Because the boats are so light, the submerged horizontal foils on the rudder and daggerboard are capable of lifting their diminutive hulls completely out of the water in even a moderate breeze. In the process they can achieve speeds of more than 30 miles per hour.

Many large offshore racers—such as the boats that compete in the Volvo round-the-world race, and monsters like the 140-foot schooner *Mari Cha IV*—are also endowed with wide, flat aft sections specifically designed to promote more efficient planing performance. In 2005, the *Mari Cha IV* broke the monohull transatlantic speed record set in 1905 by the three-masted schooner *Atlantic*, sailing from Sandy Hook, New Jersey, to Lizard Point, England, in just under 9 days 16 hours. In fact, in today's grand prix sailing world, in which monohull sailboats have been known to log more than 600 nautical miles in a single day, planing performance is pretty much mandatory to be competitive.

Even fairly conventional boats are capable of short-term planing performance if you can get them surfing down the face of a steep following wave. Years ago, during the Tartan Ten National Championship regatta in Milwaukee, we hit speeds of more than 16 knots surfing under spinnaker toward the finish line at the end of a long and brutal offshore triangle—thanks to a steady 25 knots of wind out of the west-northwest that dismasted one competitor and created waves more than six feet high. With an LWL of 27 feet, the T-10 technically has a hull speed of just less than 7 knots, but hull speed quickly becomes a non-issue in those kinds of seas!

On another occasion—my honeymoon, actually—my wife, Shelly, and I were heading north up Lake Champlain in a stiff southerly, with a sharp chop on our starboard quarter—perfect surfing conditions for our Catalina 30. I'm proud to say I let Shelly steer the entire time, because her stomach gets a bit sensitive now and then, and driving is a good way to take her mind off the motion. Talk about committing to marriage!

> *Even fairly conventional boats are capable of short-term planing performance if you can get them surfing down the face of a steep following wave.*

13

SAILING FASTER USING TELLTALES

An Elegant, Low-Tech Means of Achieving Perfect Sail Trim

WHEN I WAS a kid, I was a terrible sailing snob. As far as I was concerned, if it wasn't a stripped-down racer or a lean wooden classic, it wasn't really a boat—on the contrary, it was little more than a waterborne abomination. (Never mind that many of the boats I admired back then included hull and rig features so distorted by IOR rating-rule loopholes that they really *were* abominations!) Since those callow years, however, good fortune has plunked me on the decks and behind the helms of a wide enough assortment of boats that I can now appreciate a much broader variety of virtues.

That said, there is one area in which I remain a snob, and that's sail trim. Some say the difference between cruisers and racers is that cruisers set their sails and go, while racers are inveterate "tweakers"— continually adjusting their sails for maximum efficiency, even when they're just out daysailing. If that's the case, I'm a confirmed racer, win-loss records notwithstanding! Although I'm sure my sail trim is far from perfect most of the time, I find it jarring to see a sailboat in poor trim—jib flapping, main backwinded—or worse yet, motoring in a perfectly decent breeze. After all, part of the fun of being a sailor is achieving a certain mastery over the elements, not just raising sails when the mood strikes.

I remember a cruise when I had a heck of a time sailing east into the Sir Francis Drake Passage on our way around St. John's, in the U.S. Virgin Islands. Beating against the strong northeast trades, we had to tweak and trim for all we were worth to make it through the narrow channel between Mary Point and Great Thatch Island. While we worked, at least half a dozen boats passed us, heading both up- and downwind, with sails furled and their auxiliaries churning. Downwind? Come on! I ask you, who do you think felt better at anchor that evening, chatting about what they'd accomplished that day?

Part of the fun of being a sailor is achieving a certain mastery over the elements, not just raising sails when the mood strikes.

Telling the Tale

So how do you ensure that your sails are drawing as they should? In a word: *telltales*—bits of yarn or strips of light sailcloth attached to the leading edge of your jib and the trailing edge of the main. Simply put, they allow you to "see" the wind flowing—or not flowing—over your sails, thereby offering a direct and easy means of maximizing boat speed. Some people use short lengths—around 8 inches—of brightly colored yarn for telltales. Others prefer premade, bright orange nylon telltales from a ship's chandler like West Marine. In my experience, yarn telltales are forever getting caught on a sail's stitching, which can be a real pain, especially in light air. Nylon telltales also look very cool—reason enough for me!

Oddly enough, some sailors think telltales are ugly or funny looking and don't belong on a well-found boat. I find such an idea utterly incomprehensible. Telltales are standard issue on the best-sailed racing boats on the planet. They're simple and effective, even elegant in their conception, and they allow you to get in touch with the wind flowing over your sails in a way that's simply impossible in their absence. Ultimately, they represent the very essence of smart sailing and competent seamanship. What could possibly be *more* aesthetically satisfying than that?

Telltales and Headsails

Most jibs need three pairs of telltales: one near the tack, one at mid-luff, and one near the head. Each pair consists of a telltale on each side of the sail, and all three sets are located a few inches aft of the luff. Store-bought telltales come with convenient adhesive discs for attaching to sailcloth. Alternatively you can use a piece of Dacron sticky tape of the kind used for sail repair. Some racing jibs have little clear plastic windows in their luffs so you can plainly see the telltales on the windward and leeward sides at all times. In practice, however, Dacron sailcloth is pretty translucent stuff, allowing you to see both telltales of each pair in all but the most marginal conditions.

Telltales allow you to see whether the airflow over the sail is smooth or turbulent—an especially critical ability when beating, but important when reaching as well. In both cases, a smooth, laminar flow is crucial for the sail to create the air-pressure differential that makes it work. A poorly trimmed sail causes the air to separate, which creates turbulence on the surface of the sailcloth, compromising the sail's ability to generate lift. When the leeward, or outside, telltales are fluttering, or "lifting," the sail is trimmed too tightly, and its angle of attack is so great that the airflow is separating from the leeward side. When the windward telltales are lifting, the sail isn't sheeted in enough, and the leading edge is angling far enough to leeward that you're getting turbulence on the inside, or upwind side, of the sail. When the telltales on both sides are streaming smoothly aft, the sail is sheeted in correctly.

The best way to keep your telltales streaming depends on whether you're beating or reaching. When beating, you trim your sails to the correct angle of attack and shape them to the proper draft and draft location for the conditions. Then it's the helmsman's responsibility to ensure that the sails are drawing with maximum efficiency. If he or she is steering too low for the wind direction, the effect is the same as if the sails were sheeted in too tightly. In essence, the boat is trimmed for a beat but sailing a close reach—*stalling* the sails—and the helmsman needs to steer a slightly higher course to get the leeward telltales streaming again. If, on the other hand, the boat is sailing too high, or *pinching*, the windward telltales will begin lifting and fluttering, and the helmsman needs to change the course to a slightly lower heading.

Whatever you do, if you're *not* the person at the helm, don't be too hard on the person who is. I can assure you, he or she is well aware that the course needs some adjusting. What the helmsman *doesn't* need is a modern-day Greek chorus muttering, "Pinching a little, stalling, pinching, pinching . . ." every time he or she strays a couple of degrees from the ideal course. Alas, I was a dreadful nagger in this respect, until one day when I was doing rail-meat duty (serving as human ballast on the windward side of the boat) with a local sailmaker during the Chicago Yacht Club's annual Verve Cup regatta. Instead of giving voice to his concerns, this fellow would simply angle his hand a little to windward when the skipper was steering too low or cup his fingers in when we were pinching. It took a while to figure out exactly what he was up to, but when I did, it struck me as the ultimate in cool. (This was a hotshot *sailmaker* after all!) I have tried to limit myself to similar hand movements ever since. For one thing, it helps take one's mind off one's sore tushy. For another, I can give expression to my obvious superiority without necessarily tempting others to do the same when it's my turn to drive!

Speaking of fair play, those who always seem to end up driving can take heart that the roles are reversed when sailing on a reach. Now the helmsman simply sails a straight course while the rest of the crew adjusts the sails to the wind. In a racing situation, this can mean continually adjusting the headsail—trimming in or easing—with every puff and shift, while the occasional trim or ease is generally sufficient when cruising. No matter what your sailing style, telltales will serve you well on every point of sail from close-hauled to a broad reach. Only on a run or near run, when the sails are acting more like wind scoops than foils, will telltales no longer be able to help you.

Whether you're on a reach or a beat, telltales can also help you determine the correct jib lead angle. Let's say, for example, that you have a rather narrow jib set on a jib lead well aft. In this situation, sheeting in will have a much greater effect along the foot than it will toward the head of the sail. The result will be a leech with a good deal of twist, falling off to leeward toward the head. This, in turn, means that when you ease out, the upper portion of the sail will fall out of trim before the lower portion. In fact, it may be impossible to get the entire sail in the correct trim.

Luckily, this sorry state of affairs will be easily recognizable if your headsail is equipped with telltales. As you ease out, the upper windward telltale will start fluttering first, well before the windward telltales lower down. As you sheet in, the lower leeward telltale will stall out first because the lower portion of the sail is so much flatter and closer to the centerline. In short, the telltales will not break evenly, and the jib lead needs to move forward.

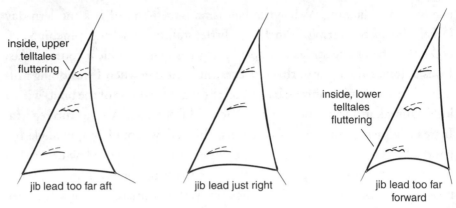

inside, upper
telltales
fluttering

inside, lower
telltales
fluttering

jib lead too far aft

jib lead just right

jib lead too far
forward

Using telltales to set the jib lead correctly.

Similarly, if the jib lead is too far forward, the sail will have too little twist and too aggressive an angle of attack aloft. The lower windward telltale will lift first as the sail is eased, and the upper leeward telltale will lift first as the sail comes in. In this situation the telltales indicate that the lead needs to move aft.

Telltales on the Main

The most important place to fly telltales on the mainsail is off the leech. Some sailors put telltales in the middle of the mainsail, but these aren't necessary unless you're sailing a boat without a headsail—like a catboat or Laser dinghy—in which case you can use telltales on a main as you would on a jib. On a sloop, even if your trim is perfect, getting telltales to fly in the body of the main can be highly problematic because of the turbulence coming off the mast—so they aren't really worth the trouble.

Back along the leech, however, it's a whole different story. A single telltale attached near the opening of each batten pocket can be invaluable in helping fine-tune twist on a close reach or beat. As a rule of thumb, when sailing to windward, the boom should be more or less parallel with the boat's centerline, and the top batten should be parallel with the boom. After that, fine-tune your trim with the help of your telltales. The goal here is to get the upper telltales, in particular, streaming aft. By doing so you ensure that the air is flowing smoothly off the leech. They'll still disappear from time to time behind the leech—but that's okay as long as they spend most of their time out where they belong.

What you really want to avoid is a situation in which your upper telltales are disappearing from view and then remaining hidden for substantially longer than they're visible. This means the leech is in too tight, and the air flow is separating off the leeward side of the sail. To remedy this, ease the mainsheet a bit to induce some twist, allowing the leech to relax a little. Doing so should get your telltales streaming again.

Telltales are invaluable in this situation, because otherwise your sail will look full, even as you're in the process of choking the poor thing. In light air in particular, it's all too tempting to strap your sails in tight, creating the illusion of power. But don't be fooled—you need to do everything you can to keep the flow moving. When in doubt, let it out—your sails need to breathe if they're going to get you anywhere in a drifter.

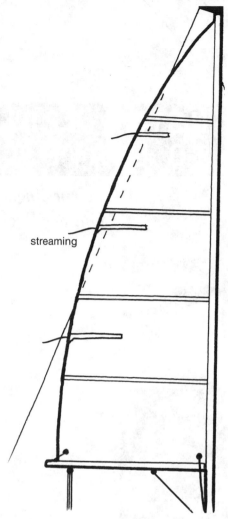

streaming

When the main has the right amount of twist, the upper telltales will stream aft from the leech, occasionally dipping behind the sail.

14

USING SPRING LINES TO LEAVE A DOCK

Harnessing a Botta Secreta to Get You Out of a Tight Spot

BACK WHEN MEN of valor were in the habit of settling their differences with swords—think Montagues and Capulets—fencing masters would often attract students by claiming to have developed something called a *botta secreta*. This was a super-secret attack, a special lunge or feint that was "indefensible," something that would automatically get you out of even the worst jams when facing the pointy end of another guy's rapier.

I like to think that using lines to get underway when you're pinned against a dock by wind or current is similar.

I remember one time provisioning at a waterside chandlery just west of Pensacola, Florida, and watching a couple try to motor away aboard a shiny new 50-footer. We were on the eastern edge of a low-pressure system centered in Texas, and a stiff 20-knot wind was blowing off the Gulf of Mexico over nearby Perdido Key. The dock faced south, directly into the wind, and the couple was hemmed in by boats forward and aft—in other words, they were well and truly pinned. Fortunately, their boat was equipped with a *bow thruster*—a small, electrically driven propeller set in a hollow tube running athwartships in the bow, just below the waterline. Unfortunately, their bow thruster didn't have quite the oomph to break them loose. The husband would gun the thing for all it was worth, and the bow would move just far enough from the dock for him to make a break for freedom. The moment he did so, however, the wind would push his bow back down and he would have to drop his main engine into reverse to avoid hitting the motorboat in front of him.

These poor people eventually got away, but it wasn't pretty. I can still hear the screech of that bow thruster on the verge of blowing itself to bits. Our own boat was only 35 feet long and offered a much smaller target for the wind—not to mention a lot less weight to manhandle—but I was still plenty worried as the crew and I went about taking on fuel and loading the last of our groceries—"Let's make that two bottles of scotch." Luckily, we were able to get away without any problem, thanks to our *botta secreta*.

The Old-Fashioned Way

How exactly does this *botta secreta* work? First, let's review how most sailors escape the clutches of the dock under less arduous circumstances: by pushing out either the bow or the stern and then motoring clear in forward or reverse.

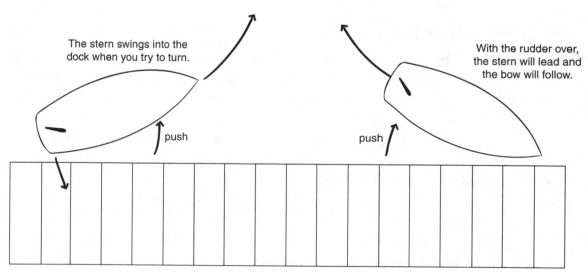

The stern swings into the dock when you try to turn.

With the rudder over, the stern will lead and the bow will follow.

push

push

The two standard ways of leaving a dock.

Many sailors prefer pushing out the bow, but this approach can be highly problematic. For one thing, once you're underway, any attempt to steer the bow farther away from the dock will cause the stern to swing inward—which may not be possible if there's another boat docked close in front of you. In addition, as was the case with the couple on that 50-footer, the bow is often vulnerable to being pushed around by the wind.

The stern-out approach, on the other hand, often works much better, because the reverse thrust of the propeller forcibly pulls the stern away from the dock—directly countering any wind or current that might be trying to push it back in. The bow also tends to stay out of trouble when turning in reverse. Basically, the stern pulls you directly where you want to go, as opposed to your having to pivot the boat around the keel or the hull's center of lateral resistance, as is the case when going forward.

Of course, when going anywhere in reverse, remember the effects of prop walk. With a standard right-handed propeller, the prop will want to pull the stern to port. If you're tied up with your starboard side to the dock, great!—prop walk will pull you that much more rapidly into the clear. If you're tied up with the dock to port, however, you may find the prop walk pulling you back in. This may not be an especially great problem aboard a modern boat with a high-performance spade rudder and a skinny keel—but it may constitute a real challenge aboard a heavy, full-keel boat with a propeller dating from the Nixon administration.

The *Botta Secreta*

The "rub" then—both in the Shakespearean and the literal sense—is to get either the bow or the stern far enough from the dock to power away with impunity. That's where the *botta secreta* comes in—by allowing you to swing out the bow or stern without having to depend entirely on the rudder.

To do this, first remove all your dock lines except the forward spring—the one running from the bow aft. Also, hang a couple of fenders forward so the dock won't damage the topsides there. Because you need to be able to release your spring quickly, use an extra-long line—one that will run from the bow cleat to the cleat or piling onshore and then back to the bow. That way, when the boat is ready to back away from the dock, you can easily undo or "slip" one end of the line, pulling in on the other end to get it back aboard. As you're doing so, make sure the line doesn't get tangled in the propeller.

If a bunch of line *does* go into the water, stop the propeller immediately. On the ugly scale, even the most embarrassingly inept docking maneuver imaginable pales in comparison to having to free a tangled prop!

Once these preparations are complete, begin the maneuver by putting the engine in forward—not too fast now!—and angling the rudder toward the dock. The forward pressure of the propeller will cause the boat to pivot around that last attachment point up at the bow, while the prop wash against the rudder helps push the stern away from the dock. What could be simpler?

Once the stern is clear of the dock, have the crew forward slip the spring line and pull it in around the cleat, piling, or bollard you've been using as an attachment point. Because the bow is right against the dock, this should be a piece of cake. Little, if any, of the line should even have to get damp. Once the spring line is cast off, pop the engine in reverse and away you go. Even when you're fighting a little prop walk, there should be no problem. In contrast to when you simply used brute force to push the stern away from the dock, you now have plenty of wiggle room—motoring away is no longer a touch-and-go game of inches.

To go out bow first, the procedure is pretty much the same, only with everything in reverse—both figuratively and literally. This time cast off everything except the stern spring—the line running forward from a stern cleat to a point on the dock roughly forward of amidships. Hang out a fender or two

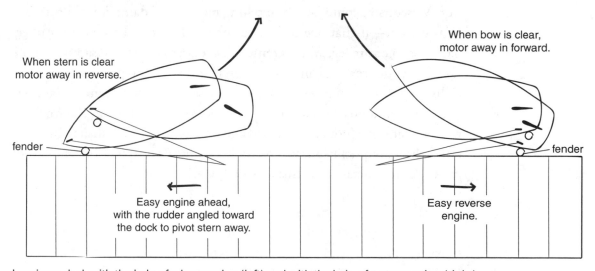

Leaving a dock with the help of a bow spring (left) and with the help of a stern spring (right).

to protect the hull where you expect it to rub against the dock. Then, when everything is ready, gently drop the engine into reverse—giving it just enough throttle to start swinging out the bow, while keeping the rudder amidships. When your boat is pointing out into the channel, shift the engine into neutral, slip the stern line, and then power ahead. Life is good. You're on your way!

No matter how you ultimately decide to leave the dock, always double-check to make absolutely sure you have disconnected all lines, shore-power cords, hoses, and other connections. Hard as it is to believe, it's surprisingly easy to forget that bright yellow cable plugged into that waist-high electrical tower back on the dock—yes, the same one you and the rest of your crew were stepping over time and again as you were getting ready to leave!

Also, before heading out, be sure to check for traffic. Again, you've got a lot to think about prior to casting off, and an otherwise slow-moving boat can sneak up on you surprisingly quickly, even in a no-wake zone. The last thing you want is to get your bow or stern away from the dock, just where you want it, and find yourself staring into the bow of a 40-foot power cruiser!

Finally, whenever you execute these kinds of maneuvers, always be sure you and your crew remain clear of any dock lines under load. If, say, a cleat was to let go, the recoiling line could instantly be transformed into a potentially lethal missile. The only time anyone ever really and truly yelled at me when I was a merchant sailor on the Great Lakes was when I stood with one foot resting on a dock bollard at the moment the first mate started taking in on a forward steam winch. I suspect the entire town of Superior, Wisconsin, could hear him telling me what a "damn idiot" I was, but he was right—if that one-inch wire rope had parted, I would very likely have lost an entire leg. Always remember that your personal safety and the safety of your crew and anyone else on board is *the* top priority—an especially important point when you have passengers who aren't as familiar with boats and boating as you. It's the most natural thing in the world to want to put out a foot or a hand to fend off an imminent collision, but it's a reflex that can quickly put you or your crew in the hospital. No amount of gelcoat or fiberglass is worth a broken bone!

WHY SAILS ARE TRIANGULAR

And Why So Many Sailboats Have Two of Them

WHY DO SO MANY modern sailboats have two sails? Why are nearly all modern sails cut in the shape of a triangle? The modern sloop rig is now almost universally accepted, and yet as recently as the early twentieth century triangular mainsails and sloops with a single headsail were not just the exception—they were downright rare. Whatever happened to effect such a change? In a word, technology. Modern engineering has given naval architects and boatbuilders concepts and materials that were beyond their forebears' wildest dreams.

First, let's take a quick trip back through time and review the state of sailing before the Industrial Revolution. Basically, you had boats made of plant material, with a smattering of iron here and there if you were lucky. Even the most magnificent ships of the age were built almost entirely of vegetable matter. Admiral Horatio Nelson's flagship *Victory* may have carried dozens of cannon, some weighing three tons apiece, but the hull itself was held together with thousands of wooden dowels known as treenails, or *trunnels*. Rigs were no different. By the time Nelson was spanking the French and Spanish off Spain's Cape Trafalgar in 1805, rigs included plenty of small iron fittings, but their spars, cordage, and sail materials were still entirely organic.

This dependence on stuff growing out of the ground imposed serious limitations on riggers and boatbuilders. Aboard larger vessels in particular, today's high-aspect fin keels were a physical impossibility, which means that sailors had to put up with a lot less righting moment and a lot more leeway when sailing to windward. Internal ballast—stones or chunks of lead or iron stowed down in the bilge—was the rule. In any kind of a seaway, outside ballast on a fin keel would have simply torn out the vessel's bottom.

As for the rig, although wood is remarkably strong and resilient for its weight, organic rope—with its tendency to stretch—makes for lousy shrouds and stays. Before the advent of steel wire and synthetics, spars had to be a lot heavier than they are today if they were to keep from going over the side. This makes for a rig that is a good deal more difficult to handle. The extra weight aloft also exaggerates a boat's tendency to pitch and roll in a seaway.

In response to these realities, riggers in the Age of Sail came up with a number of different sail types, including sprit sails, lug rigs, dipping lugs, gaff rigs, staysails, sliding gunters, square sails, and lateens. They then mixed and matched these sails in various ways to create such rigs as barks, barkentines, schooners, topsail schooners, ships, yawls, ketches, hermaphrodite brigs, brigs, cutters, luggers, sloops, and xebecs—to name just a few. Despite their radically diverse profiles, these rigs shared three important attributes: First, they subdivided the sail plan into a number of smaller, more manageable pieces. Second, they lowered the rig's center of effort in order to keep heeling forces to a minimum. Third, they were set up so that in rough weather their crews could easily lower the rig's center of gravity.

A Survey of Rigs

The classic ship rig, for example, is a good deal more adaptable than it first appears. Each mast is made up of three separate masts—a mainmast, a topmast, and a topgallant mast—all attached roughly end to end. With the onset of heavy weather, one of the first things a captain would do is have his crew "strike" the topgallant masts, lashing them safely down on deck where they couldn't cause any trouble. Likewise, in anticipation of heavy weather, many a topmast schooner captain would strike his upper spars to reduce weight aloft, creating what was known as a *winter rig*.

This strategy could also be applied to small boats. With the exception of boats built exclusively for use in sheltered waters with light air—like the boats that once plied their trade exclusively up and down the Nile and Ganges rivers—rigs in the Age of Sail were almost universally squat, with low centers of gravity.

First and foremost among these old configurations was the *lug rig*. For centuries, this low-aspect setup served as the workhorse for sailing craft of all sizes, and it can still be found aboard many small "classic" sailboats today. Cut in the shape of a quadrilateral, with the luff cut shorter than the leech, the head of a lug sail is laced to a gaff that extends forward of the mast. On a *dipping lug*, the tack runs to a point forward of the mast—often the stem—and the gaff has to be lowered and then re-hoisted on the other side of the mast every time you come about. On a *standing lug*, the tack runs down to a point on the mast and the gaff always stays on one side. Neither lug has a boom—the mainsheet simply runs from the clew of the sail to some point in the stern—the picture of simplicity. A *balanced lug*, on the other hand, has a boom that extends the foot of the sail a short distance forward of the mast. Like the standing lug, it also keeps the gaff on the same side of the mast at all times. The classic example of this kind of sail is the fully battened lug sail found on Chinese junks.

The beauty of a lug rig is that, as the sail is reefed—which is done by gathering in the foot and tying it off with reef points—the gaff moves down the mast, lowering both the center of gravity and the center of effort.

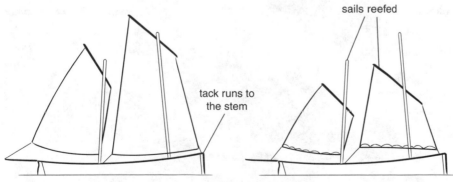

sails reefed

tack runs to the stem

A two-masted lugger with a dipping lug on the mainmast and a standing lug on the mizzen.

Remember, we're talking about a solid piece of wood here, not some lightweight aluminum or carbon-fiber tube. The effect is even more dramatic when the sail—with its gaff—is stowed completely.

The *lateen rig*, carried for centuries aboard Arab dhows, is another widely used configuration with a low center of gravity. The lateen is basically a balanced lug with an oversize gaff, a tiny or nonexistent luff, and a long leech. In addition to reefing down the same way as a lug, it needs remarkably little mast to support a substantial amount of sail, because its sharply angled gaff holds the sail's peak aloft. By way of an example, look no further than the modern-day lateen carried by the wildly popular Sunfish dinghy. While the boat carries plenty of sail, the mast is shorter than that of pretty much any other dinghy afloat. Again, it's the gaff that elevates the peak of the sail and gives it its shape. When it comes down, so does the center of gravity.

The *spritsail* also employs a distinctly diminutive mast, and is still used on the ever-popular Optimist dinghy. There's no gaff, and the head of the sail flies free with a long, light spar called a *sprit* supporting the peak of

The lateen-rigged Sunfish. (Vanguard)

the sail at the top of the leech. The lower end of the sprit lies secure in a short length of line, called a *snotter*—surely one of the finest bits of maritime nomenclature in existence—running off the mast. Spritsails serve wonderfully aboard small vessels that double as rowboats, because there's so little weight aloft once the sail is down. Heck, once the sail is down there's little if any "aloft" left—one of the reasons they were often used aboard whale boats.

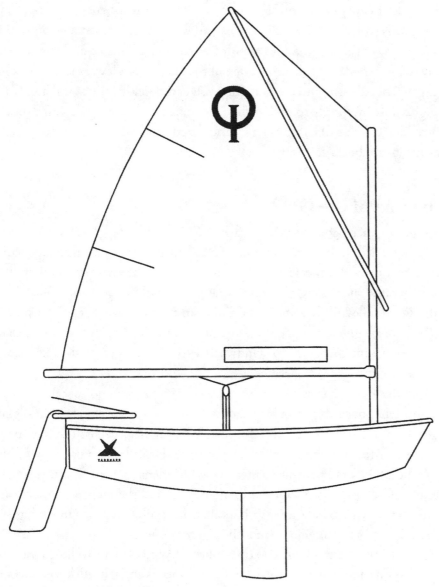

The spritsail on an Optimist dinghy.

The last thing you wanted was a big, heavy mast in the way when you were hooked into a whale and screaming off on a "Nantucket sleigh ride." Sprits were also widely used on old English sailing barges.

Finally, there's the modern *gaff rig*, in which the gaff is secured against the back of the mast with a fitting called the *jaw*. The modern gaff rig represents a major advance because it facilitates tacking, and it's noteworthy for its low center of gravity. The schooner rig, for example—for all its grace and beauty—is a pretty squat rig, especially when you take away its topsails (which, incidentally, gives you what is also called a *bald-headed schooner rig*). Taking in a reef, you lower the peak halyard and the throat halyard attached to the leading edge of the sail, which lowers the gaff as in a lug rig. Better still, in an emergency you can quickly reduce sail area and weight aloft by simply releasing the peak halyard so the entire gaff droops off to leeward. A sail that's been "scandalized" this way ain't pretty to look at, but it sure beats capsizing.

The End of the Gaff

Things began to change in the early 1800s, with the advent of modern yachting. Although sailmakers continued to use organic materials, sails quickly improved, especially in the latter half of the century. As they did so, it became increasingly obvious that twist could not be controlled in a gaff-rigged sail while beating—there was simply no way to keep those pesky gaffs from angling off to leeward. It also became increasingly obvious that boats sailed much better to windward with high-aspect sails—i.e., sails that were cut high and narrow.

To this day, some sailors insist that gaff rigs are superior because of the magnificent power they provide on a reach, and they're absolutely right—gaff rigs are powerful on a reach. But the bottom line is that a gaff rig can't compete to windward. As with water flowing over the keel, the laminar flow of air near the luff of a sail becomes increasingly turbulent as it travels aft. A squat, broad gaff sail gives you a lot more sail area aft and therefore a lot more sail surrounded by turbulent air. With a tall, thin triangular sail, a much higher percentage of the foil enjoys smooth, laminar flow, so you get more lift per square foot of area. You can also do a much better job of controlling twist.

Toward the end of the century, as centerboards and true fin keels became increasingly common—and in the process enabled boats to sail closer to the wind than ever before—rigs began to change in earnest. Smaller experimental craft—sailing canoes, in particular—began flying all kinds of exotic creations, including *batwing* sails, in an effort to compensate for the failings of the rigs they'd relied on just a few years earlier. An increasing number of small boats also began carrying a rig called a *sliding gunter*, on which the gaff is peaked so high it's almost indistinguishable from the mast.

By the last decade of the nineteenth century, racing boats of all sizes began carrying what sailors today would recognize as modern rigs. The lightweight tapered masts that supported these sail plans were increasingly made of steel, and eventually aluminum, aboard bigger vessels like those that competed in the America's Cup. In the United States, the newfangled setups were called *Marconi rigs*, because the stays and spreaders bore a striking resemblance to

The sliding-gunter rig provides performance when sailing to windward, but still offers the advantages of a gaff. (Chesapeake Light Craft)

When fully raised, the gaff on this Passagemaker Dinghy from Chesapeake Light Craft looks like an extension of the mast. (Chesapeake Light Craft)

the antennas on the wireless sets invented by Guglielmo Marconi. Others called it the leg o' mutton rig. In Britain, sailors prefer the term *Bermuda rig*, in reference to the small island boats that have carried triangular sails on a single solid mast since the 1600s. As with sails and hulls, construction of these new rigs was possible because of new materials and machining techniques. Like the wireless set for which it was named, the Marconi rig would have been a technological impossibility only a couple of decades earlier.

By the 1920s and 1930s, the Marconi rig was appearing not only in new designs like the Lightning, racing canoes, or the International 14 class, but in older boats that were rerigged to keep up with the changing times. In his book *Sailing, Seamanship, and Yacht Construction*, Uffa Fox notes how, in 1922, the 112-foot cutter *Nyria* made the transition to a steel-masted Bermuda rig, the first large yacht in Britain to do so. "Everyone [was] saying what a mistake it was, yet soon afterwards all large yachts followed her lead. Now all racing vessels, from the largest to the smallest, have Bermudian rigs, for there is no doubt that it is the fastest to windward yet evolved, and racers stand or fall according to their ability to windward."

Similarly, in 1931 the 122-foot royal yacht *Britannia*, originally a gaff-rigged cutter, was rerigged as a Bermuda sloop to maintain her competitive edge in the "Big Boat" arena of the day. "The noticeable thing is the increased height and reduced base of the sail plan," Fox writes, commenting on her new, high-aspect rig. "Her gaff with all the halyards and blocks attached to it is gone, and her mainsail has now a parabolic curve from truck to boom, whereas before it was flattened at the gaff, and the topsail on one tack was flattened as it pressed against the peak halyards. So, with the saving of weight aloft and the increased efficiency of the mainsail, *Britannia* is far better to windward than she was."

It is interesting to note that Fox, writing in 1936, was still not entirely comfortable with this new way of sailing. A veteran cruiser, he was well aware what the sea could dish out in a rough mood. Nonetheless, he could see that for the gaff rig, the writing was on the wall.

"It will be some years before the tall Bermudian rig on these large cutters will be properly understood, and until such time we shall not see *Britannia* able to storm across the [English] Channel at 12 knots in a nasty sea as she did in 1893 against the American *Navahoe*. . . . Those who, like myself, sigh over the loss in hard weather ability must be patient, and remember that in *Britannia*'s early days the larger cutters [also] sometimes carried away their short mainmasts, which showed that they were not properly understood then, so the time will come when these tall Bermudian spars will be as strong or stronger than the old short gaff cutter mainmasts, for with increasing years comes increased knowledge and improved materials. . . . When the day dawns that sees their one weakness strengthened every lover of the sea will rejoice."

Sure enough, today the Bermuda rig is truly king, and for good reason. It provides the best control of sail shape and the best performance with a minimum effort. In addition, today's reliable aluminum and carbon spars and stainless steel fittings have made the rig both light and utterly reliable when properly maintained.

Indeed, today's Bermuda rigs have reached proportions that would have been beyond comprehension in Fox's day. The largest sloop ever built, for example—the 247-foot *Mirabella V*—boasts a carbon-fiber mast measuring a whopping 290 feet tall and weighing more than 10 tons! The boom measures some 90 feet long. Granted, *Mirabella V* is an extreme boat—even the owner, former Hertz CEO Joe Vittoria, says he won't ever build a boat so big again—but it's certainly a testament to the power and reliability of today's Bermuda rigs.

In recent decades, thousands of Bermuda rigs large and small have crossed oceans and weathered countless storms; they've been neglected, bashed, modified, and rolled; they've been struck by birds, water balloons, and lightning—all this, and still they soldier on. Some sailors decry the fact that the Bermuda rig has become so omnipresent. They seem to feel it has somehow created a less interesting world—but that's simply absurd. There's nothing *wrong* with gaff rigs, junk rigs, or any other kind of rig—but the bottom line is that, for most purposes, the Bermuda rig wins out because of its efficiency and ease of use. Any sailor who seriously argues otherwise is being silly.

Why Just Two Sails?

Not only did the sailing craft of old lack triangular mainsails, they nearly all flew multiple headsails—at a bare minimum, a staysail tacked to the stem of the bow and a jib tacked to the end of a bowsprit. A few small craft flew a single triangle forward of the mast, but this was more the exception than the rule, and on larger craft it was unheard of. Staysails, inner jibs, outer jibs, flying jibs, "floaters"—the variety of headsails staggers the imagination. As late as the 1930s, the massive Marconi-rigged J-class boats that competed for the America's Cup—great towering vessels like *Weetamoe*, *Ranger*, *Endeavour*, *Yankee*, and *Shamrock V*—all carried two and sometimes three headsails, depending on the year and the conditions. The question, once again, is why?

The answer: winches. Quite simply, while sailmakers in years past could have made bigger headsails, there was simply no way on earth anybody would have been able to trim them in. Granted, sailors have been using block and tackle arrangements for centuries, but this strategy works only to a point. A *gun tackle*, on which two lines attach to the moving block, provides a 2-to-1 advantage. A *luff tackle*, on which three lines attach to the moving block, provides a 3-to-1 advantage, cutting the load by two-thirds. After that, though, as you start adding more moving parts, you quickly begin to experience limiting returns because of friction, especially when using high-friction organic rope and wooden blocks made without ball bearings.

Modern winches are just that—modern—and the precision machining and high-strength materials they require precluded their use aboard sailing vessels until the early 1900s. Among the first modern sailing winches ever used was a set aboard the Herreshoff-designed *Reliance*, which defended the America's Cup against Sir Thomas Lipton's *Shamrock III* in 1903. Designed and built by Captain Nat Herreshoff himself, these winches were considered a godsend to the job of trimming the 201-foot boat's massive sails—which in all encompassed a whopping 17,000 square feet.

Think about it: What happens when you tack a modern overlapping headsail? As the boat turns through the wind, there's little you can do until the sail blows through the foretriangle to the new leeward foredeck. By that time, sheeting in—even with a big multispeed winch—can be a bear, to say the least. One spring I was aboard an old 40-foot IOR-style sloop during a race on Puget Sound. Although the Pacific Northwest is known for its light air, that spring it always seemed to be blowing stink, and as a consequence tacking could truly be hell. Much as I loved that big beautiful sloop with its sloping reverse transom and powerful overhanging bow, at times I thought my arms would fall off. Imagine what it would be like to grind in a big genoa on *Reliance* without the help of a couple of big winches!

Also, never forget the fact that large sails are a bear to hoist and douse, especially when wet. Modern Dacron absorbs little if any water, but the same cannot be said of cotton and flax. Those old paintings and photos that show a bunch of deckhands strung out along a cutter's bowsprit and taking in sail look cool, but it must have been a damn hard piece of work getting in even a relatively narrow headsail. Getting in a big overlapping genoa in any weather except light air would have been physically impossible.

Such limitations left little choice but to subdivide a large sail area into many bits and pieces. A classic example of this Age of Sail strategy is the ship rig, with its profusion of square sails set on three, four, or five masts. Breaking a large total sail area into small squares not only made hoisting and dowsing easier, it also made the rig much easier to trim. The first glance at a picture of a ship-rigged vessel may suggest that the several yards hung on a single mast all moved as a single unit, but that would have been impossible. Instead, each yard had its own set of lines called *braces* controlling its angle to the wind—a manageable job with strong men using block and tackle.

Another advantage of subdividing a sail plan was that, if something like a block or a piece of vital cordage gave way, you wouldn't lose all your sail—just some of it. The rigs of old, with their numerous small spars, were expressly designed to lose the smaller, lighter ones first in a blow—much as small, inexpensive fuses protect the more expensive parts of a modern electrical system. Obviously no sailor *wanted* to crack, or "spring," a topmast or a royal mast, but it surely beat losing the entire rig. The downside of the Marconi rig is that it's an all-or-nothing proposition: when it's up, it's up, but when it's down, it's *really* down. Spars made of carbon fiber, in particular, don't just bend, they explode into thousands of sharp little shards when the rig falls—not a pretty sight!

Finally, it helps to have multiple headsails in a storm because you can progressively take them in and create a more compact sail profile. Think about what happens when you roll in part of your jib or switch to a smaller headsail on a modern sloop. True, you reduce your sail area, but the situation is far from ideal, because your remaining sail is where you least want it—at the very front of the boat, where it's hard to get to if something breaks and where it exercises a lot more leverage to muscle around your bow in bad weather.

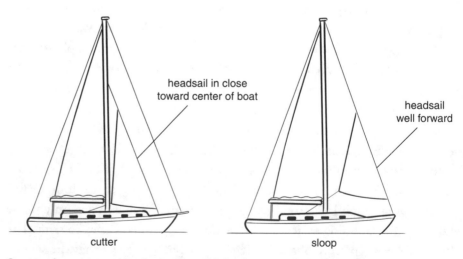

On a modern cutter, taking in the jib and flying just a staysail creates a compact and seaworthy sailplan. With a sloop, the headsail is always well forward, even when reduced in size.

In contrast, when you start to reduce sail on, say, an old racing cutter battling a squall in the English Channel, the first thing that comes in is the flying jib, or jib topsail, set way off on the end of the boom. Phew! What a relief to have that crazy thing in! Already the width and height of the sail plan are significantly reduced. Next to go is the jib, set on another stay running out to the end of the bowsprit. Now you're down to just a staysail, and your rig is dramatically more compact than it was moments earlier. Bring in the topsail and topmast, reef the main a couple of times, bring in, or "reef," the bowsprit so it's lying safe and sound on deck alongside the mast, and you're ready for anything. It's for this very reason—reducing sail to a compact sail plan—that many deepwater cruisers continue to employ the cutter rig, albeit one without a topmast, to this day.

Unfortunately, there's a downside to all that extra security. First and foremost, having to drag a jib across that inner forestay every time you come about is just that—a drag that can be hard on crew and gear. Second, an extra stay adds weight aloft and creates additional windage. It also creates added expense and maintenance. Finally, except when you're fighting your way through a gale, that staysail provides only marginal performance, especially on a beat. Unless you need a staysail to help get you through the occasional storm, your boat will be faster and easier to handle with a single large headsail. With this in mind, many cruising sailors make a provision for a removable inner forestay, hoisting it only when things get rough, but otherwise leaving it below and out of the way. And what does that leave you with? A modern sloop rig.

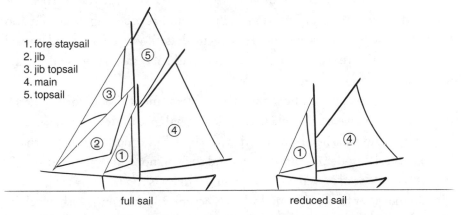

1. fore staysail
2. jib
3. jib topsail
4. main
5. topsail

full sail   reduced sail

The racing cutters that plied the stormy English Channel in the late 1800s were expressly designed so their rigs could be dramatically reduced in heavy weather.

Ketches and Yawls

Of course, not all modern boats are sloops. In addition to a fair number of cutters, you will also encounter the occasional yawl, schooner, or ketch. In a schooner rig the mainmast is aft and is as tall as or taller than the foremast ahead of it. The mainmast of a ketch or a yawl, on the other hand, is forward, and there's a smaller mizzen back in the stern. The mizzen of a yawl is usually little more than a tiny spar perched aft of the rudderpost, in the extreme stern. The mizzen of a ketch is generally larger and located forward—sometimes markedly forward—of the rudderpost. In either case, the mizzen's performance is often severely compromised when sailing to windward, because it's affected by backwash off the main.

In many cases, if not most, the reason for choosing a modern two-masted rig is largely a matter of aesthetics. Many sailors simply prefer the look of a boat with more than one mast. They may also enjoy pulling "strings," in which case two masts provide that many more strings to pull. This isn't to say there are no practical advantages to these less-common rigs. As in years past, dividing the rig into smaller parts makes it easier to handle, especially if you're shorthanded on a larger vessel. Veteran bluewater voyager Steve Dashew, for example, has made a name for himself designing powerful and fast boats specifically intended for shorthanded offshore passagemaking. Among these are a number of ketches, including a 78-footer named *Beowulf*. On a ketch of this size, Dashew is able to put some space between the two masts, giving the mizzen some "breathing room" and thereby increasing its effectiveness.

Many bluewater cruisers also elect to go with a ketch or yawl rig because it provides the option of lowering the main and proceeding under jib and mizzen alone in bad weather. This tactic has, however, received mixed reviews over the years, and it can't be assumed that, say, a yawl will handle rougher conditions better than a sloop.

In the words of Uffa Fox, the "greatest argument of all" for the ketch rig is that in bad weather she will handle and balance under jib and mizzen, "but when the weather is damned bad, she will do nothing under them, neither will she under mainsail alone, and she will not stand mainsail and jib even if the mainsail is well reefed, for all the drive is too far forward."

On the other hand, Captain Joshua Slocum's 38-foot *Spray*, with which he made the world's first solo circumnavigation in 1895–1898, was a gaff-rigged

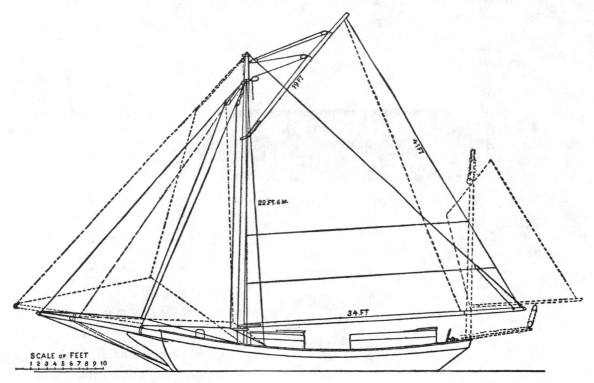

The gaff-rigged yawl configuration on Joshua Slocum's *Spray* proved remarkably versatile on his round-the-world voyage. Note that the dotted line on the main shows how the sail was cut down to accommodate the mizzenmast. *Spray* was originally rigged as a gaff sloop.

yawl with a lug sail for a mizzen, and Slocum had nothing but good things to say about both the boat and her rig.

Interestingly, many sailors think of the ketches and yawls of the mid-twentieth century—the Golden Age of "Corinthian," or amateur, sailing—as the quintessence of tradition. In fact, they were "rule beaters" designed to exploit a loophole in the rating rules developed by the Cruising Club of America (CCA) that held sway in the 1950s and 1960s. Specifically, the CCA rules didn't include a staysail hoisted on a mizzen stay in a boat's measured sail area. In other words, you could hoist all the additional canvas you wanted and it would not count against your boat's handicap rating. Most famously exploited by a yawl named *Finisterre*, designed by Olin Stephens, the rules allowed cunning sailors to hoist additional sail without adding anything to their time allowance. Seaworthiness or practicality had nothing to do with it.

16

SOME THOUGHTS ON HEAVY WEATHER

The Way of the Windjammer Is Still the Best

ONE DAY YEARS AGO I was hammering away at my job as a reporter for a newspaper just outside of Milwaukee when my boss said a man named William Stark was out front, claiming to have rounded Cape Horn aboard an old-time square-rigger. Baloney, I thought—square-rigged ships were ancient history.

Well, next thing you know, I was sitting there talking to old Mr. Stark and looking at his photos, realizing I couldn't have been more wrong. He had indeed done what he'd said—rounded Cape Horn aboard the Finnish four-masted bark *Pamir* on a passage from Port Victoria, Australia, to Falmouth, England. The article I wrote about it not only marked the beginning of a life-long interest in old-time square-riggers, it also proved to be instrumental in my becoming an editor at *Sailing* magazine.

Mr. Stark went on to publish an account of his voyage, titled *The Last Time Around Cape Horn: The Historic 1949 Voyage of the Windjammer Pamir.* Having battled depression his entire life, however, he committed suicide just before the book made it to print, a tragic end to an adventurous life. Mr. Stark and I met twice in his office, and I always found him to be a kind, extremely articulate gentlemen—and extremely patient with a reporter who was still wet behind the ears. Mr. Stark had also been a merchant sailor on the Great Lakes—a trade I too had tried my hand at—and we had a fine old time swapping stories. I like to think that, despite his personal demons, Mr. Stark's life was a fine and even noble one, in the best sense of the word. I very much envy Mr. Stark's adventure aboard the *Pamir*. The things he saw, the things he did—for me, they are the stuff of dreams.

Windjammers and Heavy Weather

The reason I mention Mr. Stark and the *Pamir*—in addition to paying tribute to a fine old sailor—is because, in studying the ways of the old windjammers, I'm continually struck by their systematic approach to bad weather. These were sailing craft whose sailors actively sought out some of the roughest waters of the world—the Roaring Forties and Furious Fifties latitudes of the Southern Ocean—which in turn required weeks of preparation, bending on special heavy-weather sails, rigging lifelines, and checking and rechecking gear. It also meant *sailing* through bad weather, as opposed to just battening down and hoping for an end to the blow. Obviously, there was a strong financial incentive for this approach—faster passages meant better returns. Nonetheless, *sailing* the ship also allowed these sailors to maintain a much better awareness of what was happening around them. It meant that, in everything but the very worst conditions, they would always possess at least a modicum of control.

Alas, just recently there was a tragic example on Lake Michigan of what can happen when you don't conduct yourself correctly while sailing in heavy weather—of how quickly things can fall apart if you don't stay on top of the situation. (I use this example not out of disrespect or to attach blame, but as an object lesson to us all. The boat in question had an experienced crew doing the best it could in extremely difficult conditions. I've had far too many close calls of my own in similar situations to pass judgment on others.) A crew of four was delivering a 35-foot sloop from Chicago to a boatyard about a dozen miles south when they encountered 30-knot winds out of the north and 9-foot seas. Although these were hardly "survival" conditions, the skipper decided to take down the small jib he had flying before running the channel into the sheltered waters of Calumet Harbor. Midway through the takedown, a crewmember who'd gone up on the foredeck without a safety harness fell overboard, which meant performing a man-overboard rescue with the harbor breakwall only a short distance to leeward. Somehow, the three sailors still on board managed to get hold of their comrade—an extraordinary feat of seamanship considering the conditions—but they were unable to haul him back on deck. Worse yet, by this time they were caught in the confused seas bouncing off the breakwall—estimated at a height of 12 feet—and because they no longer had any sail up, they were entirely dependent on their auxiliary power to get free. Unfortunately, this proved inadequate. A few minutes later the boat ran up onto the breakwall, and the skipper and crew were forced to abandon ship. By the time U.S. Coast Guard divers arrived on the scene—having been dropped off by helicopter on the protected side of the breakwall—three of the four men were dead from hypothermia. "Three people died because, first, someone went forward without a harness, and second, why would you take your sails down in the first place?" said another sailor, who'd been on the lake at the time, in an interview with *Sailing* magazine. "Someone made a terrible mistake."

Preparing Your Boat

So what does it mean to have a boat that's prepared for heavy weather? That depends on the kind of sailing you plan to do. If all you have in mind is daysailing, your primary concerns are making sure your boat is mechanically sound, that you can reduce sail in the event the wind pipes up, and that your crew all has life jackets.

Of course, like so many other things, there's daysailing and there's daysailing. Going out for a jaunt on chilly, blustery San Francisco Bay, you would be well advised to wear a safety harness and run *jacklines*—taut lengths of wire or nylon webbing strung along the deck, to which you can clip a tether. Always remember that no matter where you are—whether on the open ocean or an inland lake—a man-overboard situation is by its nature extremely dangerous. Simply keeping track of a person floating in the water can be incredibly difficult in a seaway—precisely the situation in which a man-overboard emergency is most likely to happen. Then there's the question of pulling the person back on board once you've reached him or her. Sailing literature is replete with stories of even fully crewed vessels that managed to reach a person in the water, only to find it so difficult to pull the individual back on deck that he or she perished anyway.

When installing jacklines, it's vital to keep them snug, with little slack. As for the tether that attaches your safety harness to a jackline or padeye, it should not be overly long. I know of at least one case in which a sailor went over the side and drowned at the end of an overlong tether. Because hauling a fully dressed adult out of the water and onto the deck of a sailboat with even moderate freeboard is so difficult, there are now a number of cranes and hoists on the market designed exclusively for doing such a job. If your boat has a fair amount of freeboard, one of these can serve as a nice bit of insurance—otherwise, going over-board in rough weather is essentially a death sentence.

Beyond that, heavy-weather preparedness includes—first and foremost—sails that won't shred in the wind. Also be sure to check your shrouds regularly and replace them whenever necessary. When isolated from the air—say, between the strands of a shroud and a swaged fitting—stainless steel can break down in a process known as *crevice corrosion*, an especially insidious form of degradation because it's hidden from view. Sometimes you will see a telltale streak of rust running out from the affected area, but don't count on it—do a thorough inspection!

Heavy-weather preparedness includes—first and foremost—sails that won't shred in the wind.

In addition, keep your steering gear well maintained and be sure to have sturdy running rigging. If you have an emergency tiller on board, make sure it's readily accessible and practical to install. You should also inspect a roller-furling, roller-reefing headsail on a regular basis to ensure that the top and bottom bearings are in good shape and the furling line isn't frayed. The last thing you want is to have a furling line snap, allowing the entire headsail to unfurl in a gale—with no means of getting it back in. Nor do you want the upper or lower swivel to blow up just as you're rolling in the sail in anticipation of that big, black squall line up ahead.

It goes without saying that the hull must be sound—especially the hull-to-deck joint, keel bolts, rudder bearings, through-hull fittings, gud-geons and pintles, the maststep, and the mast itself. Be especially sure to periodically examine any and all cleats, screws, bolts, and other pieces of hardware attached to aluminum spars. These fittings are often fabricated from stainless steel, which can generate galvanic corrosion when in contact with aluminum as the electrons in one metal flow to the other. Ideally, all stainless steel fittings will be electrically isolated from the aluminum in the mast, but the reality is that the two metals are often in contact.

Finally, a mechanically sound boat has a reliable, well-maintained auxiliary, clean fuel, and clean tanks. Dirty tanks in particular have caused many an unpleasant experience, as the accumulated sludge at the bottom works itself loose and then kills the engine as the boat pounds through the waves. Whether you're motorsailing back to the harbor before a thunderstorm or using your engine in combination with a heavily reefed main and jib to claw your way off a lee shore, a dead engine can be a *big* problem. Never forget that when the chips are down, auxiliary power isn't just a convenience—it's an important safety item.

Heavy Weather and Offshore Sailing

The goal of handling heavy weather inshore is simply to keep body and soul together as you run for shelter—no mean feat, given the number of yachts that have cracked up against harbor breakwalls and reefs over the years. When handling heavy weather offshore, however, you have to be prepared to ride things out come what may, which means outfitting your boat with some special equipment.

First and foremost you need purpose-built storm canvas in your sail inventory, generally a storm jib and trysail.

First and foremost you need purpose-built storm canvas in your sail inventory, generally a storm jib and trysail, which are often made from bright orange sailcloth to promote visibility. Many cruising boats simply carry a heavy-duty roller-reefing jib and a sturdy main with three sets of reef points, but this approach is inadequate for truly heavy conditions, especially in the headsail department. When a roller-reefing jib is reduced to a minimum, it inevitably carries a substantial amount of draft and even starts looking baggy. This is exactly what you *don't* want when doing your utmost to depower the rig. A storm jib, on the other hand, is cut as flat as possible, with the tack secured by a short length of wire called a *pendant* (pronounced *pennant*), so the foot will be a few feet above the deck and any waves that crash on board will pass harmlessly underneath. The idea is to have a headsail that will allow you to control your boat in extreme conditions without overpowering it.

Many sailors set the storm jib on a removable inner forestay that runs from a point in the middle of the foredeck to a point partway up the mast.

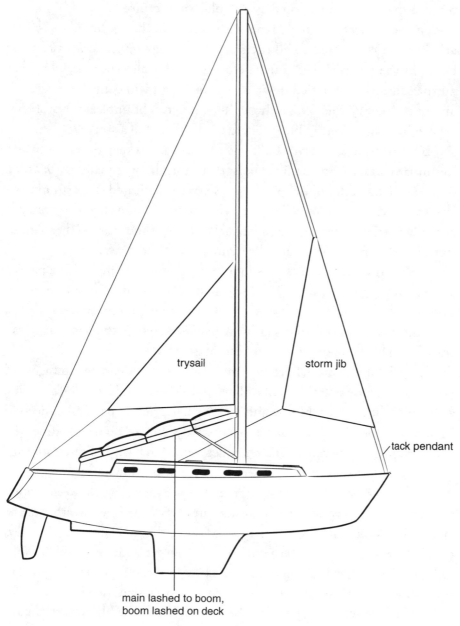

A storm jib and trysail.

This brings the headsail close to the center of the boat, creating a compact sail plan that will impart an easier motion through the waves. If you plan on adding an additional stay, you will likely need to reinforce the foredeck and add running backstays to accommodate the load. With a double-headsail rig like a cutter, you can simply use the staysail as a storm sail—one of the reasons this rig remains popular with bluewater cruisers.

Farther aft, a triple-reefed main is effective in theory, but it's problematic in practice because of all the sailcloth already bunched up along the boom by the two reefs that came before it. There's also the possibility that all the sailcloth you've tied down along the boom will come loose again if any of the reefing lines chafe through—a downright unpleasant problem, especially in a prolonged blow. Chafe can be brutal in a storm.

By hoisting a flat, heavily built trysail instead, you keep the rig clean and minimize windage. Some sailors hoist their trysails on the same track as the mainsail, but a better option is to use a separate dedicated track running all the way down to deck level. That way you can bend on the trysail before you actually need it and store it in a bag at the base of the mast. When conditions demand it, simply attach the main halyard and heave.

Unlike the main, a trysail is loose-footed and trimmed with a pair of sheets running to a pair of blocks well aft. The head goes only partway up the mast, while the tack is secured to a strong point on deck with a pendant. With the trysail up, lash the main securely to the boom and lash the aft end of the boom down and out of the way.

A well-equipped offshore boat must also have adequate stowage and lashings to ensure that things like plates and fire extinguishers don't become airborne in heavy seas. House and starting batteries, in particular, need to be securely bolted down, while items normally stowed on deck—dinghies, dodgers, grills, jerry cans, winch handles—need to have dedicated stowage or be secured so they won't go overboard in a knockdown.

Speaking of stowing and lashing, don't forget your crew. Between motion sickness and the exertion required to take care of the boat, heavy weather can be exhausting. Make sure you have sturdy lee cloths that can be quickly installed on all sea berths so those who aren't on watch can get some sleep without worrying about being pitched onto the cabin sole. When enduring a prolonged bout of heavy weather, there's nothing like being able to get some decent rest.

Finally, a well-equipped boat will remain completely watertight for the duration of even the heaviest blow. This means having secure, sturdy portlights and hatches. Companionway hatches in particular need to remain secure, since the alternative is a great gaping hole. Beware of sliding hatch boards, which can be floated out of their tracks and washed away when the cockpit fills.

Before Conditions Really Start to Deteriorate

Let's say you're confident in your boat—the rig is sound, your steering gear is in good shape, and your storm sails are close at hand. You've been monitoring the weather radio, weatherfax, and SSB radio, and you've been watching the immediate weather conditions, including barometric pressure—basically, you know you're about to get spanked. Now what?

The first thing you need to do is make sure everything is ready, both below and on deck. When lashing things down, you need to be concerned about both the wind and the waves—which, in extreme conditions, represent the greatest danger. Seawater weighs 64 pounds per cubic foot, and fresh water only slightly less. Imagine the volume and weight of water contained in a large wave sweeping up and over your foredeck.

Also be sure to prepare what you and your crew need well in advance. Have any and all foul weather gear close at hand, and be sure to have everyone put on their harnesses and life jackets—*before* going on deck, please! If you don't already have them up, rig the lee cloths, making sure they're securely anchored. The weather can get nasty very quickly, and taking measures like these before the stuff hits the fan is immeasurably easier than it will be when the gale is upon you and the boat is on its ear.

While you're at it, allow a few minutes to plan some simple, nourishing meals and gather the utensils you'll need to prepare and eat them. In a recent article in *Sail* magazine, veteran cruisers Duncan and Irene Gould recommended "dog-bowl cuisine"—simple, bland meals like cream soups that you can eat with spoons from big plastic bowls, for maximum safety. Oddly enough, windjammer sailors often lacked such sensibilities when dealing with storms. Working for hours on end while subsisting on salt pork and hard tack and dressed in wholly inadequate gear, the men at times would be little better than zombies. I can't help but wonder if many of those who were lost off the pitch of Cape Horn were just too tired to give a damn anymore.

Finally, get one last fix on your position and whatever land or other hazards are in the area—and be sure to recheck your position regularly with your GPS receiver or chartplotter. In the event of a prolonged blow, you need to be sure a windshift or unexpectedly fast rate of drift doesn't suddenly put your boat in danger.

Keep Sailing

You could fill a small library with all the books and articles written on the subject of storm tactics—and if you're planning on crossing any oceans in the future, I recommend giving at least a couple of them a thorough read. They cover everything from wave structure and behavior to the details of how best to rig a sea anchor—all valuable information.

For now, however, here are a few basics.

First and foremost, *keep sailing*. Even if it's only a scrap, having some canvas up will ensure that you have a backup in the event your auxiliary fails. The wind pressure against even a small sail will also smooth out the boat's motion considerably in the building waves.

First and foremost, keep sailing.

If you're thinking of making a dash for the nearest harbor, be aware that this course can be fraught with danger. In fact, if you're at all unsure of your ability to make it in, seek shelter elsewhere or head back out so you can ride out the storm with plenty of sea room. If getting in closer puts you in the lee of the land, great—go for it—but if there's an onshore breeze, beware! As bad as the seas may be in that moment, they're going to be a whole lot worse closer to the shore.

Years ago, when I was returning a boat after the 197-mile Hook Race to northern Wisconsin, I was hit by a series of squalls midway down Lake Michigan. By the end of the day my partner and I were exhausted—both from the race and the weather conditions—so we decided to duck in and spend the night at Two Rivers Harbor. Unfortunately, as bad as things were a couple of miles out, they became truly scary as we drew closer to the breakwall. We were motorsailing under reefed main alone, and I was trying to pick out the red and green lights marking the harbor entrance, when all hell broke loose. The waves reflecting off the shore suddenly began mixing it up with the waves coming in off the lake, creating huge peaks and troughs in the blink of an eye. Eventually I was able to pick out the harbor entrance lights against the city lights in the background, but it was a close call. It was all we could do to thread our way into calmer water without getting shoved into the pierheads on either side of the dangerously narrow channel. I hate to think what might have happened if an errant wave had grabbed our stern at just the right—or wrong—moment. We surfed in on a breaker, and watching the portside pierhead go rushing by in the fading light, I couldn't help thinking how lucky we were that I'd been able to pick out the entrance in time. Later we heard there were squalls packing 60-knot winds on the lake that night. Pretty ugly stuff—but in retrospect, in spite of making it in, it probably would have been the wiser course to stay out on the open lake.

Heaving-to

Had we decided to stay offshore, we very likely would have spent at least part of the time hove-to. *Heaving-to* is a time-honored tactic whereby you sheet the jib to windward and trim the main for a beat, while at the same time lashing the helm so the rudder keeps you headed into the wind. In this configuration, with the two sails working in opposition to one another, the boat will drift slowly to leeward while remaining more or less on a beat or close reach. This is an excellent position to be in, because it allows the sturdiest part of the boat—the bow—to meet the waves. The steadying force of the wind on the sails and the fact that you're merely holding your position—as opposed to trying to move forward through the waves—means your boat's motion will be much smoother as well.

To heave-to, simply tack the boat as you normally would, but keep the headsail sheeted as you come around, as opposed to letting the sheet run free. Once you've come around, trim in on the main and adjust the helm until the boat is balanced. This maneuver can be a bit tricky, so it pays to practice heaving-to sometime when you're out on a heavy-air daysail, playing around with various sheeting angles and helm positions to see what happens. Most full-keel boats will heave-to with a minimum of

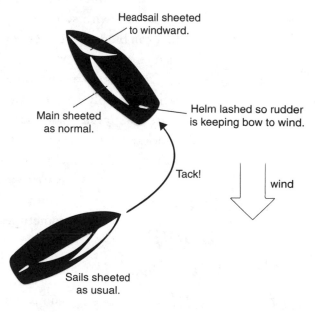

Headsail sheeted to windward.

Main sheeted as normal.

Helm lashed so rudder is keeping bow to wind.

Tack!

wind

Sails sheeted as usual.

Heaving-to.

effort, but some fin-keel designs can be tricky. After experimenting with different sail and rudder combinations in merely blustery conditions, you will be that much better prepared in the event you find yourself having to contend with heavy weather.

If your boat simply refuses to heave-to, the next best thing is to employ a similar tactic called *forereaching*. With this approach someone needs to be at the helm at all times, as opposed to simply letting the boat take care of itself. Basically, you reef down or hoist your storm sails, and then sail more or less on a close reach so the bow meets the waves. I say "more or less," because in practice it's often necessary to steer a slightly lower course in the troughs to build up the speed you need to successfully meet the next crest. This is critical—you don't ever want the seas to gain the upper hand and start pushing your boat backward, or you'll lose steerage—which in turn will leave you at the mercy of the waves. The downside to forereaching is that it can require a tremendous amount of crew effort, which can be especially hard if you're shorthanded—a big reason so many deep-water cruising sailors prefer sailboats with full keels that heave-to well.

Again, in extreme conditions, the real danger is waves wresting control of your boat or smashing into its topsides. Worse yet, if the waves are powerful enough, they can completely roll your boat, forcing your mast underwater and your keel into the air. At the very least, you and your crew can end up with some pretty serious cuts and bruises. At the worst your boat can be dismasted or your hull can sustain such serious damage that it's no longer seaworthy.

The chances of sustaining such damage are surprisingly low. Although yachts certainly do "go missing" from time to time, today's oceangoing sailboats are so well made that unless they actually hit something solid—say, a rock, a floating cargo container, or another boat—they rarely go to the bottom. In fact, in a number of instances, such as the tragic 1979 Fastnet Race, boats that were abandoned by their crews were found drifting safe and sound after the storm passed, sometimes days afterward.

For this reason, you should *never* abandon ship unless your boat is actively sinking—and I mean *actively*, as in, with the floorboards floating out the companionway. Lifeboats are miserable places to be, even in the best of conditions, and in storm conditions

> *You should never abandon ship unless your boat is actively sinking.*

they have been described as utter hell. They also can be damned hard to get into, especially when the night is pitch black or you're in a roaring seaway. If a portlight gives way or water is finding its way in by some other means, start bailing and *find that leak*. Whatever you do, don't just give in—fight to save your boat! There's an old adage, "Always step *up* into a life raft"—in other words, only abandon ship when there's little—if anything—left to abandon.

Speaking of life rafts, it's important to be aware that not all life rafts are the same. Some are sturdy enough and equipped with the necessary equipment for a prolonged time afloat in rough, cold water. Others are rated only for "coastal" use. The type of life raft you need depends on the type of sailing you do. It's also important to have a life raft that's big enough—without being too big. A good rule of thumb is to have a raft with room for two more people than you have on board. A life raft is cramped and unpleasant enough as it is without trying to cram in more people than it's designed to hold. On the other hand, an overly large life raft that has too few people in it will be more prone to capsize. With fewer bodies in it than it was intended to hold, it will also be harder for the crew to keep themselves warm.

It also pays to always have a ditch bag ready and close at hand—just in case. A well-supplied ditch bag contains such essentials as a watermaker, signal mirror, first aid kit, flares, handheld radio, instant meals, a 406 MHz EPIRB signaling device so rescuers can find you more easily, and a little money and a copy of your passport and boat documentation. Some of these items may also be contained in your life raft. The main thing is that everything you need to survive until you are rescued is close at hand. Not having the right equipment when you are adrift on the open ocean can mean the difference between life and death.

When the Going Gets Really Tough

In the event the weather becomes truly extreme, you may find that heaving-to or forereaching is no longer adequate for the conditions. The problem is not necessarily the first breaking sea that grabs your bow and sets it off to leeward—it's the second one, the one that comes smashing into your now-exposed topsides, maybe even rolling you over, before your boat has a chance to recover.

When things get truly bad, many sailors recommend dropping all sail and running out a sea anchor off the bow. A sea anchor can consist

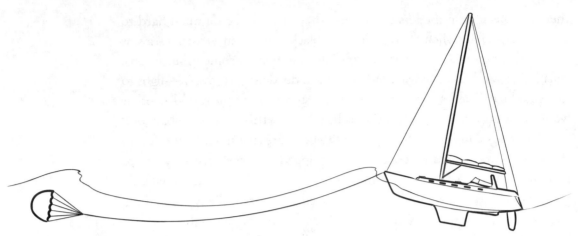

Parachute sea anchor.

of anything from a purpose-built, heavy-duty underwater parachute to a jury-rigged jumble of spars and fenders at the end of a long, stout line. No matter what you use, the idea is to have something dragging through the water that will keep your bow pointed into the wind and the seas. Chances are, at this point, you've long since stopped caring that you're wet and miserable—now the goal is survival.

Alas, while simple in concept, sea anchors can be extremely difficult to deploy and control. Among other things, the forces involved are truly awesome, so you'll need to make sure you've got some sturdy gear installed. You'll also need a *very* long nylon rode—hundreds of feet long, in fact—to help absorb the shock of having your boat brought up short as it smashes its way through those larger waves. There's also the matter of chafe, which can cause the loss of your sea anchor if the rode parts after rubbing for hours against the bow pulpit, the anchor gear, or even the chock through which it was purposefully led. In addition, some boats will "sail around" a sea anchor—just as some boats "sail around" when at anchor—with the wind causing them to swerve from side to side. In fact, the behavior of your boat at anchor is predictive of its behavior on a sea anchor. If it sails around the former, it will sail around the latter.

Another tactic sailors try in extreme conditions is running off, or turning tail and sailing in the same direction as the wind and waves under bare poles or a storm jib. Some sailors will also run the engine at fairly low revolutions in an effort to help maintain steerage. The philosophy behind running off is that, by sailing in the same direction as the wind and waves, you substantially reduce their destructive force, especially that of waves.

The danger is that you can get going so fast down the leading face of one wave that your bow drives into the backside of the wave in front of it, bringing the boat to an immediate stop and allowing the crest of the wave astern to overtake you with a vengeance. At the very least it will grab your stern and heave you around broadside to seas following close behind. At worst it can pitch-pole the boat, causing the stern to flip up and over the bow.

To avoid such a disaster, many sailors recommend setting out a kind of sea anchor over the stern called a *drogue*, with the idea of keeping your forward motion under control while keeping your stern facing the waves. Be prepared to deal with chafe, the forces the drogue will impose on any attachment points, and the challenge of deployment and recovery. Some sailors recommend attaching a stern drogue to a bridle, with the two bridle lines running through snatch blocks to the boat's two jib winches—a configuration that not only spreads the load between two purpose-built strong points, but makes it possible to fine-tune your riding angle after the drogue has been deployed.

Another option is something called a *series drogue*. Developed by retired aeronautical engineer Donald Jordon, it consists of dozens of small sailcloth cones spread along a long, nylon rode to better spread the load. The reviews are good.

Whatever tactic you ultimately choose to employ, the important thing is that you think it through and even practice it ahead of time. The time to prepare for heavy weather is when the sun is still shining—not when the barometer is plunging and black clouds are boiling on the horizon. Sometime when you're daysailing in boisterous conditions, try heaving-to or deploying a sea anchor or drogue. Bend on your trysail and hoist it along with the storm jib to see how they perform. As you are doing so, try steering with the emergency tiller. You may be surprised by how difficult some of these tasks are. Imagine what it would be like figuring them out for the first time in the middle of a gale.

Looking back on some of the first offshore races I took part in, I'm shocked at how little prepared we were for bad weather. Like most people,

> *The time to prepare for heavy weather is when the sun is still shining.*

we were lucky and nothing terrible happened. But I hate to think what would have happened if our luck had run out. Every year, sailors do get into trouble, and all too often the ending is unnecessarily tragic because the boat isn't up to the task or the crew isn't prepared. Being prepared for heavy weather is as much a part of good seamanship as sail trim or being able to tie a good bowline. Take pride in the fact that you are ready for whatever Mother Nature might throw at you, even if you're never put to the test.

THE MAKING OF A GOOD BOAT

17

Functionality, Like Beauty, Is in the Eye of the Beholder

BEFORE WE GET started, I'd like to have you all take a seat please—and stop sharpening those knives! That includes you, sir, with the calloused hands and wood shavings in your beard!

For some reason, boat talk can bring out the ogre in some people, which is too bad. One of the great things about sailing is the incredible diversity of boats to do it in: big boats, little boats, wide boats, skinny boats, monohulls, multihulls, wood boats, fiberglass boats, steel boats, aluminum boats—even boats made of cement! The number of boat types that continue to be built and sailed, even today, is truly incredible.

My own "breakthrough" in appreciating boat diversity came a few years ago on a bareboat charter cruise on Lake Erie with my wife, Shelly. As I've intimated elsewhere, there was a time when I wanted nothing to do with any boat that wasn't either a racer or an old classic with heartbreaking overhangs. Then along came this charter aboard a 34-footer of the type I had always dismissed as being the epitome of a soulless "plastic" cruiser.

Each design has to be judged on its merits and in the context of the boat's intended purpose.

In fact, I had barely set foot aboard that trim little vessel before I realized how wrong and even downright ignorant I'd been. The marina was as crowded as a shopping mall on the day after Thanksgiving, but we backed that handy little sloop out of her slip and turned toward the channel pretty as you please. A couple of hours later, a line of thunderheads rumbled in from the northwest, and we had to reef down for a bit of a squall, but again, there was no problem—in spite of some hail and about 35 knots of wind. That night we relaxed in the comfortable cockpit, slowly working our way through a bottle of wine. Then we went below for a good night's rest in the boat's spacious aft stateroom. The next morning we awoke refreshed, had breakfast, and then headed back out onto the lake, ready and eager to do it all over again. In short, we had an absolutely wonderful time, and the boat performed splendidly in every way. It really was a revelation, both the quality of the boat and the realization of my own pig-headedness.

This is not to say that all boats are good for all purposes. Deepwater cruisers need to meet certain criteria that make them markedly different from top-flight racers. Same goes for daysailers and coastal cruisers. The point is, each design has to be judged on its merits and in the context of the boat's intended purpose. Assuming the builder has successfully executed the design, whether or not the boat is a good one ultimately depends on the sailor.

What Makes a Good Bluewater Cruiser?

When it comes to crossing oceans, you obviously need a sturdy, reliable boat in the event you meet a serious gale. The ideal bluewater cruiser, however, can't be simply a waterborne tank—otherwise, it will take forever and a day to get anywhere, and you'll be sitting duck for any storm heading your direction. In addition, the ideal cruising boat needs to take care of its crew on days when it *isn't* blowing stink—days that far outnumber the stormy ones. It also needs to provide a comfortable place to rest and relax at the end of a day's sail—not a trivial consideration, as even the most dedicated cruiser spends substantially more time at anchor or tied to the dock than out on the briny. Even an aggressive circumnavigation schedule will generally allow the crew two days in port for every day of sailing.

Finally, a bluewater cruiser needs to be both seaworthy *and* seakindly in its design and construction—that is, it must be able to both stand up to the rigors of heavy weather and spare the crew undue fatigue in the course of a typical passage. This is a boat that sails well but doesn't require tremendous effort to keep it in trim. It's a boat that tracks well—i.e., it's steady on its helm—and has easy motion, so the crew doesn't get banged up every time the weather starts kicking up some waves.

A number of books extensively address the question of what makes a good offshore boat. Among the best are *Nigel Calder's Cruising Handbook* and *How to Sail Around the World*, by pioneering cruiser and solo racer Hal Roth. Nigel Calder is both a veteran sailor and a gearhead—in the best sense of the term. His book provides a wealth of formulas and tables to help divine the seakeeping qualities of pretty much anything afloat. Another good resource is *The Complete Guide to Choosing a Cruising Sailboat*, by Roger Marshall.

What follows is a short list of characteristics that make a good bluewater cruiser.

STRUCTURE AND EQUIPMENT INSTALLATION. To be truly seaworthy, a boat must be structurally sound and its equipment correctly installed. The hull-to-deck joint must be well made, and all bulkheads and other interior structural elements should be securely bonded to the underside of the deck and inside of the hull. Equally important, items like hatches, rudder bearings, and steering gear need to be robustly constructed and robustly installed, so they can withstand the force of a crashing sea.

On deck, a deepwater cruiser should have tall stanchions set in sturdy bases. It will often have bulwarks—or at the very least, toerails—to brace your feet against if you ever find yourself sliding down the deck when the boat is on its ear. There should be plenty of sturdy handrails along the cabintop, so that you never have to make any kind of "leap of faith," lunging from one handhold to the next when moving forward to the mast or foredeck. There should also be adequate *side deck* space between the cabin trunk and the bulwarks or toerail so that going forward isn't a struggle. And, of course, the side decks and foredeck should be surfaced with aggressive nonskid. Beware of stylishly molded cabin trunks—their gracefully curved surfaces can be treacherous in rough weather.

HULL DESIGN. The hull of a good cruising boat should have relatively low freeboard to minimize the impact of windage in extreme weather. It should also have a moderate beam, a bit of forefoot beneath the waterline, and a full keel or a moderately proportioned fin keel to help with heaving-to. The cockpit should be large enough to be comfortable in normal conditions, but not overly large—if you're ever pooped, a too-large cockpit will hold that much more water, the weight of which can depress your stern and make you vulnerable to being pooped again. All deepwater boats should have a bridgedeck "step" of sorts between the front of the cockpit and the companionway leading below, so water from a flooded cockpit won't slop into the cabin. The cockpit should also be equipped with large drains to allow water that comes aboard to leave as quickly as possible.

Finally, a deepwater cruiser must have a safe limit of positive stability (LPS)—at least 120 degrees, although higher is better—to prevent it from capsizing in heavy seas. As we saw in Chapter 10, LPS is the heel angle at which the hull and keel stop resisting the capsizing forces of the wind and waves and actually abet them, until the boat is completely inverted. In addition, the LPS dictates how stable a boat will be when it's upside down—in other words, how easily the boat will re-right itself. As Calder explains, a boat with an LPS of 100 degrees will, in theory, remain inverted for about 5 minutes before it's righted again by wave action. A boat with an LPS of 120, on the other hand, should right itself in about 2 minutes, and a boat with an LPS of 140 will theoretically pop right back up almost as soon as it goes over. Think about how long you can hold your breath—and about how long your hatches, hatchboards, vents, and portlights will hold when the boat is upside down in surging conditions. A couple of minutes could make all the difference in the world. For the record, Calder believes an LPS of 115 degrees is acceptable on an offshore boat.

COMFORT AND EASE OF SAILING. Many of the features that make for a seaworthy boat also make for a seakindly one. A boat with a moderate length-to-beam ratio, a bit of forefoot, and a full keel or moderately proportioned fin, for example, not only heaves-to well but also tends to track better. Granted, the boat might not be the fastest thing on the water, but what cruising sailor wants to continually tweak and trim to eke out that last fraction of a knot of boat speed anyway? Likewise, a solid masthead rig with moderate sail area will get you where you want to go without springing any nasty little surprises. In Calder's words, "On a cruising boat, it is a fundamental mistake to gear the concept of fast passagemaking to maximizing the absolute speed potential of a boat at the expense of ease of handling, comfortable motion, stability, security and other highly desirable attributes. Exhilarating performance can be fun in the short term, but extremely fatiguing in the long term. Instead, the goal should be to achieve good sustained performance in all kinds of conditions in an environment that is as relaxing and as much fun as it can be."

Many of the features that make for a seaworthy boat also make for a seakindly one.

A deepwater boat should have V-shaped sections in the bow that will allow the hull to slice through the waves on a beat or close reach, instead of slapping and pounding. It should also be stiff enough to carry sail, but not so stiff that it has a "snappy" motion when coming off a swell—which calls for a moderate L/B to ensure adequate but not too much form stability. In this same vein, a boat with a moderate to heavy displacement-to-length ratio—unlike a featherweight speedster—tends to pass smoothly through the waves instead of bouncing over them or simply bobbing on top of them like an oversized cork.

ACCOMMODATIONS. The list in this category is pretty exhaustive. An ocean is a big place, but for the crew of a sailboat on passage it's essentially no bigger than the boat's LOA. Nonetheless, the short list includes adequate sea berths, a galley that can be safely used in a seaway, plenty of storage, and a cockpit that's comfortable and safe for watch keeping.

When it comes to sea berths, simpler is better. Each berth needs to be a little more than 6 feet long and located no farther forward than around amidships. The motion in a forepeak berth in any kind of seaway will make sleeping impossible. Berths should also be parallel with the boat's centerline, not angled dramatically inward. Otherwise, either your head or feet will be higher whenever the boat heels while you're trying to sleep. Finally, sea berths should be straight to avoid cramped shoulders or feet. This consideration may seem obvious, but many modern cruising boats are equipped with curved or angled *settees*—those seats in the saloon that double as sea berths underway—which look great at boat shows but can be absolutely miserable for sleeping.

In the galley you need a cooking area that not only includes the necessary equipment for preparing meals—stove, microwave, oven, cutting board, and the like—but a layout that will make cooking safe and as easy as possible when the boat is sailing on its ear. The key is a wraparound layout, in which the counters form a U or G shape, so you can brace yourself against an opposing counter or in a corner and free your hands for cooking. Sinks should be deep and as close to the centerline as possible, where the motion is less severe. *Fiddles*—the little walls or barriers surrounding the countertops to stop things from sliding off—need to be tall and perpendicular, not low and artistically rounded. The galley should be located as close to the companionway as possible for ventilation and ease of passing snacks or coffee to crewmembers on deck. A location near the companionway also puts the galley well aft, where hull motion is easier.

STORAGE. You can never have too much storage. Extended cruising requires a tremendous amount of storage space—for everything from charts to food to spare engine parts and toothpaste—and unless your boat is 50 feet or longer, there's rarely enough room for everything. Not only that, storage space can be surprisingly scarce even in larger cruisers, as designers struggle to shoehorn in more and more accommodations per foot of LOA. The double-size quarter berths tucked under the cockpits of many newer boats may look great, but the only way to fit them in is to eliminate a voluminous amount of storage that is otherwise available under the cockpit seats. Large staterooms in the bow take away hull volume that could otherwise house wet lockers for storing damp foul-weather gear, and "sugar scoop" transoms with those oh-so-convenient swim steps leave no room for lazarettes—those wonderfully spacious lockers located aft of the cockpit. Next time you're at a boat show, do a quick inventory of that 45-foot beauty with the multiple heads and staterooms. See what's behind some of those lovely cherry-finished doors, and tally up the total storage area—including those "cabinets" that are so tiny they're essentially useless. You may be surprised that a "big" boat can actually have remarkably little room for putting things away.

COCKPIT. The cockpit should be the right size to "enclose" the on-watch crew—usually one person, unless the boat and crew are very large—so he or she doesn't have to worry about being washed around in heavy-weather conditions. A cockpit's width and length are key; there are few things in this life more reassuring than tucking yourself in where the cockpit seat meets the cabin trunk and having your feet braced against the cockpit seat or seat back to leeward—an unrealized comfort if the cockpit is too wide. In addition, all the necessary control lines should be close at hand. The helmsman shouldn't have to let go of the wheel or tiller when trimming either the main or the jib sheets. The cockpit should also have several strong points where you can secure a safety harness and easy access to jacklines without having to expose yourself to the waves.

To reiterate, these are just a few features of a good cruising boat—albeit critical ones. The real key is to find a boat that's functional and moderate in the areas of sailing and accommodations: fast but not too fast; roomy but not too roomy; and in which everything has a purpose. After all, crossing an ocean in a tiny sailboat is serious business—tremendously satisfying, but business nonetheless.

What Makes a Good Inshore Yacht?

At the other end of the sailing spectrum are the daysailer and the coastal cruiser. I lump these types together because (1) they're used exclusively in or within easy reach of sheltered waters, and (2) they're used for a few hours or, at most, a few days at a time. You don't have to worry about surviving extreme storm conditions or enduring days of difficult steering. LPS, in particular, becomes largely irrelevant—no matter how strong the wind, it will never be able to knock your boat beyond 90 degrees of heel. Only breaking waves can do that—and it's highly unlikely that you'll encounter those in sheltered waters, unless you happen to run your boat up on the beach. Without these worries, daysailers and coastal cruisers offer a generous assortment of performance and accommodation possibilities.

If you don't mind a little clutter, for example, you can limit the amount of storage in favor of accommodations. Also, because you will never be on passage for days or even weeks on end, it's no longer critical that your boat have an especially seakindly hull shape. Suddenly, fin keels, and hulls with flat, shallow sections forward and aft are within the realm of possibility—hello, boat speed! Heck, you may even like a little crash and bang when sailing to windward—makes you feel like a real "rock star" racer.

If, on the other hand, you're not in pursuit of that kind of adventure, a hull with a little displacement, moderate beam, a longer keel, V-ed sections forward, and plenty of deadrise may be more to your liking. Remember, even "sheltered" waters can get pretty bumpy on occasion: Think San Francisco Bay or an inland lake during a squall. Then again, you may sail in an area where underwater hazards like rocks and shoals prevail, as is the case along the picturesque coast of Maine or among the Florida Keys. If so, you probably ought to reconsider that deep, high-aspect fin keel and look for a hull that's suitable for "thin" water and will stand up to a hard grounding, should you experience one. You might consider a longer shoal-draft keel with a skeg or even a full keel, with the rudder hanging safe and sound from its trailing edge.

The point is, when you shop for an inshore yacht, the decisions are no longer a matter of life or death. There are plenty of sailors for whom a great day on the water means sitting in the cockpit and sipping a cool drink at the dock, without ever casting off the lines—sailors who prefer to take things easy. Other sailors can't wait to get underway as soon as they step aboard, the more wind the better. The key is to find a boat that suits your sailing style and to understand that you can't have everything.

You want voluminous accommodations and enough beam in that 34-footer to fit a ping-pong table? Great! But be aware that your boat will likely be a bit slow sailing to windward, and if you sail in a light-wind area, you'd better have a reliable engine and plenty of fuel tankage for extended motoring—chances are you're going to need it.

On the other hand, if you want a 30-footer that goes like a rocket, be aware that there's no way its accommodations will rival those of your neighbor's heavy-displacement floating "condominium."

How Much Sail Is Enough?

Which brings us to the question of size—the size of the hull and size of the rig. Let's start with the rig. In recent years, sailboat rigs have been getting progressively bigger, thanks to the stiffer hulls and better sail-handling gear that characterize today's boats. Years ago, a sail area to displacement ratio (SA/D) in the upper teens was considered powerful—but today even "cruisers" can be found with SA/Ds in the low 20s. The thinking is that a bigger rig gives you more flexibility: When things go light you have plenty of horsepower to keep the boat moving; when things get rough, all you need do is reef down. There's also more than a little marketing at work here. Yacht brokers figured out long ago that a bigger "engine" under the hood helps close boat sales—just as with cars.

The downside of this trend is that, even with modern sail-handling gear, bigger rigs mean more work. You may be a burly old sea dog, and your idea of a good time may be to grind winches and get doused with spray as you take in yet another reef—but what about your poor husband? What about your friends? The idea of "shortening sail" sounds great, but the reality can be a little more complicated. For one thing, puffs can be notoriously sneaky. For another, if you have clouds of sail up, even a moderate increase in wind velocity can have a pretty dramatic—sometimes downright scary—effect on your boat's behavior. One moment you're ghosting along on a close reach with your full SA/D 25's-worth of working sails up. The next, the wind pipes up to a hurricane 15 knots and you're on your ear. Of course, now the loads on the sheets and control lines have all ramped up exponentially, as have the loads on the helm. "Take the wheel!" you cry, but your poor husband—who at that same moment was making his way up the companionway with a tray of sandwiches—just stares at you, eyes as big as saucers. By the time you finally get things under control, you're winded, your husband has spilled the drinks, and your friends are sitting there shaking their heads. "So this is how you relax?" one of them asks incredulously. So much for the leisurely daysail.

This is not to say that performance cruisers and daysailers should be undercanvassed in the interest of safety—on the contrary, there are few things more aggravating than bobbing motionless in the water while the rest of the world goes ghosting by, pretty as you please. When I lived in Milwaukee, I occasionally saw an old Westsail 32, a storied deepwater double-ender with a displacement-to-length ratio of well over 400 and an SA/D of 15. It was stirring as hell to see this kind of ocean-crossing barky tooling around Lake Michigan, but it was soon evident why there were so few of them in the area—the hapless thing needed half a gale to get anywhere. Sailing over for a close look was rarely a problem, because it was barely moving.

Ultimately, the best course for most of us is one of moderation, which means an SA/D in the upper teens—say 17 to 19. My family's old 23-foot Ensign *Cortship II*, for example, had an SA/D of 18.8 and was truly a joy in light air, despite its full keel. I have many fond memories of ghosting in and out of the basin at Edgewater Yacht Club in Cleveland as a kid, hiking out to leeward under main and No. 2 jib. If a puff hit, no problem—with her full keel, 1,200 pounds of lead ballast, and D/L of 282, she would just heel a bit and dig in. If worse came to worst I could always reef the main, but by that time I would be about the only boat remaining on Lake Erie—besides the odd 700-foot ore freighter—and it was probably time to head home anyway.

The pantheon of "classic plastic"—older fiberglass boats that have stood the test of time—is replete with boats that have SA/D ratios in the upper teens. The C&C 27 has an SA/D of 17.87; the old Catalina 30 has an SA/D of 15.1; the C&C 35 has an SA/D of 19.1; the Tartan 30 has an SA/D of 16.99; and the Pearson 30 has an SA/D of 17.3—just to name a few. These boats were the "performance cruisers" and "racer-cruisers" of their day and have proved themselves time and again both on passage and

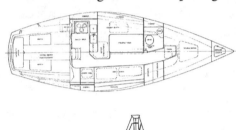

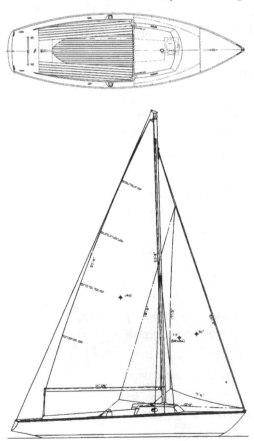

The Pearson Ensign.

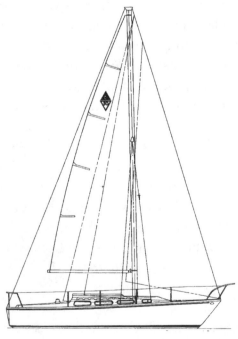

The Catalina 30.

on the race course. They didn't sport smaller rigs because their owners weren't competent sailors, but because they had different hull forms and lacked such modern conveniences as line stoppers, reliable furling gear, and powered winches. Granted, you and your spouse can "handle" far more sail than couples could in the past—but before getting all googly-eyed over that shiny "racer-cruiser" with the towering carbon-fiber mast, be sure to ask yourself whether all that sail is just a want or a genuine need. Are those acres of Dacron cloth overhead really going to enhance your sailing experience—or could they ultimately just end up getting in the way?

How Much Boat Is Enough?

Which brings us to hull size and complexity. Years ago, the rule of thumb was to buy as big as you could afford, but with the advent of ever-larger cruising boats, this rule is increasingly called into question—or at least it should be. Although hefty for their time, the classic-plastics I list above would now be considered midgets. Today's "cruising couples" are regularly encouraged to invest in boats with LOAs of 50 feet or more, and modern "daysailers" have grown exponentially. The Alerion line, for example, includes a very reasonable 20-footer, but it also boasts a "day boat" with 6,000 pounds of ballast and an LOA of 38 feet 3 inches. Morris Yachts of Bass Harbor, Maine, builds an S&S-designed 36-footer "intended for short or single-handed" daysailing. Hinckley recently unveiled its own daysailer, a sloop that displaces 14,000 pounds and has more than 42 feet of LOA! Heavens! Whatever happened to the good old 17-foot O'Day Day Sailer or the classic Rhodes 19?

The problem is that big boats, like big rigs, are a lot more work. They're also a lot more expensive and complicated to maintain. Dockage fees, haulout fees, bottom cleaning—these services are generally priced by the foot and can increase dramatically at the top end of the range. The costs of sails, spars, and hardware also tend to increase exponentially. I recently bought a new main halyard and jib halyard for our family's 16-foot Wayfarer dinghy— around 70 feet of $^3/_{16}$-inch Dacron braid—for a total cost of about $35. I also picked up a used mainsail that still has plenty of life in it for a whopping $40! That's less than the cost of a new snap shackle for a 40-footer.

I'm not saying everybody needs to sail a dinghy, but for most casual sailors—which is really what most of us are—I sincerely question the value of going much over 30 feet, unless you're a regular cruiser with a genuine need to accommodate a lot of friends and family. There are plenty of smaller boats out there with cockpits that are fully capable of holding four, five, or even six people. Back in high school I would regularly take three or four buddies for a daysail in our Ensign, and I've had plenty of great sails with four and even five people in our old Lightning. The Colgate 26, the Sonar 23, the old H-12^1/$_2$ (designed by Nat Herreshoff and loved by classic boat fans), the Precision line, the Harbor 20, the Catalina 22, and any one of a number of catboat designs, including those built by Com-Pac Yachts of Clearwater, Florida, or Marshall Marine of South Dartmouth, Massachusetts—these are boats that provide all the cockpit and performance you could ever want for a jaunt under sail. The 19-foot Flying Scott—practically impossible to capsize despite being a centerboarder—is rumored to have room for as many as eight people!

Of course, some sailors really do need—and use—their larger boats on a regular basis. In an article in *Sail* magazine, one sailor presented a number of compelling reasons why bigger is better—if you're the right sailor. Having recently upgraded from a 30-footer to a 57-footer with a 50,000-pound displacement, he pointed out that his new boat not only offers a much greater sailing range because of its higher speed, but is also much more comfortable for nonsailors. He reported that his wife had gone from being a reluctant participant to an enthusiastic supporter, and his teenage daughter had actually begun asking if she could bring friends along. "Big is easy. Big is stable. Big inspires confidence," he wrote, and he's right. "She rarely does anything abrupt or unsettling. Electric winches, powered roller furling and a large but simple sailplan make everything eminently manageable. There are two jib sheets, an outhaul and one mainsheet. That's it. Four lines. Basically, she is a huge dinghy."

Fair enough—and for those who have the ability and financial wherewithal, I say have at it. Really, I'm not being sarcastic here—if you have the money to maintain all those systems and the ability to get yourself in and out of that slip, then maybe a bigger boat is for you.

The bottom line, though, is that if you hang around any yacht club or marina long enough, you will start to notice a pattern: even as all those little boats are continually coming and going, there's precious little activity among the 50-footers. Whether this is because, labor-saving devices aside,

Com-Pac Yachts' 14-foot Picnic Cat (Brian Gilbert)

there's still something a little daunting about taking out a great behemoth of a sloop short-handed, or whether it's because the owners of those bigger boats are too busy making money, I couldn't say—but it's a fact.

In my own experience, the maximum workable length for a couple is around 35 feet, and you can have a perfectly fine time coastal cruising aboard something much smaller. My wife and I have cruised on a number of boats, ranging in length from around 20 to 40 feet, and we have never had any complaints with any of them—save the 40-footer. Not that there was anything "wrong" with the boat, it's just that, as we got up to 40 feet, things started to get a lot harder for Shelly. The mainsail, for example, was too much for her to hoist without working up a sweat. She could do it, but it wasn't fun. It was also physically impossible for her to furl the main, because the boom was simply too high for her to reach. My wife is a pretty tough woman—a former competitive skier and 3:30 marathoner, among other things—but there's no getting around the fact that the average woman is not as tall and simply can't compete in terms of arm strength.

One of the best cruises I can remember is the time Shelly and I spent the better part of a week tooling around New Zealand's Bay of Islands in a little pocket cruiser measuring all of about 22 feet. For our honeymoon, we spent five days cruising Lake Champlain and never felt the least bit cramped aboard our 30-foot Catalina. At no time did either one of us ever feel we weren't up to handling the rig.

My point here is not to beat up on sailors who prefer boats with a little more length and displacement. There are plenty of sailors for whom a larger, well-appointed yacht serves as a means of reaching more distant cruising grounds or spending more time offshore on passage. For other sailors, larger yachts serve as a kind of waterborne beach house in which they can spend the weekend—and that's great! Big boats have plenty of room for guests. They have comfy heads and spacious galleys—and when it comes time to tack or jibe, you don't have to worry about the boom banging your head.

Nonetheless, it's important to think through all the implications before graduating to this kind of sailing. Do you really need all that space, all that power, all those accommodations? Do you really need a boat that big to have fun? Or are you simply entranced by the idea of all that LOA for the sake of having more LOA?

What Makes a Good Racing Boat?

There are two basic requirements of a racing boat: windward ability and an easy-to-manage rig. It's also nice to have a large, well-arranged cockpit, so the crew isn't continually bumping into each other during mark roundings and sail changes.

One thing a racing boat does not necessarily require is boat speed—seriously. In fact, for all but the topmost echelon of grand prix racers, striving for outrageous boat speed is actually *counterproductive* to a good racing experience. The reason most of us race is simply to get out on the water, to match wits against the competition, to hone our seamanship, and to revel in the magnificent spectacle of a group of well-found vessels sailing in close proximity to one another. Obviously, it's important to go fast relative to your competitors—it's also nice not to sail a complete dog—but going fast in the absolute sense of the word is secondary. In this, the twenty-first century, even the fastest sailboats are pretty much slugs. In a hurry to get somewhere? Go bicycling.

Despite all the different types of boats on the water, there are just three kinds of sailboat racing: one-design, handicap, and development class. In one-design racing all the boats are identical, and the first across the finish line wins. Many of today's best-loved boats compete as one-designs—many of them explicitly created for this purpose. These include everything from state-of-the-art racing machines like the Farr 40 to the wildly popular 7-foot 9-inch Optimist dinghy. Others might surprise you, like the 86-year-old Beetle Cat, a classic catboat with a 12-foot LOA, gaff mainsail, and oversize "barn door" rudder—it has a devoted and very competitive following in New England. The 26-foot Folkboat, a hardy little boat from Sweden, is also still actively raced in a number of areas, including windy San Francisco Bay.

Development class racing is like one-design racing in that the first boat over the finish line wins. In a development class, however, the competing boats are no longer exactly the same. Instead, they're built to a design rule, a formula that includes things like LOA, sail area, and displacement. The 12-meter yachts of America's Cup fame, for example, were all built to

> *Despite all the different types of boats on the water, there are just three kinds of sailboat racing: one-design, handicap, and development class.*

a formula called the International Rule, in which the number 12 represents the required result when you plug things like length and sail area into the formula. Similar formulas were calculated for the smaller 6-meter, 8-meter, and 10-meter boats, which were equally competitive in the early twentieth century.

Modern examples of development class boats include those that compete in the Volvo Ocean Race, International America's Cup Class racers, and the Open 60 and Open 40 boats that compete in numerous solo and double-handed long-distance events. In the latter two, pretty much anything goes as long as the boats are within a certain length. Smaller development classes include the experimental Moth class and the International 14-footer, in which the boats are almost universally high-priced, cutting-edge racers—many of them horrendously expensive. Some of the older classes still welcome "classic" designs into their competitions—but it's still pretty pricey, rarefied racing.

Finally, there's handicap racing, in which wildly different boats—including everything from grand prix racers to family-friendly cruisers—are able to compete through the use of time ratings. Basically, a group of boats starts at the same time and then the individual times are carefully recorded as the boats cross the finish line. After everyone has finished, the race committee calculates a "corrected" time based on the distance sailed and each boat's time rating. The boat with the best corrected time wins.

Note that in every one of the cases above, raw boat speed is not necessarily a prerequisite for being competitive. To win you need only sail your boat quickly and efficiently compared to the competition. In a one-design boat or development class, you need not sail faster than that crazy 70-footer, only faster than the other boats in your class. In handicap racing, you need only sail better than your own rating. The key is seamanship, not sail area

The important thing is that you have a boat that sails well and fits your sailing style.

or LOA. In fact, the annals of handicap racing are replete with examples of smaller, "slower" boats coming home winners. In 2000, for example, the winner of the 600-mile Millennium Mackinac race from Port Huron, Michigan, to Chicago, was a 1965 Cal 40, and a brand-new 80-footer came in second: never mind that the 80-footer beat the Cal to the finish line by some 36 hours.

Granted, there's a certain class of sailor that revels in being the "scratch" boat (the one with the most punitive rating in the fleet) or in taking "line honors"—in other words, being the first over the finish line and ratings be damned—but this kind of sailing is hardly a prerequisite for having a good time. Dennis Conner, for example, may be "Mr. America's Cup," but he has also spent years racing aboard 23-foot Stars. New Zealander Russell Coutts, in addition to winning three America's Cups, also won an Olympic gold medal racing 14-foot Finn dinghies. The important thing is that you have a boat that sails well and fits your sailing style. Personally, I much prefer being out on the water to writing checks for new gear or laboring aboard some great behemoth in a boatyard. I have raced on boats from 8 feet to 70 feet long and had a great time on every one of them. I have never once finished a race—especially one that went well—and been disappointed because the boat I happened to be on somehow wasn't big enough. I've always been far too busy having fun!

HOW FIBERGLASS BOATS ARE BUILT

And Why They Are Magnificent

18

ALMOST FROM their inception, a terrible prejudice has existed against fiberglass boats. Nathanael Greene Herreshoff's son, L. Francis, famously referred to them as "frozen snot," and wooden boat aficionados forever refer to them as Clorox bottles. Even some owners seem to feel a little guilty, as if their fiberglass boats were somehow inferior to "real" boats made of wood. Years ago I reviewed a book about wooden boats for *Sailing* magazine, in which the author—not an especially experienced sailor, mind you—repeatedly stated that fiberglass boats are basically junk, claiming at one point that they have hulls that can "shatter like an eggshell." Later, he had the temerity to suggest that fiberglass boat owners don't *really* love their boats, but simply sail them as a matter of convenience. "You never tried to save an old fiberglass boat—what was the point? Broken or old, she was only plastic—dump her. It wasn't like she was a great old wooden boat, a boat with a soul."

Well, I'm here to tell you that just isn't true—not a word of it.

Not that I have anything against wooden boats—far from it. I'd be the first to admit there are plenty of beautiful wooden boats out there, and I'm glad there are people willing to both build and maintain them. Nonetheless, I get tired of hearing that wooden boats are "better" simply by virtue of having been constructed from recently dead trees. Who dares say an Etchells 22 or a Soling isn't a damn fine looking boat, or that modern Star boats are somehow less sleek or sexy looking than their wooden predecessors? For that matter, what about the many fine C&C boats that have been built over the years, the sleek fast creations built by such companies as J/Boats, Baltic Yachts, Hinckley, Oyster, Hanse, Sabre, Dufour, and Finland's Nautor—just to name a few? Today's builders and designers are continually creating wonderful, functional yachts that not only break new ground aesthetically and technically but are just as seaworthy and beautiful as their wooden predecessors. To argue otherwise is to be willfully ignorant of ongoing tradition.

Today's builders and designers are continually creating wonderful, functional yachts that not only break new ground aesthetically and technically but are just as seaworthy and beautiful as their wooden predecessors.

Not only that, boats made of "frozen snot" have introduced countless people to sailing who might otherwise never have discovered it. Wooden boat fans may dismiss today's "mass-produced" boats as cheap wannabes, but what about the masses of sailors who use them? How many fiberglass dinghies—Lasers, El Toros, Sunfish, Lido 14s, Flying Scots, Optimists, and countless others—have you seen lying neglected for months or even years alongside beach houses, only to spring into action the moment they're needed? How many classic plastics have lain similarly neglected, only to spring back to life with the help of a little elbow grease?

Years ago, my wife's Grandpa Scott bought a 16-foot fiberglass Wayfarer dinghy, which he sailed on Lake St. Clair, part of the waterway connecting Lake Huron and Lake Erie. Grandpa Scott was career Navy, a World War II veteran who'd been on Corregidor when it fell to the Japanese and once served as a diver aboard Navy submarines. He passed away about fifteen years ago, and it seemed no one wanted to take care of that old dinghy. For years it sat on a trailer in Michigan. Then somebody hauled it halfway across the country, and it sat in Sante Fe. Finally, my wife's Aunt Beth dragged it back to Evanston, Illinois, and I decided to see if I could get it sailing again. I confess, I had concerns—but I had no reason to worry. The fiberglass hull was as solid as ever, and so were the aluminum mast and Dacron sails. The only things that needed any real work were the teak cockpit seats, the oak mast step, the mahogany cockpit sole, and the mahogany centerboard—in other words, the parts made of wood. I refinished the woodwork, changed out the gudgeons on the transom so that I could hang a new rudder, installed new running rigging, and we were ready to go sailing again. The boat was essentially as good as new.

Here's another story: years ago, when he was young and adventurous and hadn't yet begun writing for *Sailing* magazine, a fellow by the name of John Kretschmer and his buddy Ty Techera decided to sail a fiberglass Contessa 32 named *Gigi* around Cape Horn, from New York to San Francisco. The pair made it, as related in Kretschmer's book, *Cape Horn to Starboard*. Kretschmer eventually lost track of *Gigi*, but she was rediscovered in Galveston, Texas, and fully restored by Jeremy Rogers Yachts, the same company that built her back in the 1980s. Kretschmer had a chance to revisit *Gigi* during the 2007 Whyte & Mackay Earls Court Boat Show in London, and I asked him about it afterward.

"Stepping into the main hall I spotted *Gigi* right away. . . . My first thought was, 'How did we sail that little toy around the Horn?' As I moved closer and took in the full measure of the boat, though, I thought, 'Wow, what a great boat to sail around Cape Horn.' *Gigi* was the perfect boat for a bluewater bumbler like me. I was a kid, longing to do something that would be remembered 25 years hence, and Cape Horn was calling. I'd read all the books, but I didn't know what I was doing. Neither did Ty. We were just game, and we were lucky—we picked the perfect boat. And now she was back in her full glory. If only the same thing could be done to me!"

To quote L. Francis again, "While it is possible that some individuals do not appreciate beauty, it is an indisputable fact that nearly all highly developed and nicely perfected objects are beautiful. It makes no difference whether it is a gun, violin, automobile, aeroplane, or a vessel; and I myself do not despise a beautiful woman."

I would add that the specific material used to construct any of these objects is irrelevant—assuming it's up to the task. Fiberglass boats not have souls? Ridiculous!

What, Exactly, Is Fiberglass?

Now that I've used up my allotted time on the soapbox, it's time to answer a pressing question: what is fiberglass, anyway?

Technically, fiberglass is a mixture of tiny strands of glass encased in a plastic resin, a "matrix" of glass-reinforced plastic (GRP), also called fiber-reinforced plastic (FRP). The resin alone, although great for making complicated shapes, isn't especially strong. Add the glass fiber reinforcing strands, however, and you get a material that's both easy to form and extremely tough—kind of like adding rebar to concrete for building dams, bridges, and office towers.

First developed in a marketable form by Owens-Corning in the late 1930s, the glass strands used for boatbuilding come in a number of forms. *Fiberglass cloth,* for example, is a smooth, woven fabric, whereas *woven roving,* though similarly constructed, has a coarser weave comprised of thicker, heavier bundles of strands. *Chopped strand mat* (CSM), or simply *mat,* is made of roughly 2-inch-long strands of fiberglass randomly pressed and held together with a binder, or seizing material, to form an even rougher kind of cloth. Fiberglass is also available in *unidirectional cloths* in which all the fibers run parallel to one another, maximizing the fabric's strength along the axis of the strands. You can also shoot short bits of fiberglass onto sticky resin using something called a "chopper gun."

Most of the fiberglass used in boats these days is tough, affordable E-glass. Stronger and more expensive S-glass, used in the aircraft industry, is a less common option. Boatbuilders use woven roving for strength and mat—which is easily saturated, or *wetted out,* with plastic resin—for binding multiple layers of roving so they won't delaminate. Because of its fine weave, fiberglass cloth creates a smooth finish for exposed and fussy surfaces—and also for repairs—while unidirectional cloth is used in high-load areas of the hull, where the strands can be oriented to oppose a specific force—such as the load created by chainplates.

Surprisingly, the fiberglass-resin matrix is not particularly stiff, and can in fact be quite bendy for its weight. Therefore, boatbuilders often insert an inner

The idea is to keep the deck as light as possible to maintain a low center of gravity, while supporting the often-substantial weight of the boat's crew and passengers.

layer, or *core*, of balsa wood or stiff, closed-cell foam to increase the total thickness of the hull—and therefore its rigidity—without making it much heavier, a technique that's especially common in decks. The idea is to keep the deck as light as possible to maintain a low center of gravity, while supporting the often-substantial weight of the boat's crew and passengers.

Alternatively, builders can use stronger fibers such as those made of carbon fiber, Kevlar, or Nomex. Because these materials are extremely expensive, however, they are only used on cutting-edge racers or selectively on some production boats. A number of bluewater cruisers, for example, include some Kevlar in the bow to resist puncturing in the event of a collision with rocks, docks, or errant shipping containers.

The long-time industry standard in plastic resins has been polyester, which comes in two forms: isophthalic and orthophthalic. Although both are used for boatbuilding, isophthalic polyester is increasingly popular because it resists abrasion better and is less prone to blistering. Blistering occurs when traces of water migrate into the matrix and mix with specks of dirt or chemicals in the plastic itself to form tiny pockets of acid. Over time, these blisters can increase in both size and number, especially if the boatbuilder wasn't careful or used inferior chemicals in the boat's layup. Most blisters merely create a cosmetic problem, but in some cases they become so big and deep that they compromise the strength of the hull. Even benign blisters can be extremely time-consuming and expensive to fix.

In part because of the blistering problem, boatbuilders have started using vinylester and epoxy resins in their layup, especially on the outer surfaces of hulls or below the waterline. Vinylester and epoxy are also tough and adhere well to an already-hardened polyester surface, making them an excellent choice for repairs or for bonding bulkheads and other structural elements to a hull. Alas, for all their usefulness they're also expensive, and polyester remains the industry standard.

No matter what the plastic resin, it generally arrives at the boatyard in two parts: a resin and a catalyst. The builder adds the catalyst to the resin to initiate the chemical reaction that converts the resin from a liquid to a solid, a process referred to as *curing*, or *kicking*. The polyester resin catalyst comprises only a couple of percent by volume of the resin mixture, and its proportion can be adjusted to hasten or retard the cure. The epoxy catalyst, more properly called a *hardener*, constitutes 10 to 50 percent by volume of the mixed resin, and its proportion can't be adjusted on the job.

Rather, you must buy a formulation that gives you the cure properties you seek.

Boatbuilding with Fiberglass

In theory at least, building a fiberglass boat couldn't be simpler—the devil is in the details.

First, the builder makes a full-scale mockup, or *plug*, of the hull he or she wants to build, along with a second plug for the deck. From these, the builder makes a set of concave, or "female," molds that he or she will use to create the actual hulls and decks. These molds—also made of fiberglass—are extremely expensive and time-consuming to build, in large part because their inner surfaces need to be carefully smoothed, or *faired*, and then polished so the hull and deck surfaces of the finished boats will be absolutely perfect. The builder also needs to reinforce the molds with braces on the outside so they can withstand the rigors of a long production run. In fact, so valuable are these molds that many of them endure as a valued commodity long after the boatbuilding companies that created them are dead and gone.

Once the hull and deck molds are finished, the builder coats their highly polished interior surfaces with a chemical release agent so that the resin-fiberglass matrix won't stick and can be easily removed when the hull or deck is complete. After that, the builder sprays on a layer of *gelcoat*, a mixture of resin and pigment that will serve as the shiny exterior surface of the hull or deck. Although thin—generally less than a millimeter thick—this gelcoat layer is quite tough and resists water penetration, chemicals, and the harsh effects of the sun. With regular cleaning and waxing, a well-formulated and well-applied gelcoat layer will last for years.

After the builder applies the gelcoat, he or she begins *laying up*, or *laminating*, the fiberglass—often alternating layers of mat and roving—which is then impregnated with resin to form the GRP matrix. If the order, or *laminate schedule*, of these layers calls for a core or for longitudinal strips of reinforcing stringers—often made of foam—these are installed

With regular cleaning and waxing, a well-formulated and well-applied gelcoat layer will last for years.

> *In addition to providing partitions, bulkheads often serve as structural members, making the hull that much stiffer under sail.*

as well. In years past builders applied the resin manually, using rollers to thoroughly wet out the various layers and squeegees to remove excess resin. In recent years, however, the process has become increasingly sophisticated.

Using a technique called *vacuum bagging*, for example, builders encase the entire layup in a sheet of plastic and attach a vacuum both to force resin into every nook and cranny, and to suck away the excess. Another option is the Seemann Composites Resin Infusion Molding Process (SCRIMP). For this technique, builders encase the dry layup in a plastic bag and draw in the activated resin by vacuum. The technique provides excellent control of the wetting-out process and protects workers from volatile organic compounds (VOCs), which can be nasty and even dangerous when breathed. In a traditional manual layup, boatbuilders aim for a matrix of about 35 percent fiberglass and 65 percent resin. Using vacuum techniques, however, builders can reduce the resin proportion to 50 percent or less, creating a much stronger matrix for a given weight.

In another innovation, boatbuilders can use fiberglass reinforcements that are pre-impregnated with catalyzed resin to ensure optimum wetting. On the downside, they must keep the material frozen to prevent kicking—but they no longer have to worry about resin-free voids.

After the resin cures, the builder pops the deck and hull out of the molds, trims the edges, and starts installing hardware—anchor rollers, stanchions, hatches, portlights, lights, plumbing, toilets—you name it. Many builders install a reinforcing grid at the bottom of the hull to make it more rigid and to create a foundation for the cabin sole, bunks, storage tanks, and so on. In addition to providing partitions, bulkheads often serve as structural members, making the hull that much stiffer under sail. To simplify the work, most builders wait until after the accommodations are installed to attach the deck to the hull. Similarly, they don't bolt on the keel until the very end. When that's done, all that remains is to step the mast, install the running and standing rigging, bend on sails, and make sure all systems are functioning correctly—then you're ready to go sailing!

The Details

While it may sound simple, executing these hardware installations quickly and effectively requires skill and planning. The same goes for the creation and execution of an effective layup schedule. Just because they aren't a bunch of fellows in flannel shirts working with odd-looking, razor-sharp tools doesn't mean today's boatbuilders exhibit less skill, dedication to quality, or expertise than the boatbuilders of old. As I said, the devil is in the details.

A good hull-to-deck joint, for example, is critical to ensuring that a boat will remain structurally sound and watertight after years of heavy use. Far too many boatbuilders—especially back in the 1960s and 1970s—fell short in this detail. Ideally, the upper edge of the hull should have an inward turning flange, upon which the deck can rest and against which it can be secured. The deck is mated to the hull with a strong, flexible adhesive such as 3M 5200 (a polyurethane adhesive-sealant), and reinforced with stainless steel through-bolts spaced every 6 inches or so. Aware of the extraordinary strength of 3M 5200, many boatbuilders use self-tapping screws in lieu of through-bolts, because they're easier and less time-consuming to install. Be warned, however, that because self-tapping screws work by cutting a thread in the fiberglass that makes up the flange, they're nowhere near as strong as bolts that have been secured by a washer and nut. Another approach is to use several layers of fiberglass to bond the joint together, forming a single, unified structure.

Whatever method the builder uses, it's a good idea for the hull-to-deck joint to be readily accessible for inspection and repairs. It's not unusual for older boats to develop leaks that can be both aggravating and difficult to fix. Given the increasingly complex accommodations going into today's boats—as well as the increased use of fiberglass *liners*, interior structural components into which everything from settees to wiring runs might be molded—the joint is often almost completely inaccessible.

The attachment method used for through-hulls and deck hardware, especially on cored hulls or decks, is another area of critical importance. Through-hulls are basically holes in the hull, either above or below the waterline, and include the raw-water intakes for the toilet and the engine's cooling system, mounts for such sensors as your speedometer and depth sounder transducers, and drains for the toilet, galley sink, cockpit scuppers, and so forth. Each water-conducting through-hull should include a quarter-turn seacock valve, ideally made of bronze, which can be easily shut off. Otherwise, something as simple as a ruptured tube or failed hose-clamp might send your boat to the bottom. Quarter-turn valves are best, because they're simple and sturdy, and it's immediately evident whether they're open or closed: a handle in-line with the hose signifies that the valve is open; a handle perpendicular to the hose is closed. Gate valves, in which turning the handle raises or lowers a disk that stops the water flow, are unacceptable because the mechanism is prone to corrosion and it's impossible to tell at a glance whether they are open or not. Especially if you're going offshore, you should attach a tapered wooden plug, or *bung*, that can be hammered in place to stop the flow of water in the event the through-hull fails. Needless to say, all through-hulls and seacocks should also be easily accessible. A situation in which water is pouring into your boat while you try in vain to reach the offending quarter-turn valve through intervening junk or furniture is one you don't even want to *think* about!

In a cored layup the through-hulls must be bedded in such a way that water will not be able to seep into the core even after years of hard use—this is critical. The best way to accomplish this is to remove the core from the area around the through-hull so that it will be attached to and surrounded by solid fiberglass. Balsa cores, in particular, need to stay dry. Otherwise they will rot away to nothing, compromising the strength of the laminate. Modern builders use *end-grain balsa*—basically hundreds of small, thin squares of balsa cut across the grain—or closed-cell foam cores so water can't migrate as easily, but a "wet" hull can still develop, adding unnecessary weight and compromising hull strength.

All deck hardware should be through-bolted with hefty backing plates—preferably aluminum—to help spread the load. This is especially important with such heavy-duty items as steering pedestals, mooring cleats, winches, and anchor windlasses. Ideally, if a boat has a cored deck, these high-load items will be installed in an area that is solid fiberglass, as with your through-hulls. On some boats, the attachment points for high-load hardware such as chainplates are located on raised moldings so water will quickly flow away, instead of pooling, reducing the chance of any sneaking inside. It's also a good idea not to seal off the backing plates and bolts on the underside of the cabintop. That way, if a leak develops, it will be immediately apparent and much easier to access and fix.

Another indicator of quality is how bulkheads are attached to the interior surfaces of the hull and decks. Bulkheads must remain firmly bonded in order to function effectively as structural members, and that means bonding them with multiple layers of fiberglass that are wide enough to withstand heavy-weather loads and flexing. Inshore yachts often make do with bulkheads that are simply dropped into place in slots molded into an interior liner, but that's wholly inadequate if you intend to set sail for points unknown.

In Nigel Calder's words, "Anyone who ventures more than a day or two offshore faces the risk of being caught in a gale. If you intend to cross oceans, it is not a matter of 'if' but rather 'when.' The average production sailboat, which was not designed for these conditions, almost always comes through OK—thousands have gone around the world in all kinds of conditions. But then there are some that don't make it. Speaking for myself, if I am to go offshore, I won't bet the life of my family on a boat not purpose built for the task."

Amen to that!

Thankfully, one area in which quality doesn't vary much is the keel attachment. Most modern fin keels are cast with a number of sturdy stainless-steel J-bolts in them. The curved portions are firmly embedded in the fin, and the straight, threaded portions stick up where they can be bolted through the bottom of the hull. Because of the crucial nature of this attachment, it's pretty much always done correctly, with a narrow margin for error. To ensure corrosion resistance, the bolts should be made of 316 stainless steel, not the 304 stainless steel commonly used for standing rigging. Strong, corrosion-resistant silicon bronze is even better, but it's almost never used for this purpose.

The manner of installation of all the other things a boat needs—stanchions, portlights, water tanks, fuel tanks, batteries, accommodations, and the like—depends on a number of factors, including the kind of sailing you have in mind and what you're willing to pay for it. If you intend to cross the Pacific Ocean, for example, your requirements will be dramatically different than if you plan to simply daysail. There are those who decry an apparent lack of "quality" in many modern yachts because of their perceived inability to handle the worst conditions nature can throw at them— but what's the point of spending a whole lot of extra money on equipment and capabilities you'll never need?

If you anticipate doing some serious passagemaking, offshore portlights should be securely installed with through-bolts of the highest quality—only then can you be confident they will stand up to serious waves. But it makes

> **There's no excuse for poor construction.**

> *When the boat heels to the gathering breeze, and the sailor casts his eye to windward, gauging what is to come and how best to meet it, it makes no difference whether the horizon shows a familiar coast, an exotic landfall, or unending sea.*

little sense to install bombproof portlights if you never plan to subject them to that kind of abuse. The same goes for heavy-duty, all-chain anchor rodes and oversize standing rigging. As with the design and construction of the boat itself, offshore gear isn't "better" than inshore gear—it's just designed for a different purpose. Lightly built river craft like the old trading sloops that used to ply the Hudson River would not have stood up to a moderately powerful gale in France's Bay of Biscay. Similarly, a narrow, shoal-draft sharpie ketch of the type that originated in the sheltered waters of Long Island Sound would be a poor choice for sailing on blustery San Francisco Bay. But who cares? That's not what they were made for.

That said, there's no excuse for poor construction. Batteries—including those that start the engine and those that power such "house draws" as lights and radios—need to be securely installed so they won't break loose in the event of a knockdown. So do water tanks. Likewise, stanchions and mooring cleats need to be securely installed, and there should be easy access to things like fuel filters, water filters, water pumps, and the shaft seals where the propeller shaft exits the hull, so that a boat's auxiliary power and drive can be easily serviced.

Nonetheless, if all you plan to do is coastal sailing, there's no reason to have a boat built like a brick, uh, outhouse. The vast majority of boats never go more than 20 miles offshore, and that's *fine*. Part of good seamanship is knowing what your boat is capable of doing. Good seamanship also means paying attention to the weather and knowing what to expect wherever you sail. There's a good reason why many production boats look similar—because they deliver the kind of performance sailors want at a price they can afford. Do these sailors want to cross oceans? No. Do they want to spend hours maintaining their boats or bending on sails in preparation for a spin around the harbor after a hard day at work? No. Do they want comfort, speed, and ease afloat? Absolutely—and there's nothing wrong with that.

All sailors take part in a pastime and tradition that stretches back to the dawn of human history. They leave behind cars, televisions, and other modern conveniences to venture onto the water under sail. On the Chesapeake Bay or off Cape Horn, they assume responsibility for their welfare and the welfare of their crew to a degree that is rare in our times. When the boat heels to the gathering breeze, and the sailor casts his eye to windward, gauging what is to come and how best to meet it, it makes no difference whether the horizon shows a familiar coast, an exotic landfall, or unending sea.

19

KEEPING FROM RUNNING AGROUND

The Wealth of Information on a Nautical Chart

FIRST A CONFESSION: In the eyes of many an old salt, I'm not really a cruising sailor. Why? Because many believe you're not a true cruiser until you've had firsthand experience with running aground.

Actually, I *have* touched bottom on a number of occasions and have had my share of close calls—some of them very close. Cruising along the Intracoastal Waterway just east of notoriously shallow Mobile Bay, for example, I would inevitably find myself spending the night at anchor with the keel comfortably planted in the muck at the bottom of some steamy little hurricane hole. A couple of buddies and I also did some tense "sailing by Braille" one time as we bumped our way over a half dozen little tongues of silt on our way down a narrow inlet out onto Chesapeake Bay.

Nonetheless, I have never experienced a true grounding on a reef or sand spit, one in which the crew has to wait hours for the tide to rise—hoping and praying that there will be enough water to float them free. Nor have I ever had to run out an anchor to pull, or *kedge*, myself into deep water or engaged in any of those other fine adventures that make such great yarns later—which is fine with me. I like to think that my "luck" has come in no small part from careful sailing.

I'm not saying that cruisers who have had hair-raising groundings are by definition less skilled. Many of them were simply pushing the envelope, exploring harbors and coves where charted depths—if a chart even existed—were approximations at best. Still, many groundings have occurred because sailors simply didn't know what they were doing, while many others have occurred because the skipper or navigator was dead certain that the location shown on his chart plotter or GPS receiver admitted no possibility of error. As Joshua Slocum once observed after a rendezvous with a steamship in the North Atlantic, "I admired the businesslike air of the *Olympia*; but I have the feeling still that the captain was just a little too precise in his reckoning. . . . Over-confidence, I believe was the cause of the disaster to the liner *Atlantic*, and many more like her. The captain knew too well where he was."

With this in mind every sailor should have a grasp of at least the rudiments of piloting—the art of knowing where you are and how to get where you want to go—without the help of modern electronics. Whether it's a nineteenth-century chronometer, a handheld GPS, or an elaborate four-color computer chart plotter, all technology is susceptible to error—human or otherwise. By having multiple means of keeping track of where you are, you can avoid unpleasant surprises and unnecessary insurance claims. Ultimately, piloting—like anchoring, steering, and sail trim—is just plain-old good seamanship. In many ways it's the essence of being a sailor. Perhaps that's so why many sailors—myself included—find it so satisfying.

> *Every sailor should have a grasp of at least the rudiments of piloting.*

Nautical Charts: The Compass Rose

Piloting, the art of navigating close to shore, is all about three simple things: knowing where you are, knowing where you want to go, and knowing how to get there without bumping into anything. There are many books available on the subject, and I highly recommend giving at least one a careful read if you plan to do any bareboat chartering in an area that has challenging tides or an abundance of reefs. Still, you can get pretty far with just a few basics.

First and foremost among piloting tools is the nautical chart, a wonder of human creativity. Elegantly beautiful, charts are also packed with useful information, once you know how to read them. Let's start with the compass rose, water depths, and the scale.

The *compass rose*, which is generally printed in multiple locations on a chart, shows not one but *two* norths. The first, shown on the outer graduated ring, is *true north*—the exact direction of the geographical north pole as agreed upon by mapmakers. The other, on the inner ring, is *magnetic north*, the direction a compass "thinks" is north when it's functioning correctly. The difference between the two is called *variation*—something that vexed navigators for centuries and was a factor in any number of past maritime disasters. Variation exists because the earth's magnetic field is not perfectly aligned with its axis of rotation. In fact, the magnetic north pole wanders slowly (and, fortunately, predictably) through the high Canadian arctic and is at present hundreds of miles from the geographic north pole. The magnitude of the resulting variation (i.e., the angular separation in degrees of the two north poles) depends on where on earth you happen to be. The two poles might be aligned from your location (zero° of variation), or they might be widely separated (up to 50° of variation). In most tropical and temperate waters, however, the variation is less than 20°. Further, the variation might be westerly, which means the compass needle points west of true north; or easterly, which means the compass points a few degrees east of true north. As if that isn't enough, as already mentioned, the local variation fluctuates gradually over time.

Fortunately, all this is carefully illustrated by the compass rose. Looking at Chart No. 14839 of my old stomping ground, Cleveland Harbor—as put together by the National Oceanic and Atmospheric Administration, or NOAA, a part of the U.S. Department of Commerce—the compass rose indicates 8° of westerly variation for the year 2002. In addition, according to the chart, the variation is increasing by 4 (minutes) each year, so that in 2008—as I write this chapter—it stands at 8°24′ west.

To adjust, or *correct*, a magnetic heading to obtain a true heading you *subtract* a westerly variation and *add* an easterly variation. For example, if you're sailing parallel to the breakwall and toward the east entrance light of Cleveland Harbor on a magnetic heading of 065°, you would need to subtract about 8° to arrive at a true heading of 057°. Over the years, sailors have come up with various mnemonic devices to help them remember

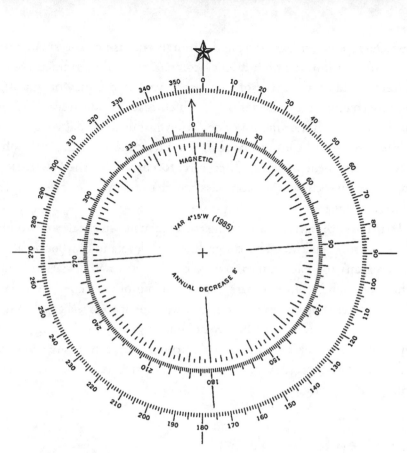

A standard compass rose from a NOAA Chart. Note the 4°15' of westerly variation for the area when the chart was made.

which way to add and which way to subtract, but I find them all utterly useless. Instead, whenever cruising in a new area, I just study the variation and the way the true and magnetic headings on the compass rose are oriented, and refresh my memory that way. You can also simply go "all magnetic," navigating without correcting, which works fine as long as you're consistent and are on the alert for bearings that may be printed or listed in degrees true and therefore need to be corrected.

In addition to variation, there is also something called *deviation*, which is similar but most definitely not the same. While variation is the same for all nearby boats, deviation is unique to each boat and is caused by onboard magnetic influences that deflect the compass from magnetic north. When deviation is present, more likely than not it's caused by the presence of metal or possibly magnets in the vicinity of the compass—things like engines, loudspeakers, navigational instruments, and current-carrying wires. Deviation can be controlled through the use of the small tuning magnets found in most high-quality compasses. Only a trained compass adjuster should do this kind of work, and even then it may be impossible to remove that last bit of deviation, in which case the adjuster will create a deviation card with the amount of deviation east or west that your compass exhibits on various headings. Bear in mind that these are deviations from the correct *magnetic* heading. Therefore, to correct all the way to a true heading, you first correct the compass course to the magnetic heading, and then correct the magnetic heading to the true heading.

To make sure things are working correctly you can check your compass against a number of known headings, like the Cleveland Harbor breakwall. If things aren't too bad, you can try to create your own deviation card. If, on the other hand, your compass is seriously out of whack and you plan to explore new cruising grounds, it's money well spent to hire a good compass adjuster to make sure that, when you're piloting, you're obtaining the best positional data possible. For practical purposes you can ignore a deviation of less than 2 or 3 degrees, because no one can steer a boat more precisely than that in any case.

How Deep Is the Water?

To read water depths on a nautical chart, first figure out the unit of measure that was used to record the depths and the *vertical datum*, or the point from which the depths are measured. NOAA charts for the Great Lakes, for example, indicate depths, or *soundings*, in feet based on *Low Water Datum*—the shallowest that part of the lake will be at the lowest point in the year. Charts for the U.S. east and west coasts also indicate soundings in feet, but the reference point is *Mean Lower Low Water*—the average height of the lower of the two daily low tides the area experiences. Charts made outside the United States indicate soundings in meters and also typically use different datums, such as *Lowest Astronomical Tides*—the lowest tidal level that will occur under normal astronomical and average weather conditions.

If this seems confusing, don't worry—everything is made clear in the chart title, which is always prominently displayed in an area free of geographic or nautical features. For example, the title on NOAA Chart No. 13276 for just north of Boston, Massachusetts, looks like this:

SALEM, MARBLEHEAD AND BEVERLY HARBORS
Mercator Projection
Scale 1:10,000 at Lat. 42° 31'
North American Datum of 1983
(World Geodetic System of 1984)
SOUNDINGS IN FEET
AT MEAN LOWER LOW WATER

What could be simpler? The scale of 1:10,000 means that an inch of distance on the chart is the equivalent of 10,000 inches—so the 72,913 inches in a nautical mile translate to about 7.3 inches on the chart. The North American Datum of 1983 and the World Geodetic System of 1984 refer to the *horizontal datum* used for the chart. This is the real esoterica of global mapmaking, and we need not delve into it. The main thing to remember is that you need to make sure your GPS is set to work according to the chart's horizontal datum. Fortunately, the chart datum is the same no matter where you are in North American waters, and this is generally the default setting on any GPS instrument sold in the United States. Otherwise, your readings could be off by dozens of feet—no laughing matter in a narrow channel!

Of course, soundings change continually due to the rising and falling of the tides. Generally there are two high tides and two low tides every 24 hours 50 minutes—with each rise and fall lasting a little more than 6 hours. This pattern of *semidiurnal tides* is the norm because the moon and sun's gravitational attractions in combination with the centrifugal force of the earth-moon couple raise two bulges of high water on opposite sides of the globe, and the planet spins through both bulges each day. (Actually, since the moon completes 3.3 percent of its orbit during one 24-hour rotation of the earth, any given spot on earth is directly beneath the moon every 24 hours 50 minutes.)

In the absence of other effects, each spot on earth would experience symmetrical, semidiurnal tides. But the tides that occur in a particular body of water are profoundly influenced by such geographical features as depth, seabed topography, and shoreline morphology—including the presence or absence of channels or other bottlenecks. These have the effect of magnifying tides in some places (up to 40 feet or more in Nova Scotia's Bay of Fundy), dampening them in others (to hardly anything at all in the Caribbean, for example).

Some areas experience irregular, or *diurnal*, tides in which there is only one low tide and one high tide per day. Others experience *mixed tides*, in which the range of one of the day's two tides is only a fraction of the other. Even where the semidiurnal pattern prevails, the two low tides and the two high tides are usually not quite equal to one another.

Exaggerated *spring tides* occur when the sun, moon, and earth are in alignment and the sun and moon are therefore working together to raise the tidal bulge. This happens when the moon is either full (directly opposite the sun as viewed from earth) or new (between the earth and the sun).

More moderate *neap tides* result when the sun, moon, and earth are oriented at a 90° angle. This occurs at the moon's first and third quarters. The sun then works at cross purposes with the moon, and though the moon prevails by virtue of its much closer proximity to earth, the tides are dampened.

To figure out how much water there will be over a particular spot at a particular time, look at a tide table. Tide tables give the times of local low and high tides for each day of the year. They also indicate the depth of the water above—and occasionally below—charted

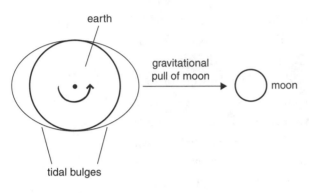

The two "bulges" that cause the world's semidiurnal tides. Although the bulge does slowly move as the moon orbits the earth, it is the rotation of the earth "within" the bulge that causes the tides experienced each day.

MARBLEHEAD

Marblehead 42°30'N 070°51'W

May Tide Chart 2008

DATE		HIGH				LOW				☀		☽
		AM	hgt	PM	hgt	AM	hgt	PM	hgt	rise	set	qtr
1	Thu	8:09	9.1	8:40	9.3	1:55	1.2	2:22	0.7	5:38	7:44	
2	Fri	9:04	9.4	9:29	10.0	2:50	0.6	3:13	0.3	5:36	7:45	
3	Sat	9:58	9.7	10:17	10.6	3:43	-0.2	4:02	0.0	5:35	7:46	
4	Sun	10:50	9.9	11:05	11.1	4:35	-0.9	4:51	-0.3	5:34	7:47	
5	Mon	11:42	10.1	11:54	11.5	5:26	-1.4	5:40	-0.4	5:33	7:48	●
6	Tue	-	-	12:34	10.1	6:17	-1.7	6:30	-0.4	5:31	7:49	
7	Wed	12:45	11.6	1:27	10.0	7:09	-1.8	7:22	-0.3	5:30	7:50	

Tide table for Marblehead, Massachusetts, the first week of May 2008.

The Rule of Twelfths

Tide tables are all well and good—if you happen to be passing over a particular shallow at the exact moment of low or high tide—but what about the rest of the day? Unfortunately, this question is complicated by the fact that the rate at which the water rises and falls varies depending on how much time has passed since the last high or low tide. Specifically, the depth changes faster around the midway point than at the beginning and end of each cycle.

To address this variation, navigators have developed the *Rule of Twelfths* to arrive at a close approximation of water depth at a particular time and place. To employ this technique, first divide the local tidal range by twelve. For example, a range of 10 feet, or 120 inches, yields 10 inches per twelfth, while a range of 8 feet, or 96 inches, would yield 8 inches per twelfth. Once you've calculated your twelfths, figure that, in the first hour after a high or low tide, the depth will change by one-twelfth of the total range; in the second hour it will change by another two-twelfths; in the third

and fourth hours it will change by three-twelfths each hour, in the fifth hour it will change by two-twelfths; and in the last of the six hours between a high and low tide it will change by one-twelfth. The twelfths are cumulative—whatever the time, add or subtract the relevant twelfths for all the hours since the last high or low tide.

For example, if you're passing over a reef for which the tide table indicates a depth of 6 feet at the last low tide, and there's a tidal range of 10 feet, there will be approximately 6 feet 10 inches of water over the reef one hour before or after low tide. Two hours before or after low tide there will be 8 feet 6 inches of water—the original 6 feet plus one-twelfth for the first hour and two-twelfths for the second hour, for a total of three-twelfths, or another 30 inches of water. Five hours before or after low tide you will have the original 6 feet of water plus eleven-twelfths of water—110 inches or 9 feet 2 inches of water—giving you a total depth of 15 feet 2 inches. That should be plenty of water to ensure a safe passage!

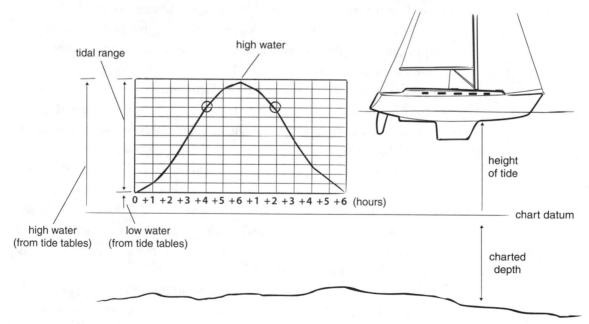

The Rule of Twelfths. This illustration shows how to derive actual depth from charted depth two hours before or after high tide.

depths for each of those tides. During the first week of May 2008, for example, the tide table for Marblehead, Massachusetts, shows that the first low tide of May was at 1:55 a.m. on May 1 and that the water level was 1.2 feet above local datum. After that there was a high tide at 8:09 a.m., at which point the water level was 9.1 feet above local datum. Another low tide followed at 2:22 p.m., during which the water was 0.7 feet above local datum, and then a high tide at 8:40 p.m. when the water was 9.3 feet above local datum. On May 2, the first low tide was at 2:50 a.m.—55 minutes later than the first low tide the day before.

Tides cause currents. That is to say, the sea doesn't simply rise and fall like water in a bathtub; when the tide rises, that added volume of water must come from somewhere. It *flows*—into and out of bays, rivers, estuaries, and channels—sometimes with the force and turbulence of a roaring rapid.

The current is said to *flood* when the tide rises and to *ebb* when the tide falls. The period of weak or nonexistent current between a flood and the following ebb or between the ebb and the following flood is termed *slack water*, and the pause in the tidal height between the rise and fall or the fall and rise is a *high-water stand* or a *low-water stand*, respectively. Though tides and tidal currents are causally related, slack water and the tidal stand are not necessarily coincident in time. A river emptying into an estuary, for example, can cause the ebb to continue as long as two hours or more after the tide has begun to rise.

For purposes of navigation, a tidal current is characterized by its *set*—the direction in which it is flowing—and by its *drift*, or speed. (Note that a northwest current is setting *toward* the northwest, whereas a northwest wind blows *from* the northwest.) Although currents are not noted on paper nautical charts, you can study them in published tidal current tables, which come in tabular form for all waters and in chart form for select waters, showing the set and drift at various tidal stages for different localities. Such data can be linked to electronic nautical charts so that, when the cursor pauses at a location on the chart, the local current set and drift for the present time are displayed.

Bear in mind that drift is not just dependent on tidal range—it can also be dramatically influenced by features such as depth, the width of a channel, landform or subsurface constrictions, and outcroppings of land.

How Far Do We Have to Go?

Finally, there's the chart's scale, which allows you to determine both distances and your own boat speed. All inshore charts are created as Mercator projections, on which the latitude and longitude are shown in degrees (°), minutes (' ; with one minute equaling $1/60$ of a degree), and either seconds (" ; with one second equaling $1/60$ of a minute) or tenths of a minute.

Mercator Projections

Named for sixteenth-century Flemish cartographer Gerardus Mercator, Mercator maps solve the problem of projecting a round earth onto a flat piece of paper by imagining the entire globe to be surrounded by a gigantic tube, which is in contact with the globe only at the equator. Every point on the globe is then projected (as if by a high-intensity light beaming from the center of the globe) onto this tube, and the result is that the meridians of longitude become vertical, parallel lines on the tube, rather than converging at the north and south poles as they do on the globe. Unwrapping and flattening the tube gives you a Mercator projection of the world.

The crucial advantage of a Mercator projection is that it enables us to plot courses and bearings as straight lines rather than as segments of circles. This system works well, but it's not without flaws—primary among them that landmass sizes and shapes become progressively more distorted as latitudes increase. Greenland, for example, appears much larger on a Mercator map of the world than it really is. For large-scale, small-area charts, however, like those used for coastal piloting, the distortion is small and immaterial.

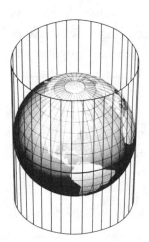

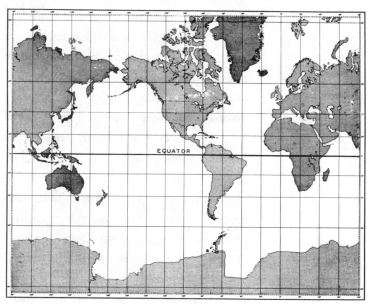

How a Mercator projection is obtained. The round earth is projected onto a cylinder; this tube is then "unrolled" to a Mercator projection.

Near the chart title there will be a legend showing feet, yards, meters, and nautical miles. But a more satisfying way of figuring out nautical miles is by looking at the latitude scale, on which one minute of latitude also happens to equal one nautical mile. (This isn't just coincidence, of course. Rather, a nautical mile is *defined* as a minute of latitude.) Better still, because a knot is a nautical mile per hour, you can also use the latitude scale to calculate speeds. When I first heard about this aspect of piloting as a kid, I thought it was just about the coolest thing in the world—and I still do!

Beware that this technique does *not* work with longitude! Latitude lines remain parallel—and are often referred to as parallels—whether you're in Sumatra or Ultima Thule. Therefore a minute of latitude is a nautical mile at any point on the planet. Lines of longitude, or *meridians*, on the other hand converge at the poles, so a minute of longitude equals one nautical mile only at the equator, and it becomes smaller and smaller the farther from the equator you get.

Everything Else

There's far more to a modern nautical chart than just the compass rose, soundings, and lines of latitude and longitude, including hundreds of standardized symbols denoting everything from underwater wrecks and cables; to sand, mud, and coral on the ocean bottom; to navigation buoys (otherwise known as floating *aids to navigation* or *ATONs*); to such on-shore features as water tanks, radio towers, and lighthouses (the latter being an example of fixed ATONs); and much more. Special conventions are used to denote the flashing patterns of lighted buoys and the heights, light patterns, and sound signals of fixed lights and major lighthouses are also noted (with further detail provided in the Light Lists maintained by the Coast Guard). Different type styles are even used to distinguish specific types of information: italicized letters denote underwater features such as reefs, channels, and bays, while regular (i.e., roman) type denotes features that stand above the sounding datum, such as islands, cliffs, towns, and boat ramps.

Books that feature information about nautical charts include NOAA's *Chart No. 1 United States of America Nautical Chart, Symbols Abbreviations and Terms* and the British Admiralty's *Chart 5011, Symbols and Abbreviations Used on Admiralty Charts. Chart No. 1* is no longer printed, but

NOAA offers it online for free download, along with a complete catalog of nautical charts. *Chart No. 1* is also still available in print form in several commercially produced versions; these include Nigel Calder's *How to Read a Nautical Chart*, which includes all of *Chart No. 1*, reorganized for clarity, as well as the equivalent international symbols (where these differ from U.S. convention) and the symbology and standards of electronic charts.

Nothing except a boat encourages dreaming more than a nautical chart.

There are also plenty of books on navigation and seamanship that include a sampling of chart symbols sufficient to get you through 99 percent of what you'll encounter on the water. John Rousmaniere's classic, *The Annapolis Book of Seamanship*, has a worthwhile color section, as does *Chapman Piloting & Seamanship*. With these resources in hand, the best way to become familiar with the language of charts is simply to purchase one at your local chandlery or find a digital chart on NOAA's online chart viewer page (http://nauticalcharts.noaa.gov), and then study its features. Take your time, take notes, and have fun—imagine the challenges of getting from place to place with the wind coming from various directions. Even a chart from waters you already know can be fascinating reading as you discover features and characteristics of the area you never knew existed.

20

KEEPING FROM RUNNING AGROUND—PART TWO

Using a Chart to Navigate

OF COURSE, nautical charts don't exist merely for dreaming. They are tools to be used in conjunction with your steering compass, a handheld compass, parallel rules, dividers, and your trusty pencil to keep both you and your boat out of trouble.

Central to these efforts is the *line of position*, or *LOP*, a line upon which you know your boat to be located. Among the many ways of obtaining an LOP, the most common is by taking a bearing on a known, charted object and then transferring the bearing to the object's symbol on your chart. A line of position doesn't tell you *where* along that bearing you are—i.e., it doesn't fix your position (see below)—but it's a darn good beginning. A bearing is simply the direction of an object relative to magnetic north (or to true north if you choose to correct your courses and bearings for variation). The best way to obtain a bearing is by sighting it over a handheld compass. These are available with pistol grips and pointers or in the shape of a hockey puck. In either case they are not only wonderfully "salty" little devices, but lots of fun.

When you take bearings, it's a good idea to become adept at calculating the reciprocal, or the bearing in the opposite direction, so to speak. This makes plotting LOPs much easier. To obtain a reciprocal either add or subtract 180° from your bearing, whichever one gets you a positive number under 360. Let's say, for example, that you sight a lighthouse bearing due west, or 270° magnetic. The reciprocal is 270° minus 180, which gives you 90°, or due east.

To transfer this line of position to the chart, first lay your parallel rules—two rulers articulated on hinges that allow them to separate and come together while remaining parallel at all times—across a nearby compass rose (most charts have three or more roses printed on them) so that one edge intersects the center of the rose and 270° magnetic on

Piloting puts you in touch with your surroundings in a way that simply isn't possible when you navigate by GPS.

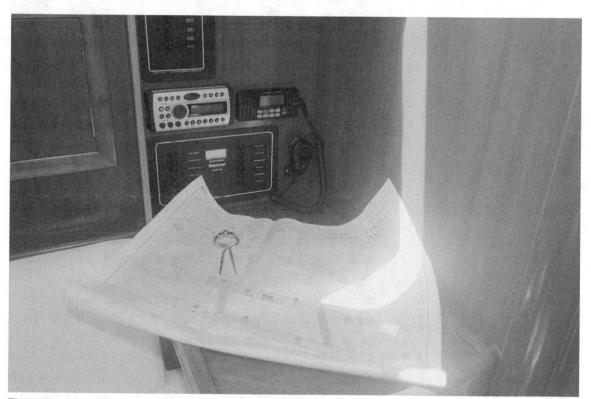

The tools of the navigator include parallel rules that allow you to "walk" your course to a nearby compass rose, and dividers, which are used to measure distances. (Erik Skallerup and Domenic Mosqueira/YachtShots, BVI)

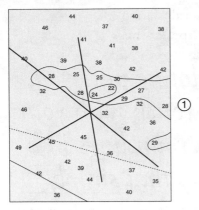

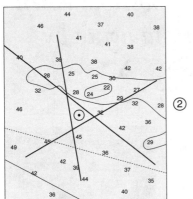

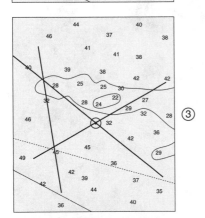

Using three lines of position to obtain a fix. Rarely, however, will all three LOPs meet at the same precise point (1). Usually they form a "cocked-hat" triangle that encloses your probable position (2). If the triangle is too large (3), it is wise to take another sight and plot another bearing.

the inner graduated ring. Then "walk" the parallel rules toward the lighthouse symbol on the chart by holding the trailing rule firmly against the chart and swinging the leading rule toward the lighthouse. If it doesn't reach the lighthouse on the first swing, hold it down firmly against the chart, relieve your pressure on the trailing rule, and swing the trailing rule ahead until it catches up with the leading rule. Then swing the leading rule again, repeating until you get there. When you do, draw a line along the rule from the lighthouse toward your location, jotting the bearing in degrees magnetic or true, along with the time of the bearing.

To find out where along that LOP you are, take a second or, better still, a third bearing simultaneously with the first, and transfer all three lines of position to your chart. The intersection of the lines is a *fix* and shows where you are. Note that these lines of position are rarely if ever perfect. Instead, when you plot three bearings, their intersection will usually take the form of a triangle, or what was once referred to as a "cocked hat." You may assume that your position is somewhere within the triangle. A three-bearing fix is more reliable than crossing just two bearings, because a significant mistake in one of the three LOPs will be obvious. With just two LOPs, one or both of them could be way off and you would have no way of knowing it. The smaller the cocked hat, the better. If the triangle is exceedingly large, it's probably a good idea to sight and plot another set of bearings.

You need not depend solely on point objects for bearings, even though lighthouses, buoys, water towers, church spires, and numerous other charted features give you plenty of point objects to choose from. Feel free to also use the ends of islands or the edges of cliffs: pretty much any charted feature that gives you a definitive direction will do. Try to avoid lines of position that cross each other at highly acute angles. Ideally your bearings will be separated by at least 60° and no more than 120°. Otherwise, you'll end up with disproportionately long cocked hats. Theoretically, the more bearings the better, but three suffice.

With this in mind, it's a good habit always to be on the lookout for good bearing targets and, like Chicago voters, perform your duty early and often. Years ago, sailing on Lake Champlain, I became obsessed with a series of rocks running up and down the middle of the lake, including Colchester Shoal, the Four Brothers, and Ferris Rock. Much to my wife's amusement, I spent the better part of the first morning taking bearings on and getting fixes off pretty much everything in sight. Buoys, radio towers, bluffs, birds' nests, shrubberies, you name it: anything and everything was fair game. Of course,

Using Ranges

A *range* consists of two fixed, easily recognizable objects that can be lined up, one in front of the other. If the two objects are charted, they constitute an instant and precise line of position. Draw a line between them on the chart and extend that line seaward in your direction. When the two objects line up from your vantage point on deck, you're on that charted line. No bearings are necessary. The objects can be manmade—navigation buoys, smokestacks, church steeples, radio towers, and so on—or naturally occurring—a headland, one end of an island, a half-tide rock, or a hilltop, to name a few.

Best of all are dedicated range marks, or lights, installed by the Coast Guard to guide watercraft along a treacherous channel or through a difficult harbor approach. These will generally consist of two large rectangular marks set on a pair of towers, one below and in front of the other. Wherever ranges have been installed, they will be clearly marked on local charts. From a distance, when the two marks line up over your bow (when you're approaching) or over your stern (when you're departing), you'll know beyond doubt that you are on a safe course.

To establish natural ranges, look on a chart of the area in which you plan to sail. If a tricky harbor approach or narrow channel lies along your planned route, look for pairs of objects that create lines along which you can sail in safety. For example, if you draw a line between a distant lighthouse and the bluff on the edge of a nearby island, does

that line extend through the charted deep water between two shoals? Great, you've now got a quick and easy means of guiding yourself in. Keep the two objects aligned on your approach, and you know you're in deep water.

If the two objects get out of line, you'll know immediately that you have drifted off your chosen course, introducing what is called *cross-track error*, or *XTE*. This can be especially dangerous in a narrow channel or when picking a course through an area fraught with underwater hazards, and you need to turn right or left immediately to bring the objects back into alignment.

If, on the other hand, you aim for a headland alone, rather than, say, a headland that is directly behind a daybeacon, you have no readily apparent way of knowing whether you've drifted off course. All you know is that your bow is pointed at the headland. Granted, you'll know something's wrong if your compass heading keeps changing, and you can always take a bearing with a handheld compass to establish another line of position and fix your position, but doing so can be difficult in heavy seas and requires time, which is in short supply when you're conning your way through hazardous waters. What you need is instant, easy-to-interpret feedback when you wander or are pushed off course. By establishing and employing a clear, unambiguous range, you know at all times the exact bearing you're sailing.

whenever I made visual contact with any of the rocks themselves—all clearly buoyed, by the way—I was sure to take bearings on them as well.

Okay, I'm exaggerating a little. But I do like to take lots of bearings, and I make no apologies for it. On the one hand, it's just good seamanship, and on the other, it's fun. What could be better than drawing a bead on a new headland or lighthouse, jotting down a compass bearing, and then marking your line of position on the chart?

This sort of piloting puts you in touch with your surroundings in a way that simply isn't possible when you navigate by GPS. Those landmarks and buoys become your guides, your allies, your companions, your friends—and no, this time I'm not being facetious. Many a poem has been written about lighthouses, or even just the flash of a distant light, and for good reason. Even those hazards you are so assiduously avoiding take on a whole new meaning. I can still vividly recall every one of the rocks I mentioned above—finding them on the chart, looking out for them underway, and confirming that they were what I thought they were when I finally found them through my binoculars. In the end, they too become good friends—albeit friends you treat with a great deal of respect!

How Do We Get There?

In a perfect world, setting a course would always be a piece of cake. Get a fix on your position, find your destination on the chart, and then check to make sure no hazards lie between you and the destination. If the coast is clear, lay your parallel rules between your fix and your destination, then walk them over to the nearest compass rose to read your course. (Remember to use the inner ring of the rose unless you're correcting for variation!) In other words, plotting a course is the reverse of plotting a bearing—instead of starting from the compass rose, you end up there. If there are any reefs, headlands, or other obstructions in your way, simply plot two or more dogleg courses around them.

Unfortunately, especially where tidal currents are strong, this process becomes a bit more complicated. Powerboats can treat pretty much any body of water like an oversized parking lot, but boats under sail often don't travel a heck of a lot faster than the currents that are affecting them. Then again, even in a current-free body of water, the most efficient sailboat in the world will make a fair amount of leeway when sailing to windward.

On a high-performance racing boat in smooth conditions you may get leeway of less than 5°, but on a heavy, full-keel cruiser in a chop, you may get twice that amount. If you aren't careful, setting a course close to windward of a submerged hazard could very easily put you aground. Keep in mind that leeway is classified differently than current. In fact, leeway is specifically defined as the difference between a boat's heading, or the course being steered, and the course the boat is actually sailing, *assuming it is not affected by current*. The key then is to figure out the course you need to steer to get where you want to go after factoring in both leeway and any currents you may experience. The following is a means of doing just that. It represents only one of many different piloting techniques out there, but serves as a useful tool in its own right and a highly illustrative example of what piloting is about.

By establishing and employing a clear, unambiguous range, you know at all times the exact bearing you are sailing.

Compensating for Current

The way to compensate for current is to create a vector plot on your chart that shows how the set (direction) and drift (speed) of the current are going to affect your course between your departure point and your destination. As a first step, pencil in a straight line between your start and end points. Then, figure out the set and drift of the current during a convenient time period—one hour makes the math a lot easier—and plot the resulting vector on the chart, starting from your departure point. (A vector in piloting is simply a line denoting direction and distance.) As you do so, mark it with three arrows, a standard convention representing set and drift. That done, take your pair of dividers and set the points at the distance you expect to cover in your chosen time period at your present speed. Feel free to use the latitude scale on either side of the chart. Place one point of the dividers on the end of the current vector and swing the other point to intersect that first line you drew. Draw a third line connecting these points and you've got the course you need to steer in order to progress along that first line—i.e., in order to get where you want to go. The point at which your course line meets the line from your fix to your destination is how far you will get in one hour.

Keep in mind that leeway is classified differently than current.

Let's say, for example, that you want to sail across a strait that is 7 nautical miles wide on a course of 049° magnetic, or roughly northeast. At the time of the crossing, you estimate the current will be roughly north, with a set of 015° and a drift of 1.5 knots. Let's also assume that the wind is blowing about 15 knots out of the south and that you should be able to maintain a steady 5 knots on a broad reach. Using one hour as your time frame, plot a vector from your starting point with a distance of 1.5 nautical miles and a heading of 015°. Now, taking the distance from the latitude scale at the side of your chart, spread your dividers to 5 nautical miles and place one point on the end of the current vector. Then swing the other point until it meets the line connecting your point of departure with your destination. Finally, plot a line connecting the end of the current vector to this same line. This is the course you need to steer to compensate for current if you want to sail a straight line to your destination. Thus, you steer 061° in order to achieve a *course made good* (CMG) of 049°. Note that in this case the current is helping to push you on your way, and you should cover a little over 6 nautical miles along your CMG in one hour. Nice!

Remember that this vector plot does not take leeway into account. In this example your leeway should be minimal because you're on a broad reach, as opposed to a beat. Nonetheless, it would probably be best to set your course a touch above 61°—say 64°—to compensate for the force of the wind in your sails.

Note, too, that current sets are tabulated in degrees true, not magnetic. To be perfectly consistent, if you're plotting magnetic courses you should apply local variation to tabulated current sets to convert them to magnetic as well. In practice, however, this is rarely necessary. Given all the estimates in your vector plot—current set and drift, your speed through the water, and your leeway—the enhanced precision you would gain from converting current sets to degrees magnetic would have little practical meaning. It might make sense if the local variation is more than 20° or so, but otherwise it's unnecessary.

Finally, remember, the line from the end of the current vector is not the course you're going to *sail*, it's the course you're going to *steer* to compensate for the fact that the water is carrying you sideways as you progress, crabwise, toward your destination. The course you're going to travel—or

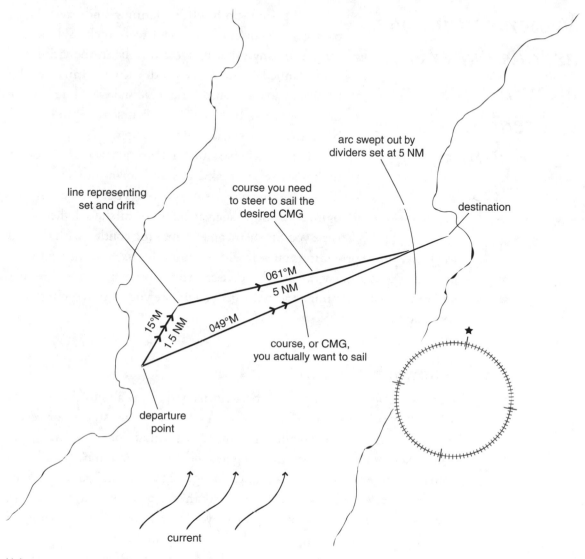

line representing
set and drift

course you need
to steer to sail the
desired CMG

arc swept out by
dividers set at 5 NM

destination

061°M
5 NM

15°M

1.5 NM

049°M

course, or CMG,
you actually want to sail

departure
point

current

Using a vector plot to compensate for current.

at least the one you *want* to travel—is that line going straight from your
starting point to your destination. Mark this desired CMG with two
arrows, and mark the vector designating your heading—i.e., the course
you're going to steer—with a single arrow. When plotting these vectors,
be sure to mark them consistently, including times, compass headings,
and whether these headings are magnetic or true. Following these time-
honored piloting conventions will help keep things straight in your head.

> *When sailing hazardous waters, it often makes sense to break a passage down into small, easy bites.*

Make sure, both when planning and executing a passage, to be on the lookout for reefs, rocks, submerged wrecks, or any other dangers that lie in the vicinity of your planned course made good. Currents can be tricky things, and your hoped-for and actual CMG may differ dramatically, so be sure to set a course that gives a wide berth to any otherwise hidden danger.

In fact, when sailing hazardous waters, it often makes sense to break a passage down into small, easy bites—linking a series of short legs between easily recognizable points such as buoys or offshore lights. Each time you finish a segment, making contact with the end *waypoint*, you're providing yourself with a good solid fix, and the next waypoint provides an easy target. This conservative approach is not only easier and more reliable, it might actually get you where you want to go faster in the long run.

Knowing What to Look For

Alas, we all know what poet Robert Burns had to say about "the best-laid schemes o' mice and men." And in the end, any course steered or vector plotted is just that, a scheme, or plan. It's vital that you occasionally get your head "out of the boat," looking around so that you don't blindly sail some well-intentioned pencil line to "nought but grief an' pain." It's true that reef-strewn waters can be scarier than the bejesus. But then again, those same "sinkers" will often provide you with at least some warning of what's up (so to speak), if you just know what to look for.

Back when I was serving in the Peace Corps in Western Samoa, for example, I used to travel from the island of Savai'i, where I was living, to the more populous island of Upolu aboard a car ferry named the *Lady Samoa*. Approaching the dock at Salelologa, the biggest town on Savai'i, meant winding through a maze of unmarked, submerged coral heads. But it was never a problem for the captain of the *Lady Samoa*, because the reefs were all clearly delineated by breakers resulting from the long, easy swells from the open ocean and the chop of Apolima Strait.

In fact, breaking water has long been used by mariners around the world as a telltale sign of shoaling waters. Explorers trying to find a route into a South Pacific atoll would often look for a patch of smooth water, much like the captain of the *Lady Samoa*, and night lookouts were regularly reminded to keep a sharp eye for breakers. In his classic *Sailing Alone Around the World*, Joshua Slocum describes how a region of breakers both awed and guided him as he tried to make his way out into the Pacific after passing through the Straits of Magellan:

> It was daylight, and the sloop was in the midst of the Milky Way of the sea, which is northwest of Cape Horn, and it was the white breakers of a huge sea over sunken rocks which had threatened to engulf her through the night. It was Fury Island I had sighted and steered for, and what a panorama was before me now and all around! It was not the time to complain of a broken skin. What could I do but fill away among the breakers and find a channel between them, now that it was day? Since she had escaped the rocks through the night, surely she would find her way by daylight. This was the greatest sea adventure of my life. God knows how my vessel escaped.

Luckily, you don't need to be off the pitch of Cape Horn or in mountainous seas—or even in long ocean rollers—to gauge depth by wave action. A low sand spit stretching out from a headland, for example, will be noticeable even with just a little chop. So will small rocks. What you're looking for is any kind of disturbance, a swirling or even just a little patch of choppy water, with little waves that are a bit sharper and shorter than they appear elsewhere. It's a little like looking for patches of wind in ghosting conditions or for a school of surface-feeding fish. That riffle you see may be nothing, but then again, it may be telling you something.

Of course, when the water is truly glassy, this approach can be problematic. At such times, however, you may be able to see the hazard itself through clear and undisturbed water. In tropical waters, especially, it is truly amazing how clear the water can be—though it's not always so. This visual approach can be especially helpful when picking your way into an unfamiliar and poorly charted little cove. Veteran cruisers will generally do everything they can to arrive at a strange anchorage with plenty of daylight. Early mornings and late evenings may be beautiful to look at with a mug of coffee or rum drink in your hand, but that same dimly romantic light makes it much more difficult to pick out any lurking coral heads. The same is true of an overcast sky.

No matter what the weather, the higher you get the better. If you have ratlines on your shrouds, this is the time to use them! Arrgh! Up you go, sailor! If your rig lacks ratlines, get up on the cabintop or the bow pulpit if necessary to spy out a suspicious-looking dark patch. Another trick, if you're having trouble with glare, is to wear polarized sunglasses. This will filter out some of the light bouncing around on the surface, making it that much easier to see what is lying beneath.

HOW RACING CAN MAKE YOU A BETTER SAILOR

Around the Buoys or Around the Harbor, the Skills Are the Same

MANY SAILORS never race, and that's too bad. Nothing will hone your skills and sharpen your awareness of what your boat is capable of faster than a little competition. As Uffa Fox famously put it, "Once you race, every fault is pointed out in the way other boats sail away from you, and when you do anything well this too is revealed as you start sailing away from the rest of the fleet."

Although you may discover a competitive streak you didn't know you had, the object here is not so much cutthroat competition as the lessons you learn from conning your boat around a race course as efficiently as possible—whether it's an offshore distance race or a quick inshore jaunt around the buoys. One of the most fascinating races I've ever participated in is the 100-Miler organized by the M&M Yacht Club in Menomonee, Michigan. Held on Green Bay, the race—which is actually about 35 nautical miles—starts off the Menomonee Marina and makes a big loop, with its farthest point near Eagle Harbor, on the other side of the bay in Wisconsin's Door County. Competitors must

Sailboat racing hones skills that will deepen your enjoyment of cruising and daysailing. (John Payne)

navigate a circuitous course of islands, bluffs, and buoys on all angles of sail, all the while trying to predict the next wind shift and turn it to advantage. It's a wonderful challenge, packing a tremendous amount of varied sailing into a single day.

Every sailor can benefit from a fundamental understanding of what happens on a race course—even if you never actually test that understanding in a race. If you do decide to give it a try, even at the most basic and casual level, I can guarantee that, win or lose, you will be a better sailor and have some great memories at the end of the day.

How a Sailboat Race is Run

A sailboat race is simple in concept. You start across an imaginary line between a buoy, or *pin*, to port and a *committee boat* (from which the race is organized and run) to starboard. After that—in the case of an inshore race

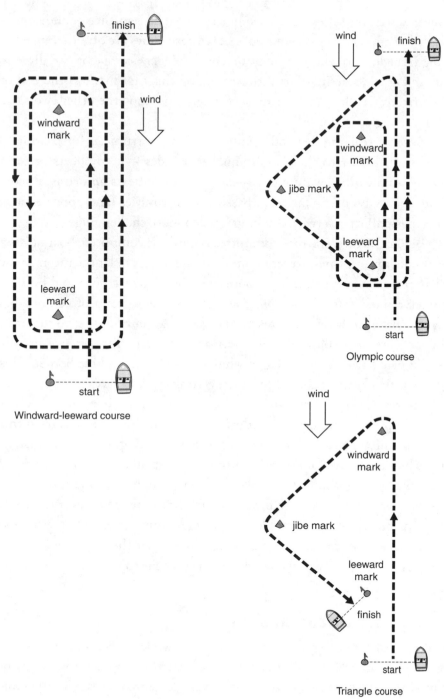

The courses used for sailboat racing are deceptively simple.

over a closed course—you sail around a prescribed sequence of buoys, generally leaving each one on your port side. These buoys are often arranged in a big triangle, with the first buoy, or *windward mark*, a mile or two directly upwind of the starting line. After rounding this first mark at the end of the first *leg*, the fleet sails a pair of reaching legs along the other two sides of the triangle.

Because reaching legs offer only limited opportunities for passing—sailors often refer to them as "spinnaker parades"—many fleets prefer a simple windward-leeward course—i.e., a series of beats and runs. Racing dead downwind offers far more passing opportunities (and opportunities to be passed!) than a reach, making it much more challenging.

Before the race, the race committee aboard the committee boat hoists a series of flags or displays a set of numbers and letters to let the racers know what course is being run. The committee then blows a horn and hoists a predetermined class, or *section*, flag to let the first group of competitors know it has exactly five minutes until its start. At four minutes to the start, the race committee blows another horn and raises a *preparatory flag*, usually a solid blue flag or the "P" flag, a white flag with a thick blue border. This gives the timekeepers aboard the boats getting ready to race an opportunity to confirm that they have an accurate countdown. At one minute to the start, the preparatory flag comes down and another horn sounds. It's at this time that life in the starting area becomes interesting, to say the least, as boats bob and weave for position within the constraints of the international rules that govern racing. The goal of each boat is to hit the line at full speed precisely at the starting signal, without inadvertently going over too early. Finally, the race committee blows a horn, or sometimes fires a gun, and at the same time lowers the section flag. With that the sailors are off and running, beating toward the windward mark at the top of the first leg.

Competitive Seamanship

Success during pre-start maneuvering and while navigating the course requires a wide range of skills, every one of which also applies to cruising or daysailing. Pre-start maneuvering, for example, employs many of the same techniques that are used when executing a crew overboard drill or docking under sail. Inevitably there will be times just before the start when it's important to slow down—maybe you're in danger of crossing the line early, or you need to let a competitor pass in front of you—which means luffing your sails yet keeping the boat under control. You also need to be able to tack or jibe crisply even when another boat is blocking your wind or you haven't yet accelerated to full speed. In other words, you need to be able to handle your boat in less than optimum conditions, often at slow speeds, sometimes making course changes when you might not otherwise want to. Runners and swimmers begin their races from a standstill, but in the last few minutes and seconds before the start of a sailboat race the competitors are in constant motion—requiring the utmost maneuverability and control.

Of course, sailboat racing also places a premium on boat speed on all angles of sail, in many ways the essence of good seamanship. In earlier chapters we talked about how to fine-tune your sails for speed, but you won't really know if what you're doing is working until you see how you stack up against another sailboat. Theory is one thing, but practice is another.

The draft depth that works best, for example, varies from boat to boat and depends on the conditions. Some boats sail best in a slight chop with a relatively flat main and jib, while others need plenty of belly. When you're sailing neck and neck with competitors, it won't take long to figure out whether your sails are shaped correctly.

Then again, you may be walking away from the rest of the fleet one moment, but then the wind changes velocity or direction and everybody starts catching up again. Clearly something needs to be done, so you start tweaking—maybe you take in on the outhaul to flatten the mainsail or let it off a little to give the sail more depth. Maybe you move the jib lead forward or aft to fine-tune the draft depth in that sail as well. If these adjustments revive your speed, great. If the competition is still gaining, keep experimenting. Maybe it's the draft location more than the depth that needs tweaking. Taking in or easing the cunningham or main halyard a couple of inches will move the draft forward or aft, respectively. Maybe you need to adjust the jib lead or the mainsheet to increase or reduce leech twist. Keep working at it, changing your settings by just a few inches and watching for a minute or two to see what happens to your boat speed. There's nothing like this kind of sailing to give you a better feel for sail trim.

Sailboat racing places a premium on boat speed on all angles of sail.

Another way to make your boat sail faster is by changing the distribution of your crew weight. In addition to hiking out to keep a boat on its feet in heavy air, crewmembers can also help maximize boat speed in light or moderate conditions. Many dinghy crews, for example, will move forward in a drifter to lift the stern out of the water a bit and reduce wetted surface area. This works especially well on boats that have wide, flat sterns for planing. Another light-air technique is to shift crew to leeward to induce a little heel. This helps the sails maintain an airfoil shape through force of gravity, as opposed to just hanging limp. It may also help reduce wetted surface area. In a drifter every bit helps!

Yet another effective technique is to heel a boat to windward when sailing downwind, both to reduce wetted surface area and to get the mainsail up and away from the water where it will catch plenty of breeze. Dinghy sailors often heel their boats so aggressively that their windward rails almost drag in the water.

Shifting crew weight to change a boat's angle of heel can have a dramatic effect on boat speed. These Optimist sailors are heeling their boats to windward on the downwind leg of their race course. (Molly Mulhern)

The effect of even a slight change in heel angle can be truly remarkable, even aboard larger keelboats. On light-air days you will see even the biggest racing boats with their crews all sitting to leeward—on the "low" side—their toes dangling just above the water as they struggle to keep the boat moving. Look at the photographs in any sailing magazine and you'll notice that racing crews cluster amidships when sailing to windward. The idea is to keep excess weight out of the bow and stern and lessen hobbyhorsing in the waves. When sailing downwind, on the other hand, crews often gather in the stern to keep the bow from digging in and lifting the rudder out of the water, possibly causing a broach.

The importance of crew weight was dramatically driven home for me in a regatta aboard a 35-foot J/105. We were doing well until everything started to fall apart on the first downwind leg of the second race. The wind was blowing around 15 knots, and we had the spinnaker up, yet nothing we tried could keep our competitors from slowly gaining. We tweaked the outhaul, played with the vang, and adjusted the spinnaker for all we were worth, but none of it seemed to do any good.

Finally our mainsail trimmer suggested we all try hiking out a little. Because we were sailing a broad reach and healing only slightly, it had never occurred to any of us that there might be anything wrong with our weight distribution; most boats like a touch of heel on that angle of sail. No sooner had we all moved to windward, though, than the boat seemed to take off. Our motion through the water became smoother—even quieter—and the boats that had been inexorably walking up on us from astern no longer did so. All of us, the mainsail trimmer included, were amazed. He told us afterward that he had suggested hiking only because he couldn't think of anything else. We all became slightly better sailors that day.

Getting in the Groove

Another key to successful racing—and another technique you can use to improve your daysailing or cruising—is playing wind shifts to windward. Wind direction is rarely steady. Instead, it moves around continually as weather systems come and go or as local heating, cooling, and topographic influences come into play. Even a "steady" breeze will tend to *oscillate*, or shift, around an average direction. Taking advantage of these shifts can mean big gains.

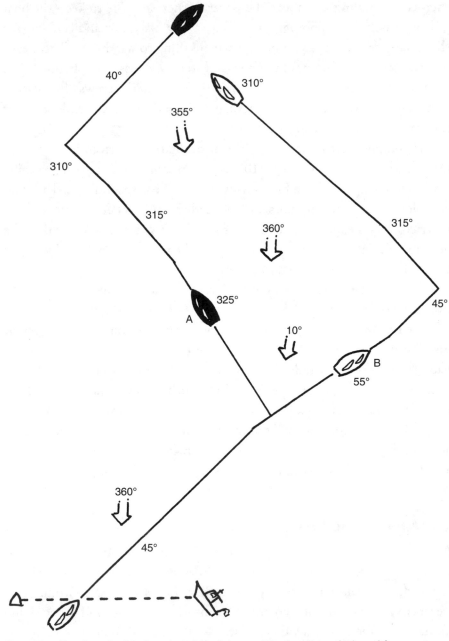

windward mark

40°

310°

355°

310°

315°

360°

315°

325°

A

10°

45°

B

55°

360°

45°

By getting "in phase" with the wind shifts it is possible to sail to windward far more quickly and efficiently than if you ignore them. Here the boat following course A ends up closer to the mark by tacking when it is headed so that it sails on the lifted tack.

Let's say, for example, you're sailing a beat and the windward buoy has been set at a bearing of 270°, or due west. Assuming a standard 90° tacking angle, you can sail on a heading of 315°, or northwest, on port tack and 225°, or southwest, on starboard. What happens, though, if the wind shifts clockwise, or *veers*, 10° north to 280°? Suddenly you find yourself sailing higher on starboard tack; you have been *lifted* and can maintain a course of 235°—10° closer to the mark than before. On port tack, however, you are *headed* and must fall down to 325°—10° farther from the mark than before. Not good!

What Boreas gives Boreas takes away, however, and a few minutes later the wind oscillates counterclockwise, or *backs*, all the way back to 260°. Now the shoe is on the other foot, so to speak. Starboard tack is headed, the highest you can sail being 215°. On port tack you find yourself sailing a lifted heading of 305°.

The key to a successful beat in these conditions is to tack with the shifts so that you spend as much time as possible on the lifted tack, thereby minimizing your distance sailed. Who the heck needs boat speed? Of course, if you can work it so that you're also on the part of the course where the wind is strongest—or where you've got more *pressure*, as racers like to say—so much the better.

Playing the shifts this way is called *getting in phase* and in many ways represents seamanship of the highest order. Clouds, headlands, other sailboats, weather fronts—an accomplished racing sailor will use any and all clues in an effort to predict wind speed and direction. America's Cup veteran Dennis Conner talks about being able to "sniff" out the wind, or of having a "hunch" that it's going to build or shift to a certain direction. But these aren't just lucky guesses. They are the product of countless hours of sailing.

Even more dramatic, and certainly more important from a cruising standpoint, are *persistent shifts*—shifts in which the wind changes direction and then stays there. You may not care to respond to every last variation in wind direction when you're daysailing or weekend cruising. But what if you're bound for an anchorage 5 miles to windward and the wind backs a good 45°? Anticipating a shift this dramatic can make the difference between arriving under sail by daylight or powering into the chop and the deepening twilight in an anxious effort to arrive before dark.

It's also possible to play the shifts while sailing on a run—one of the reasons a simple windward-leeward course is more challenging than a triangle. The goal in this case, though, is to jibe into headers, not lifts. When you sail downwind, the apparent wind is inevitably less than the true wind because you're traveling more or less in the same direction as the moving air. If, for example, you're sailing at 5 knots on a run in 15 knots of breeze, the wind on your sails will be 10 knots. By sailing at a slight angle to the wind—on a broad reach as opposed to a run—you enhance the apparent wind. This causes your boat to speed up, which hauls the apparent wind slightly forward and enhances its velocity still more, and so on in a feedback loop. Racers describe this as "heating it up" or sailing a "hotter angle." In light and moderate winds—generally 14 knots or less—it's actually faster to zigzag downwind than to sail a straight course, the faster speed more than making up for the greater distance run. In especially light air the jibing angles that make up this zigging and zagging will be as great as your tacking angles when sailing on a beat.

The End Result

The result of even the most casual sailboat racing is a greater awareness of your boat and a greater confidence in your abilities—qualities that cannot fail to improve your sailing. Some sailors contend that they are not in any hurry, that they sail in order to relax and that maximum relaxation means maximum idleness. But that's a copout. Being a sailor doesn't mean getting blown around like a paper boat on a pond. It means *sailing*. It means mastering the art of seamanship. It means conning your boat efficiently and intelligently, if for no other reason than because that's part of the fun.

Being a sailor doesn't mean getting blown around like a paper boat on a pond. It means sailing. It means mastering the art of seamanship.

No self-respecting sailor in years past would ever have *dreamed* of not sailing his boat to and from his destination as ably as possibly—whether he was aboard a sleek clipper or a Thames River sailing barge. Don't be fooled by the draft-horse lines of some old-time sailing craft. Their masters were not out there for the fun of it, but to make a living. They did everything they could to ensure that their charges—even heavily loaded—would be handy under sail.

And what about those times when you *are* in a hurry? What about when there are storm clouds on the horizon, or when the auxiliary is acting up? In addition to being tremendously satisfying, sailing can occasionally be dangerous. One of the reasons we learn and practice seamanship is to make our boats do what we want when the chips are down.

There are many kinds of racing out there. The America's Cup and masochistic ocean-racing events get most of the press, but every week of the sailing season brings dozens of races in which having fun is just as important as winning. The West Coast, in particular, seems to place an emphasis on having a good time, with events like the Baja Ha-Ha Rally, from San Diego to Cabo San Lucas in Mexico, and the Half Pint-o-Rum Race, organized by the San Diego Ancient Mariners club. The latter not only requires a bottle of rum as an entrance fee, a member of the crew must swim or run ashore and then down a tot of said elixir for a boat to officially finish.

Many class or manufacturer's associations sponsor some friendly racing during their regattas and summer rendezvous. Hunters, Island Packets, Hinckleys, Beneteaus, Catalinas, catboats, schooners—you name the boat, and it has probably been raced. Even the venerable and highly competitive Chicago Mac Race from Chicago to Mackinac Island, at the top of Lake Michigan, has an ulterior motive—it was originally organized in part to make things interesting for boatowners taking their craft north for a few weeks of leisurely cruising.

If you've never raced before, you may be surprised at how many racing boats in your area are looking for additional crew. Sailing is both challenging and time consuming, which can make it difficult for skippers to gather all the sailors they need. Take a walk through a nearby marina or harbor office and you may be surprised at the number of "crew wanted" notices tacked to the bulletin board. While you're there, why not tack up a "crew available" notice of your own? Many yacht clubs and racing fleets actively connect skippers with willing crew. Give them a call or do a little Internet surfing to see what's available. Getting into the mix may be a lot easier than you think.

> *One of the reasons we learn and practice seamanship is to make our boats do what we want when the chips are down.*

Handicap Racing

Many sailors, including casual cruisers and serious racers, compete under some kind of handicapping rule, which allows dissimilar boats to compete fairly through the use of time ratings. Under most handicapping rules, a group of boats starts at the same time and their elapsed times are then carefully recorded as the boats cross the finish line. After everyone has finished, the race committee calculates *corrected times* based on the distance sailed and each boat's time rating. The boat with the best corrected time wins. A number of "rules" have been tried over the decades, including the Cruising Club of America (CCA) rule, the International Offshore Rule (IOR), and the International Measurement System (IMS), just to name a few. Perhaps the most user-friendly and democratic rule—and the most popular— is the Performance Handicap Racing Fleet, or PHRF (pronounced *perf*). Unlike most rating and design rules, which are derived by plugging such specifications as sail area and LOA into a mathematical formula, a boat's PHRF rating is purely empirical. A committee gets together and decides how fast a boat is and then assigns it a rating—i.e., the number of seconds per mile by which a boat is assumed to be slower than a theoretical benchmark. That initial rating is then adjusted upward or downward as necessary in response to actual results on the race course over time. Most boats rate somewhere between 50 and 250. A slower boat will have a higher rating, which means that at the end of a race that many more seconds will be subtracted from its finish time to arrive at its corrected time. A Catalina 22, being a small boat, has a PHRF rating of around 270, while a Catalina 30 has a rating of around 180. This means that the C30 has to beat the C22 by 90 seconds per mile raced in order to finish ahead on corrected time. In a four-mile race, the C22 would have 1,080 seconds, or 18 minutes, subtracted from its finish time, while the C30 would have 720 seconds, or 12 minutes, subtracted from its time. The Catalina 30 would have to cross the finish line more than 6 minutes ahead of the Catalina 22 to beat it on corrected time.

WHY WE SAIL

22

Nothing Ventured, Nothing Gained

IT'S OFTEN SAID of skiing that if you don't fall down from time to time, you're either not learning anything or not trying very hard. I think this is also true of sailing (and life in general) and if you're not learning anything, what's the point?

I don't mean to say that a good sailor must run his or her boat up on the rocks every now and then—on the contrary. When I worked with a deep-sea diving company in Louisiana, we used to say that there were old divers and bold divers but no old, bold divers, and the same might be said of sailors. What I'm talking about isn't recklessness. It's pushing yourself a little, trying something you've never done before, but only after making sure that you and your boat are adequately prepared.

Is there an island on the horizon you've never seen up close? Why not pay it a visit under sail? Have you never ventured beyond the harbor when there were whitecaps on the bay? Why not snug up that lifejacket, put a reef in the main, and go splash around out there for a while? Have you never gone sailing at night, never completed a passage to that cozy little harbor 30 miles

> *You don't have to sail around Cape Horn to have an adventure.*

to the north, or never sailed competitively? Why not give these things a try? You only live once. What are you waiting for? None of us is getting any younger!

Set a goal, then do what it takes to execute that goal in a seamanlike manner. Take a close look at your boat—at its hull, its rig, and its keel—to assess its capabilities. Take an inventory of the equipment you have on board and acquire whatever else you might need for the goal you have in mind. While you're at it, make an honest assessment of your knowledge and abilities and acquire any necessary skills you lack. Read books, practice maneuvers you're not comfortable with, and daydream about what you have in mind the next time you're at home relaxing in your favorite chair. Make your goal an immediately achievable one—how about going for a sail without using your auxiliary or anchoring somewhere for an afternoon picnic?—and then achieve it. You don't have to sail around Cape Horn to have an adventure. Make your goals stepping stones. You may be surprised where they lead.

I have a confession to make: A part of me doesn't much like sailing. I'm serious. I don't know how many times I've had to rouse myself on a Saturday morning for a weekend regatta, thinking I would like nothing better than to stay in bed. I don't know how many times my wife and I have gone cruising someplace new and I've wished we could just spend the week in a hotel. What if we don't do well? What if I mess up a maneuver and damage the boat? What if I find myself in a situation I can't handle and embarrass myself in front of the fleet or the marina? I've been sailing most of my life, yet there's still something about it that I find a little intimidating.

> *Sailing is one of the few remaining pastimes that force us to deal with the wide world on its own terms.*

Nonetheless, I always get out there, and no matter what my mood when I set out from home, I'm always glad to be on a boat again—and even happier to be out on the water. To paraphrase Bob Marley, "I don't like sailing. I love it!" I'm not going to let a few prerace or precruise jitters get in the way.

Sailing is one of the few remaining pastimes that force us to deal with the wide world on its own terms, without an electrical or internal-combustion advantage. That's why sailing can be intimidating, but also why it's so rewarding.

So go out there and test yourself a little, and if things don't work out quite as planned, who cares? As long as you sail responsibly and get everyone home in one piece, mistakes are the best teacher. I've learned a lot more from those challenges that ended in failure than the ones I failed to attempt. The main thing is that you're doing it, that you've chosen to take part in an activity that is infinitely complex, infinitely challenging, infinitely rewarding, and infinitely demanding—an activity that gets better and better the more you do it and the more you learn. The main thing is that you're a *sailor*—and what could be better than that?

BIBLIOGRAPHY

Calder, Nigel. *Nigel Calder's Cruising Handbook*. Camden, ME: International Marine, 2001. From tying knots to choosing a boat and troubleshooting its electrical system, Calder covers pretty much everything a cruiser needs to know before weighing anchor—whether it's to sail away for a weekend or around the world.

Chapelle, Howard. *Yacht Designing and Planning*. New York: W. W. Norton & Company, Inc., 1936. Chapelle's classic on yacht design includes a wealth of information as well as beautiful hull and detail drawings. It remains timeless, with observations on boats and sailing that are as relevant today as when the book first came out.

Coleman, Henry. *Sailing Boats from Around the World*. Mineola, NY: Dover Publications, Inc., 2000. Originally published in 1906, this is another classic. Coleman covers everything from sloops to catboats to the galleys of the ancient world to the sailboats that once plied the Ganges River in India. It offers a fascinating glimpse of the sailing world during its transition from its pre-industrial roots to our modern era.

Cort, Adam, and Richard Stearns. *Getting Started in Sailboat Racing*. Camden, ME: International Marine, 2005. A clear, concise survey of what it takes to succeed on the race course, the book explains sailboat racing in a way that is easy for the beginner to understand while also offering insights and tips for the seasoned racer.

Fox, Uffa. *Sailing, Seamanship, and Yacht Construction*. Mineola, NY: Dover Publications, Inc., 2002. Originally published in 1936, Fox's book offers a glimpse into the golden age of Corinthian sailing in England. A designer, builder, and master sailor, Fox did it all, from winning championships in dinghies to crossing oceans, battling gales, and sailing with the king of England.

Garrett, Ross. *The Symmetry of Sailing: The Physics of Sailing for Yachtsmen*. Dobbs Ferry, NY: Sheridan House, Inc., 1996. Chock full of complex graphs, diagrams, and mathematical formulas, this book is not for the faint of heart, but it's well worth the effort since it clearly reveals how and why boats do the things they do. Study this book and you'll never see sailboats the same way again.

Gerr, Dave. *The Nature of Boats: Insights and Esoterica for the Nautically Obsessed*. Camden, ME: International Marine, 1995. An accomplished naval architect, author, and builder, Gerr makes otherwise complex maritime phenomenon surprisingly easy to understand. His obvious love all things nautical is wonderfully contagious, making this book a pleasure to read.

Killing, Steve. *Yacht Design Explained: A Sailor's Guide to the Principles and Practice of Yacht Design*. New York: W. W. Norton & Company, Inc., 1998. Far and away the best book on modern yacht design available today. The book is replete with wonderful drawings and photographs illustrating everything from how keels work to how naval architects use tank testing to verify their designs.

Knox-Johnston, Robin. *Yachting: The History of a Passion*. New York: Hearst Marine Books, 1990. A fully illustrated history of the sport of yachting by the first man to sail nonstop alone around the world. The book covers everything from the first yachts and yacht clubs to today's extreme round-the-world races.

Marchaj, Czeslaw. *Aero-Hydrodynamics of Sailing*. New York: Dodd, Mead & Company, 1980. This is another highly technical book that is not for the faint of heart. Nonetheless, as with Garrett's book, the rewards are worth the effort.

Marshall, Roger. *The Complete Guide to Choosing a Cruising Sailboat*. Camden, ME: International Marine, 1999. Not only is this book a "complete" guide, it is a practical one as well. In addition to discussing yacht design and construction in general, Marshall takes a detailed look at five different boat types, including a medium-weight cruiser, a cruiser-racer, a weekend cruiser, a single-hander, and long-distance voyager.

Perry, Robert. *Yacht Design According to Perry: My Boats and What Shaped Them*. Camden, ME: International Marine, 2008. More than just another guide to naval architecture, Perry's book looks at the *process* of bringing a new sailboat design to completion, including the personalities that are an inevitable part of every project. As the creator of such ground-breaking designs as the Valiant 40, Perry has a wealth of stories and insights to share.

——. *Sailing Designs, Vol. 5*. Port Washington, WI: Port Publications, Inc., 1999. This book is the fifth in what is now a series of six compilations of Perry's regular design-review column in *Sailing* magazine. There is simply no better way to become familiar with the various types of sailboats out there than to browse your way through this series—again and again and again. Always highly opinionated, occasionally profound, and often humorous, the reviews never grow stale.

Regan, Paul. *Eagle Seamanship: A Manual for Square-Rigger Sailing*. Annapolis, MD: Naval Institute Press, 1979. This book serves as the manual for Coast Guard cadets serving on the bark *Eagle*. It covers everything you need to know to operate a square-rigged sailing ship.

Roth, Hal. *How to Sail Around the World: Advice and Ideas for Voyaging Under Sail*. Camden, ME: International Marine, 2004. As important as Roth's advice on the practical matters of sailing is his philosophical approach to boats and voyaging. In Roth's view, sailing skill is far more important than modern gadgetry like radar and chart plotters. For Roth, basic seamanship and a well-found boat are still, and will forever remain, the name of the game.

Rousmaniere, John. *The Annapolis Book of Seamanship*. 3rd rev. ed. New York: Simon & Schuster, 1999. The ultimate reference guide to sailing, this book covers everything from mechanical systems to basic piloting to the rules of the road when in the company of cruise ships and freighters. The book includes a four-color guide to the more common symbols found on a nautical chart.

Royce, Patrick. *Royce's Sailing Illustrated, Vol. 1*. Newport Beach, CA: Royce Publications, 1993. Quirky and not especially well organized, but endlessly entertaining, this pocket-sized book packs a tremendous amount of information and brings a sense of exuberance to the subject of boats and sailing. Scattered throughout the pages are bits of information on various rigs and boats types that make for fascinating reading—truly a modern classic.

Seidman, David. *The Complete Sailor: Learning the Art of Sailing*. Camden, ME: International Marine, 1995. If a picture is worth a thousand words then this single book contains a full library's worth of information. The hundreds of clear, concise illustrations by Kelly Mulford are both informative and entertaining. The text is also clear, concise, and comprehensive—a great introduction to the nuts and bolts of sailing.

Slocum, Joshua. *Sailing Alone Around the World and the Voyage of the Liberdade*. London: Hart-Davis, 1967. Published originally in 1899, this book recounts the adventures of history's first solo, around-the-world voyage by the square-rigger master Capt. Joshua Slocum. In addition to being a heck of a yarn, the narrative includes countless tidbits on seamanship and life at sea.

Spurr, Daniel. *Your First Sailboat: How to Find and Sail the Right Boat for You*. Camden, ME: International Marine, 2004. With its clear text and many photographs and illustrations, Spurr's book takes the mystery out of how to determine if a particular boat is right for you and how to work it once it's yours.

Stark, William. *The Last Time Around Cape Horn: The Historic 1949 Voyage of the Windjammer Pamir*. New York: Carroll & Graf Publishers, 2003. A rousing, poignant tale of a young man in search of adventure: Stark not only found what he was looking for, but also a berth aboard the last commercial sailing ship to sail around Cape Horn.

Stephens, William. *Traditions & Memories of American Yachting*. Camden, ME: International Marine, 1981. A compilation of articles that originally appeared in *MotorBoating* magazine between 1939 and 1946, this is *the* definitive history of sailboat racing and cruising in the nineteenth and early twentieth centuries. It includes a treasure trove of photographs, lines drawings, and information documenting the evolution of modern yachting and the America's Cup in particular.

Villiers, Alan. *The War with Cape Horn*. New York: Charles Scribner's Sons, 1971. One of a number of titles by the veteran square-rigger master Capt. Alan Villiers, this book is about the ferocious winter of 1905 when dozens of well-found vessels were either lost or disabled off Cape Horn. If a book like this doesn't make you wish you could run away to sea, nothing will.

INDEX